Religion, literature, and
society in ancient Israel,

G. ALLEN FLEECE LIBRARY
COLUMBIA BIBLE COLLEGE
& SEMINARY
7435 Monticello Rd.
Columbia, SC 29203

RELIGION, LITERATURE, AND SOCIETY IN ANCIENT ISRAEL, FORMATIVE CHRISTIANITY AND JUDAISM

ANCIENT ISRAEL AND CHRISTIANITY

Studies in Judaism Editorial Board
Editor in Chief
Jacob Neusner
Brown University

David Altshuler	George Washington University *Ancient Judaism; Jewish Art*
Michael Berenbaum	Georgetown University *Holocaust Studies; Jewish Thought*
Marvin Fox	Brandeis University *Jewish Thought, Ethics, Philosophy*
Ernest S. Frerichs	Brown University *Biblical Studies and Archaeology*
Zev Garber	Los Angeles Valley College University of California, Riverside *Academic Study of Judaism. Holocaust Studies.*
Beverly R. Gaventa	Colgate Rochester Divinity School-Bexley Hall-Crozer Theological Seminary *Judaism in the Hellenistic World and Earliest Christianity*
Calvin Goldscheider	Brown University *Jewish Social Studies*
William Scott Green	University of Rochester *History of Judaism*
David Hirsch	Brown University *Jewish Literature in English, Yiddish, and Hebrew*
Abraham J. Karp	University of Rochester *American Jewish History*
Burton Mack	Claremont Graduate School *Judaism in the Hellenistic World; Apocryphal and Pseudepigraphic Literature*
Ivan Marcus	The Jewish Theological Seminary of America *Medieval Judaism*
David Novak	Baruch College, City University of New York *Jewish Law*
Robert Seltzer	Hunter College *Modern Jewish History*
Norbert Samuelson	Temple University *Jewish Philosophy*
Manfred Vogel	Northwestern University *Modern Jewish Thought*
Alan Zuckerman	Brown University *Jewish Political Studies*

NEW PERSPECTIVES ON ANCIENT JUDAISM

VOLUME TWO

RELIGION, LITERATURE, AND SOCIETY IN ANCIENT ISRAEL, FORMATIVE CHRISTIANITY AND JUDAISM

Edited by

Jacob Neusner
Peder Borgen
Ernest S. Frerichs
Richard Horsley

ANCIENT ISRAEL AND CHRISTIANITY

UNIVERSITY
PRESS OF
AMERICA

Lanham • New York • London

Copyright © 1987 by

University Press of America,® Inc.

4720 Boston Way
Lanham, MD 20706

3 Henrietta Street
London WC2E 8LU England

All rights reserved

Printed in the United States of America

British Cataloging in Publication Information Available

Library of Congress Cataloging-in-Publication Data

Religion, literature, and society in ancient Israel,
formative Christianity and Judaism.

(New perspectives on ancient Judaism ; v. 2)
Includes bibliographical references.
1. Judaism—History—To 70 A.D. 2. Christianity—
Early church, ca. 30-600.   I. Neusner, Jacob,
1932-   . II. Series.
BM177.N485   vol. 2   296'.09'01 s   87-23027
    [BM165]   [296'.09'015]
       ISBN 0-8191-6597-2 (alk. paper)

All University Press of America books are produced on acid-free
paper which exceeds the minimum standards set by the National
Historical Publication and Records Commission.

To

HOWARD CLARK KEE

In tribute to a definitive voice of this generation's research
into the interplay of religion and society
in the formative history of Christianity and Judaism.

His lessons on the study of Christianity
shape our understanding of our work
in the study of both his field
and also ancient Israel.

'ad me'ah ve'esrim

...to one hundred and twenty years...

CONTENTS

Preface ix

Part One
ANCIENT ISRAEL

Chapter One: '*Apiru* and Cossacks: A Comparative Analysis of Social Form and Historical Role 3
>Richard A. Horsley
>University of Massachusetts, Boston

Chapter Two: Ancient Israel's Scripture and its Religion: The Achievement of Helmer Ringgren 27
>Ernest S. Frerichs
>Brown University

Chapter Three: The Present State of Research on Joseph and Aseneth 31
>Christoph Burchard
>University of Heidelberg

Chapter Four: The Dawning of a New Epoch in Research on Christian Origins: The New English Pseudepigrapha... 53
>James H. Charlesworth
>Princeton Theological Seminary

Part Two
FORMATIVE CHRISTIANITY

Chapter Five: Jesus of Galilee and Judas the Maccabee: Hero Worship or Messianic Machinations?... 67
>John T. Greene
>Michigan State University

Chapter Six: Der biblische Hintergrund der paulinischen Gnadengaben.......... 77
>Otto Betz
>University of Tübingen

Chapter Seven: The Magi at the Birth of Cyrus, and the Magi at Jesus' Birth in Matthew 2:1-12.. 99
>Roger David Aus
>West Berlin, Germany

Chapter Eight: Thomas and Aesop...115
>John Priest
>The Florida State University

Chapter Nine: Outside/Inside: Celsus on Jewish and Christian *Nomoi* 133
>Harold Remus
>Wilfrid Laurier University

Chapter Ten: Who Is "Israel"? The Jewish-Christian Confrontation in
   Fourth Century Iran..151
                                              Jacob Neusner
                                              Brown University

Preface

Howard Clark Kee enjoys a distinguished position among his colleagues in the study of religion in late antiquity, because of his acuity in joining archaeological to literary study in search of the social foundations of religious worlds. He has spent many years in archaeological digs in the State of Israel and in Jordan, working on the Hellenistic and Roman periods. He is equally well qualified in philological and textual studies – a rare combination indeed. And the movement of his learning, from music to art and archaeology to languages to texts carried him, finally, to the social sciences, which he has mastered so as to study the relationship of religion and society in antiquity – the overall theme of this book. He is a principal voice in the study of the social setting of early Christianity in its relationships to both Judaic and Graeco-Roman culture. Less widely known is the fact that he is a trained musician, of professional quality. His colleagues join in this tribute to the learning, imagination, and insight, which, through many and important publications, serve as guide for both method and result as well. His findings therefore form a major *ouevre* of scholarly achievement, and the methods that have guided him define a principal paradigm for research. A person of remarkable breadth and sensibility, our honoree has further provided us with a model of the good colleague, interested in scholarship *sine ira et studio*, sustaining friendships far and wide, helping everyone and harming none.

Born in 1920 in Edgewater Park, New Jersey, Howard Clark Kee began not in history and religion but in language, literature, and music. He studied as an undergraduate at Temple University and received his B. A. in English and Music at Bryan College. Receiving his degree in 1940, he began his career as a professional accompanist in piano, organ, and vocal arrangements in Dallas. Music made possible his scholarly career, and the art and imagination characteristic of his learning are at one with his musical gifts. At the same time he studied at Dallas Theological Seminary and earned his Master of Theology degree, majoring in Semitic languages, in 1944. From 1947-1949 he completed the residence requirements for the Ph.D. in New Testament at Yale University, at the same time supporting himself as organist and choirmaster at Yale Divinity School. He studied at the American School of Oriental Research in Jerusalem in 1949-1950 and then joined the Drew University faculty. He completed his doctoral dissertation and received the Ph.D. from Yale in 1951. He married Janet

Burrell in that same year. The Kee children are H. Clark, Christopher, and Sarah.

His professional career, as Instructor in Classics and Religion at the University of Pennsylvania, 1951-1953, Assistant, then Associate, and finally Professor of New Testament at Drew University, 1953-1968, Rufus Jones Professor of History of Religion at Bryn Mawr College, 1968-1977, Visiting Professor at Princeton University, Swarthmore College, Franklin and Marshall College, and Andover-Newton Theological School, and, finally and at the climax and worthy conclusion to a great career, he was called by President John Silber to serve as William Goodwin Aurelio Professor of Biblical Studies and Professor of New Testament in the School of Theology as well as Chairman of the Graduate Division of Religious Studies at Boston University from 1977 to his retirement in 1986 – that career has graced important colleges, universities, and divinity schools and made a mark on each.

In addition, as exemplary citizen of the academic world, Howard Clark Kee has served in various positions in the Studiorum Novi Testamentai Societas, the Society of Biblical Literature, the American Academy of Religion, Columbia University Seminar in New Testament, Boston Area New Testament Colloquium, the Council on Graduate Studies in Religion, the Philadelphia Chamber Orchestra, the American Bible Society, and the Yale Institute of Sacred Music, among many professional affiliations. He was an editor of *Religious Studies Review,* SBL Dissertation Series, *Biblical Perspectives on Current Issues* (Westminster), the editorial board of *Journal of Biblical Literature, Cambridge Companion to the Bibl*e, and other important series.

Naturally, scholarship of the excellence and distinction of that of Howard Clark Kee has elicited appropriate response from the academic world. He has held a Guggenheim Fellowship (1966-7), has served as Visiting Scholar at Graduate Theological Union, Berkeley (1974-5), Fellow of the Wellcome Institute of the History of Medicine, London, 1984, and has held positions as Member of the Library of Congress Manuscript Project in libraries of monasteries in Jerusalem and at St. Catherine's, Sinai, and Guest Research in Hellenistic-Roman Materials of the Department of Antiquities of the State of Israel. He received the Teacher-Scholar of the year Award at Boston University in 1983-4, a National Endowment for the Humanities Summer Fellowship in 1984, and gave a National Endowment for the Humanities Seminar for College Teachers in 1986. He has given guest lectures at many universities worldwide, including Marburg, Tübingen, Brown, Colgate, Michigan State, Vermont, Massachusetts, Jerusalem, King's College, London, Dublin, Edinburgh, Durham, Aberdeen, Heidelberg, and on and on. The bibliography of his published writings completes the picture of one of the great careers of our generation, happily still in full progress.

Preface

The editors note support of The Max Richter Foundation of Rhode Island, at the instance of its trustees in expression of their respect and esteem for the honoree of this volume.

This writer and his colleague, Professor Ernest S. Frerichs, express their thanks to Brown University, which has covered many incidental costs connected with this project, and has always made possible its faculty's unencumbered participation in scholarly ventures. Further thanks are owing to Mrs. Annette Boulay, Administrator of the Program in Judaic Studies at Brown University, for her efficient help in many aspects of the organization of this book.

JACOB NEUSNER
For the editors

Ernest S. Frerichs and Jacob Neusner
Program in Judaic Studies
Brown University
Providence, Rhode Island

Richard Horsley
Department of Religious Studies
University of Massachusetts
Boston, Massachusetts

Peder Borgen
Department of Religious Studies
University of Trondheim
Trondheim, Norway

ANCIENT ISRAEL

Chapter One

'Apiru and Cossacks
A Comparative Analysis of Social Form and Historical Role

Richard A. Horsley
University of Massachusetts, Boston

Gottwald and Chaney have significantly advanced our understanding of the *'Apiru* (SA.GAZ) in Canaan during the Amarna age.[1] Prior to their work, nearly all studies of the *'apiru* were either simply analyses of the textual evidence for this poorly understood phenomenon or rather vague explanations of historical relationships. Previous attempts to discern concrete social forms of the *'apiru* phenomenon were limited. Either they did not take adequately into account the various ways in which key terms were used in the sources, or they did not accord with the wide variety of evidence now available.[2] Thus Gottwald's implicit and Chaney's explicit portrayal of the *'apiru* in Amarna Canaan in terms of social banditry enables us to discern more precisely the concrete social form taken by the *'apiru* phenomenon. Perhaps most important, moreover, the discernment of the concrete social form of the *'apiru* in comparative sociological perspective enables us to understand more precisely how the *'apiru* could have been an important factor in the process by which "Israel" emerged as an independent people in the central hill country of Palestine.[3]

---

[1] N.K. Gottwald, *The Tribes of Yahweh* (Maryknoll, NY: Orbis, 1979), esp. pp. 391-409, 474-492; M.L. Chaney, "Ancient Palestinian Peasant Movements and the Formation of Premonarchic Israel," *Palestine in Transition: The Emergence of Ancient Israel* (ed. D.N. Freedman & D.F. Graf; Scheffield: Almond, 1983), 39-94, esp. 72-83.

[2] E.g., M. Weippert, *The Settlement of the Israelite Tribes in Palestine* (SBT 21; London: SCM, 1971), 63-102, esp. 73-74, 91-92: the only possibilities to be entertained are those mentioned in the *textual* evidence.

[3] The *'apiru* are important in the "withdrawal" or "revolt" model of the origins of Israel, but not only there. See G.E. Mendenhall, The Hebrew Conquest of Palestine," *BA* 25 (1962), 66-87; *The Tenth Generation* (Baltimore: Johns Hopkins University Press, 1973); Gottwald, *Tribes of Yahweh*, 210-219; Chaney, "Ancient Palestinian Peasant Movements;" and the discussion in *JSOT* 7 (1978), pp. 2-52.

Chaney explains the *'apiru* in terms of Hobsbawm's broad comparative study of *social banditry,* which is "universally found wherever societies are based on agriculture (including pastoral economies), and consist largely of peasants and landless laborers ruled, oppressed and exploited by someone else ..."[4] Brigand groups stem largely from the mobile margin of peasant society, i.e., escaped serfs, ruined freeholders, army deserters, etc., although they sometimes also include disaffected or impoverished nobles. Although considered criminals by the official power-structure, they are usually supported and even looked up to as heroes by the peasantry. Based in remote areas such as mountains and frontier zones, brigand bands can survive best in conditions of administrative inefficiency or feudal anarchy or midst the rival jurisdictions of petty principalities. Groups of social bandits ordinarily survive by robbing and raiding. In circumstances of social-political chaos, however, they constitute a political force, however small, in their own right as "a nucleus of armed strength." Thus, especially weak states or district governors must often come to terms with such a local power group which it cannot otherwise simply eliminate. Thus, while social bandits are usually most significant as a symbol of freedom to the oppressed peasantry, they also can become part of the overall system dominated by the rich and powerful. Social banditry is not ordinarily of much greater significance than a symptom of peasant unrest. In unusual circumstances of extreme economic hardship and political chaos, however, social banditry can become a precursor of, a model for, and the cadre of widespread peasant rebellions. Chaney has demonstrated from the Amarna letters how the model developed by Hobsbawm is readily applicable to and is vividly illustrated from the *'apiru* phenomenon in fourteenth century Canaan.

Now that Chaney and Gottwald have shown the way, demonstrating the broad applicability of Hobsbawm's model, such that "social banditry" can be discerned as the apparent social form taken by the *'apiru* in Amarna Canaan, perhaps it would be appropriate to attempt a refinement in the model and its application.

Like my own work on Jewish banditry in late-second Temple times,[5] Chaney's analysis of the *'apiru* works with Hobsbawm's overall model of "social banditry." In the particular steps of his presentation, however, Hobsbawm delineates three similar but distinctive types of banditry, "the noble robber," "the avengers," and the "Haiduks."[6] Hobsbawm's comments on "the avengers" do not seem applicable to the known data on the *'apiru*. His comments on the Haiduks, however, seem particularly applicable and parallel to what we know of

---

[4]E.J. Hobsbawm, *Bandits* (rev. ed.; New York: Pantheon, 1981) 19-20. Hobsbawm's shorter statements on social banditry are "The Social Bandit," in *Primitive Rebels* (New York: Norton, 1959), 13-29; and "Social Banditry," in *Rural Protest* (ed. H.A. Landsberger; New York: Barnes and Noble, 1973).

[5]R.A. Horsley, "Josephus and the Bandits," *JSJ* 10 (1979), 37-63; and "Ancient Jewish Banditry and the Revolt Against Rome, 66-70 AD," *CBQ* 43 (1981), 409-432

[6]Hobsbawm, *Bandits;* on the Haiduks see *Bandits,* ch. 5, and "Social Banditry," 154-156.

the 'apiru, distinctly more so than some of his generalizations about "the noble robber." Hobsbawm, moreover, includes information on the Cossacks in his chapter on the Haiduks, and the more one investigates the phenomena of the Cossacks on the southeastern frontier of sixteenth to eighteenth century Russia the more striking are the parallels with the 'apiru in ancient Canaan.

Several features of "the image" of the noble robber, which define his social role and his relationship with the common peasants, do not appear to fit the evidence we have concerning the 'apiru, which is more closely parallel to that for the Haiduks. For example, the "noble robber" characteristically begins his outlaw career as the victim of some particular injustice.[7] The motive to become a Haiduk, however, is generally more economic.[8] The 'apiru, similarly, would appear to have been driven into their outlawry generally by severe economic pressures, such as debts or exorbitant taxation.[9] Moreover, although the peasants' admiration of the Haiduks is not lessened thereby, "the redistribution of wealth, the rightings of wrongs (except in the form of vengeance) and in general the championship of the poor as such, normally do *not* form a significant part of the public image of the Haiduks."[10] We have little or no direct evidence on the 'apiru in these respects. However, we have the impression that, like the Haiduks, they were "far more permanently cut off from the peasantry than the classical social bandit ..."[11]

Moreover, whereas ordinary social bandits not only were helped and supported by their people but never really left their communities of origin,[12] the ancient 'apiru (according to the evidence we have) were generally foreigners in the lands in which they had taken up their new life, perhaps hundreds of miles from their original village communities. Like the Haiduks, they had become members of new, semi-separate (if small and partial) societies. "What distinguished Haidukry from other kinds of social banditry is that its social function is consciously recognized, permanent, and to this extent it is much more institutionalized and structured than the common type of brigandage.[13] An ordinary brigand band usually centers around the magnetic leadership of a celebrated bandit, with "fifteen as the usual size for a largish group," and the group rarely lasts more than a few years.[14] Haiduks and especially Cossacks

---

[7]Hobsbawm, *Bandits*, 42.
[8]Hobsbawm, *Bandits*, 71-72; P. Longworth, *The Cossacks* (New York: Holt, Rinehart and Winston, 1969), 19.
[9]W.L. Moran, "Habiru," *New Catholic Encyclopedia* (Washington, DC.: Catholic University Press, 1967); E.F. Campbell, "Shechem in the Amarna Archive," Appendix 2 in G.E. Wright, *Shechem* (new York: McGraw-Hill, 1965), 194; Gottwald, *Tribes of Yahweh*, 407; R.McC. Adams, *The Evolution of Urban Society* (Chicago: Aldine, 1966), 60; A.L. Oppenheim, *Ancient Mesopotamia* (Chicago: University of Chicago Press, 1964), 82.
[10]Hobsbawm, "Social Banditry," 155; cf. *Bandits*, 42-45.
[11]Hobsbawm, *Bandits*, 73.
[12]Hobsbawm, *Bandits*, 42, 47-48.
[13]Hobsbawm, "Social Banditry," 154.
[14]Hobsbawm, "Social Banditry," 154-155; *Primitive Rebels*, 18-19.

formed more permanent groups with more formal structure and organization.[15] Similarly, some of our ancient Near Eastern data indicates that *'apiru* also formed semi-independent communities.[16] Indeed, in their size (often a hundred and more), their inclusion of some families and their semi-permanently settled, year-round location on their own territory, some *'apiru* groups resemble the Cossacks even more than the Haiduks, who were often simply seasonal all-male bands, who returned to their villages or towns for the winter. Like their later Balkan counterparts, therefore, *'apiru* groups appear to have been "a more serious, a more ambitious, permanent and institutionalized challenge to official authority than the scattering of Robin Hoods or other robber rebels which emerged from any normal peasant society."[17]

Finally, insofar as many *'apiru* groups were mercenaries attached to kings or emperors, they do not resemble ordinary social bandits and not even the free Haiduks, but rather that Haiduks or Cossacks who sold their services to lords as retainers or to the Tsar as border-guards.[18] In the remoter areas without the benefit of efficient maintenance of law and order by the established regime the local lords or powerful families always had to reach some economic, even "political" *modus vivendi* with ordinary brigand bands. In the case of both *'apiru* and Cossacks, however, the relationship was more formalized. The Tsars provided the Cossacks with land, supplies and privileges in order to induce them to protect, rather than raid into, the territory nominally under Tsarist rule. Our sources for the ancient *'apiru*, which are heavily weighted with diplomatic correspondence and other official documents, provide a vivid picture of how often *'apiru*, were employed as border-guards and auxiliary troops.

It would seem appropriate, therefore, to pursue Chaney's analysis of the *'apiru* in terms of Hobsbawm's model a step further in the direction of a comparison of the ancient "outlaws/refugees/mercenaries" with the Balkan Haiduks and particularly with the Cossacks in southeastern Europe in the sixteenth-eighteenth centuries. In focusing primarily on the parallels between the *'apiru* and the Cossacks, however, we will be expanding, or rather stepping somewhat outside of Hobsbawm's original model of "social banditry." Hobsbawm, in effect, excludes the "state-Cossacks" from his discussion of the Haiduk-type of social banditry. What is characteristic and distinctive about both *'apiru* and Cossacks, however, is that they occupied an ambiguous position and role between the established governments and the peasantry. They served

---

[15]Hobsbawm, *Bandits*, 74-76.
[16]M. Greenberg, "Hab/piru and Hebrews," in *World History of the Jewish People, First Series, Ancient Times, Vol II: Patriarchs* (ed., B. Mazar; Brunswick, NJ: Rutgers University Press, 1970), 194; H. Cazelles, "The Hebrews," in *Peoples of Old Testament Times* (ed. D.J. Wiseman; Oxford: Clarendon, 1973), 14; Gottwald, *Tribes of Yahweh*, 402.
[17]Hobsbawm, *Bandits*, 76.
[18]Hobsbawm, *Bandits*, 70-71; Social Banditry," 156; I. Racz, *Couches militaire issues de la paysannerie libre en Europe orientale du quinzieme au dix-septieme siecles* (Debreczen, 1964); Longworth, *Cossacks*, 33-36.

governments, or individual boyars or gentry, as border guards and mercenaries. At the same time, however, they functioned as constant magnets for peasants who were inclined to flee their oppressive circumstances and to "become" *'apiru*/Cossacks themselves.

Further pursuit of the comparative sociological approach inaugurated by Chaney and Gottwald is dictated partly by the nature of the historical material on the *'apiru*. Historical data on the *'apiru* are limited and fragmentary, much of it in the form of diplomatic correspondence which is not only hostile to the *'apiru* but limited in its interests as well. As evident in most analyses of the *'apiru*, the data are thus too limited and problematic for self-contained and comprehensive study of the phenomenon by itself. Comparative study – and more morphological analysis – therefore can provide both supplementary information and a certain external control as well for examination of the *'apiru*.[19] The following morphological analysis will proceed from delineation of significant social characteristics shared by *'apiru* and Cossacks, through comparative examination of their economic and political interaction with the larger societies on whom they were semi-dependent but whose domination they resisted, to a critical assessment of their revolutionary role and effects.[20]

Fugitives

The *'apiru* were typically foreigners and fugitives. Greenberg's survey of the

---

[19]In the past few decades there has been a good deal of sophisticated practice of, and reflection upon, comparative historical and sociological analysis. See e.g., the review essays, V.E. Bonnell, "The Uses of Theory, Concepts and Comparison in Historical Sociology," and T. Skocpol and M. Somers, "The Use of Comparative History in Macrosocial Inquiry," both in *Comparative Studies in Society and History* 22 (1980), 156-173 and 174-197 and the literature cited in both. In particular, see M. Bloch, "A Contribution towards a Comparative History of European Societies," in *Land and Work in Medieval Europe: Selected Papers by Marc Bloch* (New York: Harper & Row, 1967), 44-81; and B. Moore, *Social Origins of Dictatorship and Democracy: Lord and Peasant in the Making of the Modern World* (Boston: Beacon, 1966). The approach here is far less elaborate, comprehensive and sophisticated than in these recent studies just cited, and very limited in its purposes. Comparison with the Cossacks may be helpful simply for our hypothetical reconstruction of a more complete picture of the *'apiru* from the fragmentary evidence available. And the Cossacks, who share several key similarities with the *'apiru*, may provide a historical *model* of a concrete social form with which we can compare the *'apiru*. Comparative historical analysis thus may provide some historical credibility for the hypothesized reconstruction of the social form assumed by the *'apiru* -- i.e., a historical example of that social form elsewhere in comparable circumstances.

[20]The sources for the Cossacks are also problematic, although they are now being worked through carefully and critically by scholars such as L. Gordon, *Cossack Rebellions: Social Turmoil in the Sixteenth-Century Ukraine* (Albany: State University of New York Press, 1983). See her "Historiographical Essay" and "Bibliography," pp. 249-284. The principal other book-length treatment of Cossacks available to English readers is P. Longworth, *The Cossacks*. (New York: Holt, Rinehart & Winston, 1969). The review of Longworth's book by I.L. Rudnytsky in *Slavic Review* 31 (1972) complains principally about coverage of the Ukraine, a problem now taken care of by Gordon's circumspect and theoretically sophisticated treatment. See also G. Stoeckl, *Die Entstehung des Kossackentums* (Munich: Isarverlag, 1953).

textual evidence indicates that these characteristics prevailed from place to place and from century to century. In the Alalakh texts, for example, "in nearly every case the SA.GAZ's place of origin is other than the town in which he is found." Similarly, "most of the *'apiru* at Nuzi appear to be foreigners."[21] It is clear from Amarna and Hittite texts that many 'apiru are fugitives from the law or from the kingdom in which they had originated.[22] Once the semi-independent groups were established, moreover, they welcomed additional fugitive and renegade elements. Thus, far from being an ethnic group themselves, they were outlaws and outcasts of diverse origins who in their common plight had banded together. Moreover, there was no tribal solidarity in their background which united the various bands.[23]

Similarly, the Cossacks on the southern and southeastern frontiers of Muscovy were not an ethnic group, nor were they ever united by tribal bonds. The very early bands may have been composed largely of raiding groups splitting away from the Tatars. By the fifteenth and sixteenth centuries, the Cossack groups were composed of fugitives from Russian, Lithuanian, Polish, and other territories. A Cossack group might even include kidnapped or runaway Turkish galley-slaves. They were largely newcomers to the frontier and, as Tsar Ivan IV labeled them, "runaways from our state and from the Lithuanian lands."[24] By the end of the sixteenth century most of the Cossacks were Slavic. There was great variety, however, in background and origin. In the Ukraine, for example, "in the official Cossack register of 1581 a few Moldavians and Wallachians, one Serb, two Tatars, thirteen Muscovites, and two Lithuanians could be registered. One must recognize that there were many more foreigners whose names did not distinguish them."[25] Indeed, "the Zaporozhian Cossacks were so heavily composed of fugitives that they renamed all their members upon entry into the *sich* to avoid pursuers."[26] The Cossacks were thus continually welcoming fugitives to the "wild country" who were far away from their villages and

---

[21] Greenberg, "Hab/piru and Hebrews," 190-191.

[22] Greenberg, "Hab/piru and Hebrews," 193-194; *The Hab/piru* (New Haven: American Oriental Society, 1955), 87; M.B. Rowton, "The Topological Factor in the *Hapiru* Problem," *Studies in Honor of Benno Landsberger* (AS 16; Chicago: University of Chicago Press, 1965), 383-385.

[23] Perhaps because he is attempting to fit the *'apiru* into his overly rigid structural concept of dimorphism," Rowton, "Dimorphic Structure and the Problem of the 'Apiru-'Ibrim," *JNES* 35 (1976), 14-16, creates a confusion in this respect with regard to both *'apiru* and Cossacks. He suggests that the *'apiru* phenomenon commonly took the form of tribal splinter groups. The Cossacks, he implies, were a semi-ethnic element. The authority he cites on the "kazakh tribe" in central Asia treats the "Cossacks" as a totally different socio-political phenomenon. See L. Krader, *Peoples of Central Asia* (Bloomington: Indiana University press, 1966), 63-66, 98-99, 102; Longworth, *Cossacks*, 344, n. 4.

[24] Longworth, *Cossacks*, 18; concerning the Russian frontier, see further D. Gerhard, "The Frontier in Comparative View," *Comparative Studies in Society and History* 1 (1959), esp. 224-228.

[25] Gordon, *Cossack Rebellions*, 76; cf. W.H. McNeill, *Europe's Steppe Frontier, 1500-1800* (Chicago: University of Chicago Press, 1964), 112, 115; Longworth, 343, n. 1.

[26] Gordon, 73; Longworth, 26; the *sich* was the base community of free Cossacks south of the rapids on the Dneiper River.

countries of origins. As with the *'apiru*, the solidarity of Cossack groups clearly did not have an ethnic or tribal basis.

Economic Pressures

Both in the case of the ancient *'apiru* and in that of the Cossacks, the principal cause of flight into outlawry was apparently the increasing economic pressures brought upon the peasantry.[27] Many peasants fell into debt when they were unable to meet the demands of imperial as well as local rulers for tribute and taxes. Special factors such as the rise of chariot warfare in the second millennium only exacerbated the economic burden of the peasantry. Debtors were subject to personal seizure and sale into slavery. An old Assyrian document attests flight because of unpaid debts. In the Amarna age, the letters of Rib Adda of Byblos indicates that a local ruler could resort to sale of his peasants (in order to meet his own fiscal crises) simply in exchange for grain.[28] Gottwald suggests that in Amarna Canaan the combination of increased economic pressures on the peasants and peasant flight from those pressures created a spiraling intensification of the cycle: "To make up for the loss of human and natural resources, the cities would have to increase the burden they placed upon those who remained under their control. This in turn would increase the flow of fugitives."[29]

In eastern Europe in the sixteenth and seventeenth centuries, the peasantry was subjected to enserfment by their lords, the gentry, and the boyars, backed by the Polish or Muscovite states. This was partly due to the transformation of east European agriculture into production for trade to Western European countries. For example, in the early fifteenth century, Lithuanian peasants were obligated to an average of fourteen days' labor dues per year. By the mid-sixteenth century this had increased to about two days per week and a few decades later to a half of the week's labor, with women and children now included in the requirement.[30] Landlords' strategy for dealing with the shortage of labor power in Poland, the Ukraine and Russia was to change the peasants' obligation from payment in kind or money to labor. "This process spiraled, as the labor requirements prevented the peasants from adequately cultivating their own plots and rendered them ever more unable to pay money rents." Both peasants and lords were affected by the spiral. The heavier the obligations, "the more the number of indigent peasants grew who were unable to provide exploitable

---

[27]M. Liverani, "Social Implications in the Politics of Abdi-Ashirta of Amurru," *Three Amarna Essays*. (Malibu, CA: Undina, 1979), 15-18; "Il fouruscitismo in Siria nella tarda eta del bronzo," *Rivista Storica Italiana* 77 (1965), 315-336; G. Buccellati," *'Apiru* and *Munnabtutu* – The Stateless of the First Cosmopolitan Age," *JNES* 36 (1977), 145-147.
[28]Moran, "Habiru;" Campbell, "Sechem in the Amarna Archive," 194.
[29]Gottwald, *Tribes*, 407.
[30]Gordon, 42.

labor."[31] Simultaneously, the magnates, gentry and boyars were asserting their own control of the former common lands. Not surprisingly, many peasants fled to the frontier, to join "Cossack" groups.

To stem the flight of their peasants, the gentry and boyars obtained legislation to tie peasants to the land and specialized military forces to pursue runaways. Many a landlord was unable or unwilling to feed his peasants; but the peasants now legally tied to lord and land were willing to risk "outlaw" (and hunted fugitive) status in an effort to find a refuge with the Cossacks. One is reminded of Rib Addi's situation in Byblos: "Hostility is powerful against me, and there are no provisions for the peasants, so therefore they desert to the sons of Abdi-Ashirta and to Sidon and Beirut."[32] As Cossacks and other fugitive peasants settled the frontier, however, the Polish magnates and the Muscovite boyars and state found it all the more attractive to expand their holdings into the southwestern frontier regions, carrying the process of enserfment with them as they gradually asserted their economic and political control.[33]

This competitive process of territorial expansion, however, further exacerbated the pressure on the peasantry. The situation is parallel in certain respects to the rise of chariot warfare in the second millennium B.C. In order to pay for their expanding and increasingly expensive military machines, both the ancient and the early modern states had to raise further funds from taxation which ultimately derived from land under cultivation and peasant labor. One can easily imagine the spiraling effect as in Amarna Canaan, as decreasing labor supply led lords to increase the pressure on the remaining peasants.[34] Usually the fugitives were simply individuals or families. But the conditions were often such that entire villages disappeared.[35]

Finally, the Cossacks were by no means all fugitive peasants. Ruined and outlawed gentry also fled to the frontier, especially from the unusually large Polish gentry class, and played prominent leadership roles in the Cossack bands.[36] The Alalakh text mentioning Idrimi, a former King, as a fugitive who took refuge among the 'apiru/SA.GAZ near the coastal town of Ammiya provides the analogous phenomenon of former gentry or rulers among the hapiru.[37]

---

[31]Gordon, 43.
[32]EA 118-21-29 cited from Chaney, 75.
[33]Gordon, 20.
[34]See Gordon 43-44; Longworth, 18-19, 345, nn. 16-17; 76-78; 126-130; J. Blum, *Lord and Peasant in Russia From the Ninth to the Nineteenth Century* (Princeton: Princeton University Press, 1961). J.L. H. Keep, "Bandits and the Law in Muscovy," *Slavic and East European Review*, 35, #84 (1956).
[35]Gordon, 44; Longworth, 127.
[36]Gordon, 66, 73, 31.
[37]Greenberg, "Hab/piru and Hebrews," 190.

Status in Society

Those who were refugees and outlaws with respect to their place of origins generally occupied a special, semi-independent status once they formed or joined *'apiru* (Cossack) groups (in a new situation far from their original homes). Some ancient Near Eastern sources indicate that some *'apiru* became individually dependent, having contracted certain services to a master in return for their keep.[38] Most *'apiru,* however, apparently became members of a sizeable group which, even if it became semi-dependent upon a state, city, or powerful individual, still maintained a semi-independent status with regard to the rest of a given society or territory. For example, in the Hittite-Ugaritic treaty concerning extradition of fugitives, it is clear that the *'apiru*/SA.GAZ present in the realm of the great Hittite king occupy their own "territory" as a semi-independent community, even though they are apparently clients of the king.[39]

Some texts indicate that the *'apiru* occupy a social status somewhere between free peasants and slaves – not surprising for those who were without political rights in their society of current residence. Yet it would be inappropriate to apply the concept of "class" to the *'apiru*[40] since they were apparently not really a legitimate group or stratum in the society, but one of special position. For example, there was a town or a district called "Halbi of the *'apiru* in Ugaritic territory.[41] Thus, their role in a society or a given territory may have placed them somewhere between ranking members of the society or the ruling groups on the one hand, and the ordinary people or peasants on the other.[42] This relative importance (or actual "political" power) may be reflected in the sequence of classification in an Egyptian list of captives from Amen-hotep II's second Asian campaign (ca. 1430 B.C.); 3,600 *'apiru* are listed after the 127 "princes" and 179 "brothers of princes" and before the 15,200 ordinary Shoshu (nomads) and 36,300 Kharu (settled population from Syria Palestine).[43]

The Cossack position or status in territories nominally under Polish, Ukrainian or Muscovite jurisdiction appears to have been similar. They are almost always members of sizeable semi-independent groups. They are not part of the general peasantry, but are independent of tribute, dues, or taxation. They are even paid a certain amount of food, equipment, and horses for their services, just as were the *'apiru.* Only a very few, however, appear to have achieved a status of landlords, and that occurs only when the Polish state attempts to bring some of them into dependence on and closer cooperation with the state and ruling class. Mostly the Cossacks retain a semi-independent status as a group which is

---

[38] Moran; Greenberg, "Hab/piru and Hebrews," 191.
[39] Greenberg, 194-195.
[40] *Vs.* Greenberg, "Hab/piru and Hebrews," 194, 196; Cazelles, 9; Weippert, 65 (who relies on the older literature on *'apiru*).
[41] Cazelles, 14; Greenberg, "Hab/piru and Hebrews," 195, n. 16.
[42] Campbell, 202.
[43] Greenberg, "Hab/piru and Hebrews," 195.

not an ordinary but a special component on the fringe of the society. In the sixteenth century, some of the Cossack groups appear to have been almost independent communities out in the "wild country" of the steppe (beyond the rapids). Even so, many of these physically independent communities were under contract or agreement with the Polish state, Lithuanian/Ukrainian magnates or Muscovy to provide certain services in return for payments of some sort. The Cossacks' dependence upon the larger societies in which they had a special status on the fringe may have been more complex – the early-modern economic structure even in southeastern Europe was far more complex than was the ancient Near Eastern. Their semi-independent, semi-dependent special status on the fringe of society, however, was similar to that of the *'apiru* groups in the ancient Near East.[44]

Just as some of the Cossacks had originally been from the gentry, so some of them, in effect, became landholding gentry. First, the Polish state and later the Tsars attempted to control the Cossacks by giving their leaders a stake in the system as landowning gentry as well as military officers. The practice of having several hundred or a few thousand "registered" Cossacks still left others, the majority, in as volatile a situation as ever on the fringe of the society. The registered Cossacks, however, did have a greater stake in perpetuating the system of landholding and intensifying enserfment. Partly because of their position of leadership among the Cossack groups, some Cossacks became, in effect landed Polish/Ukrainian or Muscovite gentry.[45] Of course, their "gentrification" did not completely eliminate their Cossack sense of independence and pride and their potential as leaders of rebellion against the regime – as we shall see in the case of Bogdan Khmelnitsky.[46]

Evidence for the *'apiru* in the ancient Near East is not nearly so extensive, and the ancient Near Eastern social structure was less complex. But we have the sense that a few *'apiru* who became chariot warriors or officers of troops of *'apiru* infantry, for example, may well have occupied a status analogous to Cossacks who had become landed squires.[47]

Raiding and Mercenary Service

With regard to both the means by which they supported themselves and the role they played in ancient Near Eastern societies, the *'apiru* appear primarily as armed bands of raiders or mercenary soldiers. Some *'apiru*/SA.GAZ served as dependent servants or retainers of individual figures or families (apparently very much as Haiduks served in this way to Hungarian or Polish nobles and magnates in early modern times). The semi-independent groups of *'apiru*, moreover,

---

[44] Longworth, 21-24; 88; 128; Gordon, 72.
[45] Gordon, 89-87; Longworth, 33-34.
[46] Longworth, 98.
[47] Greenberg, "Hab/piru and Hebrews," 194, n. 14; Cazelles, 9.

undoubtedly engaged in a range of economic activities, depending upon local circumstances, such as building projects, raising of cattle and other farming, and some trading (if only of their booty). These other activities may well have been more important than suggested by our sources, which are heavily weighted towards diplomatic correspondence and other official documents. Most prominent in our sources and surely most important in ancient Near Eastern social-political affairs, however, were their raids upon cities and towns and their service as mercenaries.

The very term used to refer to these groups indicates their raiding activities.[48] The Akkadian equivalent for the Sumerian ideogram SA.GAZ is very frequently *habbatu,* or "brigand," "raider." In one of our earliest texts referring to the phenomena – a description very similar to those of early Cossacks – the SA.GAZ appear as marauders on the fringe of Sumerian society: "these people without clothes who travel in dead silence, who destroy everything, whose menfolk go where they will, whose womenfolk have spindles; they establish their tents and their camps they spend their time in the countryside without observing the decrees of my king Shulgi."[49] In texts from Mari the SA.GAZ are portrayed as highly mobile groups with donkeys who come in "from the flat country," conducting raids and seizing towns. They are clearly raiders, not conquerors, for they do not keep the towns. And troublesome as they are to the king of Mari, they are more so to the Assyrian king.[50] More prominent than their raiding in the early Babylonian texts and in texts from the Alalakh, is their service as mercenary soldiers on behalf of and supported by the kings. In groups ranging in size from fifteen or thirty to (coalitions of) 1436 or even 2000 or 3000 under the leadership of their own chieftains, they are employed as garrisons, as a combination of soldiers and workers. In return for their services, they receive rations of food for themselves and their horses, other supplies such as clothing, and their own quarters or landholdings.[51]

Again in the important Amarna texts, the *'apiru* appear primarily as mercenaries and marauders – although again we must allow for the political-military bias of sources consisting principally of diplomatic correspondence. As semi-independent armed bands, the *'apiru* appear as mercenaries/auxiliaries in the service of one king or city-state against another. They are sometimes settled on land, "doubtless partly in payment for their services and partly as a way of keeping a close watch on their activities."[52] Much of the raiding by *'apiru* bands appears to have been done to one city or king at the behest of another: For example, Mayarzana of Hazi complains that the SA.GAZ raids on his own and other, nearby cities tributary to the Egyptian Pharaoh had been carried out on

---

[48] Rowton, "Dimorphic Structure," *JNES* 35 (1976), 15-16.
[49] Cazelles, 7.
[50] Cazelles, 8.
[51] Greenberg, "Hab/piru and Hebrews," 189-191; Cazelles, 8-9.
[52] Gottwald, 402.

behalf of Amanhatbi, Prince of Tushulti, who then protected the marauders from his counterinsurgency expedition.[53] But there were also independent bands of *'apiru* in Amarna Canaan conducting raids on their own initiative.[54] In one fascinating parallel to the Cossacks who often worked and raided in the same frontier areas and, in similar fashion, to the more nomadic independent bands of Tatar raiders, a text mentions SA.GAZ alongside Shutu nomads as plunderers.[55] Hittite and Egyptian texts portray the *'apiru*/SA.GAZ similarly as raiders and mercenaries. It appears consistent with our sources, moreover, to speculate that independent raiding by *'apiru* bands likely increased in periods and areas of general political instability and areas of inter-state conflict. Such political turmoil, however, would also likely have resulted in predatory raiding by *'apiru* at the behest of one king against another.

The Cossacks present a similar picture of armed bands whose principal activities were raiding and service as mercenaries. Their principal difference from the Amarna age *'apiru* appears to be the scale of operations, both in the size of the independent bands of warriors and in the size of the states into whose service and conflicts they entered (Poland, Muscovy, the Ottoman empire, etc.) As was the case with the ancient *'apiru,* small numbers of Cossacks entered the service of individual lords or families (Polish magnates, Hungarian gentry, etc.). Most appear to have been members of larger groups which entered into various relationships with various conflicting states and principalities. Some very early Cossack groups may have started as bands of Tatar raiders who had split off from the great Horde in the steppe along the frontiers of Muscovy or in the Ukraine.[56] These bands of free warriors then raided from the wild areas of the steppe across the frontiers into border towns and settled areas of the Ukraine or Muscovy. But they were also recruited as border guards who could provide an early warning system against raids by Tatars or other bands of fellow Cossacks, or as military escorts and auxiliaries, judging from reports by Western European merchants or travelers from the fifteenth century on. The Tsar thus encouraged the bands of wandering and predatory Cossacks to settle down in border lands under at least nominal state control as tillers of the soil as well as border guards. Besides grants of land, these "town" or "service" Cossacks were given hunting and fishing rights and supplies. However there were plenty of free Cossacks left out in the "wild country." As one traveler reported: "occasionally Cossacks cut across it seeking, as is their way, some one to swallow up. For they live by plunder, are subject to no man and run across the broad and empty steppes in bands of three, six, ten, twenty, sixty and more men."[57]

---

[53] Greenberg, "Hab/piru and Hebrews," 192-193; cf. Liverani, 16.
[54] *Vs.* Greenberg, 193-194, we simply do not know their "preferred role."
[55] 5Greenberg, "Hab/piru and Hebrews," 193; and see 189 and 195.
[56] Longworth, 13-19.
[57] Longworth, 15.

Rulers and nobles whose territories were harrassed by Cossacks, however, learned that they could also use them to advantage in their struggles with other states or magnates. The Tsar, for example, paid the Cossacks of the Don to provide him auxiliary military aid when threatened by the Crimean Tatars or the Turks, and encouraged their raids against the Tatars and Turkish territories, while denying responsibility for them.[58] In the Ukraine, Cossack bands could be engaged by powerful Polish or Lithuanian nobles in their efforts to resist and indeed rival the power of the Polish state. Some of them operated as virtually independent rulers of separate principalities with the help of such mercenaries. Under their chieftains or *hetmans*, who were sometimes outlawed gentry themselves, groups of Cossacks were engaged to construct and garrison border fortresses or to conduct allegedly retaliatory or defensive raiding expeditions against Tatars or Turks.[59] Starting in the 1570's rulers along the Danube began to employ Cossacks from the Ukraine as mercenaries.[60] Like their ancient *'apiru* counterparts in the ancient Near East, the Cossacks took payment in supplies, landholdings, and certain rights allowed by the states they served, including their own independence from state taxation and control. They also surely profited from the booty raised in their raiding expeditions allowed, if not actually encouraged, by their royal or noble sponsors.[61] In their larger-scale raids, either for their patrons or for independent advantage, Cossacks were capable of capturing whole towns. Like the *'apiru*, however, they did not retain control, and retired with their booty to their semi-independent life and territory.[62]

Values of Freedom, Equality and Group Independence

As semi-independent communities of free men who were not under the direct rule of other men, the *'apiru* were surely bearers of values of freedom and independence. Our data provides little evidence directly on the values or "religion" of the *'apiru*. It is clear that *'apiru* formed independent or semi-independent communities separate from both peasant villages and the royal courts of the ancient Near East, the two other principal forms of community. From Hittite and Ugaritic texts we know that *'apiru* had towns or districts of their own.[63] Their territory was an attraction to refugees, but the kings who needed their military services allowed them to coexist semi-independently on the fringes of society, apparently as separate mini-societies. Mendenhall thinks that "characteristic of several *'apiru* groups, as attested by in Western Asiatic sources, is an established relationship between the group and a deity, usually through the

---

[58] Longworth, 80-81.
[59] Gordon, 65; cf. 89-91.
[60] Gordon, 106.
[61] Gordon, 157-158, etc; cf. the functional equivalent in Eastern Europe: besides the Haiduks in Hungary, the Szeklers in Transylvania, and the Grenzers in Austria, Longworth, 344, n. 9.
[62] Gordon, 116-118; McNeill, 78, 115-118.
[63] Greenberg, 194-195; Cazelles, 14.

mediation of a priest."[64] The particular deity would have served to preserve "the precarious existence of an outlaw group rather than for establishing the legitimacy of a government."[65] It is tempting to reason from the structural independence of the *'apiru* groups that their deities and priests were in some way expressions of their concern for their own liberty and brotherhood as groups free of city-state or imperial domination.

Such speculation is all the more justified by the parallel provided by evidence of Cossack communities' ideology of freedom and communitarian equality. Like the ancient *'apiru,* the Cossacks had established semi-independent communities (villages, brotherhoods) of free men, no longer subject to serfdom, tribute, and jurisdiction of lords and the state.[66] One of the key points at which Cossacks would form alliances to fight against the lords or state who had previously paid them as mercenaries was when those lords or state began to encroach on the independence of their communities.[67] Most Cossacks were nominally and/or politically Orthodox in their explicitly "religious" alliance or allegiance. But more importantly, they held intensely certain other values or commitments. We can discern and describe these as personal freedom, group solidarity, equality, and group independence.

The strong and persistent sense of *personal freedom* was rooted in their typical origins as escaped serfs. It continued as a fierce sense of individual independence, subject ultimately to no other man. Gordon speaks of a natural "creaming" effect that took place in the formation of Cossack groups and values: only the most free-spirited and rebellious would have left the security of village communities, where families had lived for generations, to risk their fortunes in the wild country.[68] Cossacks had always to agree individually to follow a certain course of action or campaign. Any individual Cossack was always free to leave the group and go on his own way.[69] When Bogdan Khmelnitsky sent out the call to arms against encroaching Polish domination in the Ukraine, he appealed to this traditional passion for individual freedom: "You whose fathers recognize no laws, who never subjected themselves to kings, be slaves no longer."[70]

Perhaps this intense passion for personal freedom among the Cossacks made rituals and ideology of *loyalty to the group* all the more important. Cossack bands were somewhere between a kinship group and a state in social form. Social organization was affected by their military or raiding activity. As Gordon points out, "By using kinship as a metaphor for loyalty, these groups were able

---

[64] Mendenhall, *Tenth Generation,* 131.
[65] Greenberg, *The Hab/piru,* 133.
[66] Longworth, 88, 102, 128; Gordon, 74.
[67] Longworth, 128.
[68] Gordon, 75-76; Longworth, 41.
[69] Gordon, 84.
[70] Longworth, 101-102.

to demand powerful commitments from their members." Because of their character as fighting groups, commitment to the group often involved extreme risk-taking. Punishments for disloyalty were correspondingly severe. Cossack bands engaged in great fanfare of fetishes, symbols and ceremonies of loyalty, which served to internalize the commitment. "This density of ritual is characteristic of fraternal organization."[71] Considering their individualistic origins as refugees with no previous ethnic or other horizontal social relationships, and their precarious and marginal situation socially and politically, this "density of fraternal ritual" was surely important for group cohesion and self-preservation. Although the value of loyalty to other Cossacks might appear to stand in tension with the passion for individual freedom, it could also serve to support that freedom (the two value usually were mutually reinforcing in practice). In case after case, when the state and noble magnates pressured the Cossack bands they had engaged as border guards or mercenaries to block the flow of refugee serfs, the freedom-loving Cossacks steadfastly refused, even at the risk of their own security, payments and continuing independence.

Within the brotherhood – and even with respect to those who might be expected to join – there was a strong sense of *equality* and (depending on one's viewpoint) democratic or "mob-rule" decision-making. Stenka Razin, leader of the massive revolt in the late 1660's expressed this sense of equality along with that of the passion for freedom in appealing to captive soldiers and slaves to join the Cossacks: "You who are free; you can go wherever you like ... but anyone who joins me will become a free Cossack. I'm only out to trash the boyars and the rich gentlemen. With poor and ordinary men I'll share everything like a brother."[72] The spoils from the Cossack raids were divided equally, and their land and fishing and hunting rights were held in common. Longworth cites cases from Cossack bands' dealings with receiving or sending ambassadors from/to Muscovy in which they insisted upon dividing goods equally among themselves since "there were no great men among them; all were equal"; or they collectively elected the ambassador because they had no "best people," and "all were equal to one another."[73] Even among Cossacks of the Ukraine, among whom there had been a high percentage of outlaw gentry from the beginning, this sense of equality had become strong in the sixteenth century, although it then dissipated considerably as more and more became drawn into the ranks of the landed gentry through the Register. But the egalitarian sense continued strong into the seventeenth century among Cossack bands along the southeastern frontiers of Muscovy.[74]

Cossack bands apparently made major decisions, such as the launching of a major aid or military expedition and the selection or deposition of their leaders,

---

[71]Gordon, 82-83.
[72]Longworth, 132, n. 11.
[73]Longworth, 40-41.
[74]Longworth, 132.

by process of group "discussion." Whether one labels this a form of primitive participatory democracy or simple "mob-rule," participation by the membership in a general assembly or military council (*Krug*, "circle," or *Rada* in the Ukraine) was essential as a means of self-government among bands of freedom-loving, anti-statist individualists.[75] Even when some Cossacks had attained a privileged status in the Ukraine, they still refused to accept the principle of class *rule*, i.e., that political power should follow from a title and control of land.[76]

The Cossacks, finally, steadfastly insisted upon their own *group-independence* as separate communities or brotherhoods, subject to no lord or state. For some time Cossack bands remained relatively unchallenged in their independent existence out in the wild country, a kind of no man's land, and balanced off threats of hegemony by their own dealings with various political entities. As the state and greedy landlords moved hungrily south and east to claim lands which had been settled or otherwise opened up by Cossack communities, the latter fought back, even forming cooperative alliances to resist.[77]

Role in Peasant Revolts

Many studies of the 'Apiru mention little or nothing concerning their role in popular revolts. However, Biblical scholars such as Chaney and Gottwald who find the "revolt model" to be the most intelligible way to account for the emergence of early Israel in the hill country of Palestine (in the thirteenth-eleventh centuries) explain that the *'apiru* were a crucial component in the peasant revolt or "withdrawal" which resulted in a new social order (at least in the hill country).[78] Chaney has elucidated how the *'apiru* may have contributed to the Israelite revolt by bringing Hobsbawm's comparative studies of social banditry and peasant revolt to bear on evidence from the Amarna letters. Because of both the limitations and the ambiguity of the evidence from the Amarna archives, of course, we are limited to informed conjectures on the relationship of *'apiru* bands to popular rebellions. However, this makes Hobsbawm's comparative studies and the potential parallels provided by the Cossacks all the more useful in attempting to reconstruct the origins of early Israel.

Hobsbawm found that social banditry has three kinds of relationships with wider peasant agitations (of which it may be the primitive form as well as the precursor), which Chaney has explored in connection with the Amarna evidence.[79] Evidence on the Cossacks' relations with peasant uprisings in the Ukraine and Russia provide important variations on the relationships discerned

---

[75]Longworth, 36-37; Gordon, 84; McNeill, 113.
[76]Gordon, 87.
[77]Longworth, 128.
[78]Chaney, esp. 49-57 & 81-83; Gottwald, esp. 474-492.
[79]Hobsbawm, "Social Banditry," 146-148; *Bandits,* ch. 7.

by Hobsbawm, variations which may further elucidate the possible roles that the ancient 'apiru may have played in Canaanite peasant revolts.

Hobsbawm finds, *first*, that "banditry and more ambitious types of peasant movements tend to flourish in the same areas, if not actually to live in symbiosis."[80] This generalization would appear to be applicable also to Cossacks and peasant revolts in the Ukraine and Russia, but in a somewhat different form or sense. Bandits were small outlaw bands in close proximity and relations with the peasant villages from which they originated in areas under nominal state control. Cossacks, on the other hand, were generally semi-independent communities which were sufficiently large and powerful relative to the state that the latter was forced to respect their independent existence in their own territory (usually on the frontier). Cossacks were separated from the peasant villages from which they had fled and which were still under nominal landlord or state control. As with banditry and peasant revolt, so also with Cossacks and popular rebellion, frontier areas (and areas of administrative inefficiency) were especially susceptible to increased flight of peasants into the ranks of the Cossacks and to cooperation between outlaw bands and peasant villages. In joining or leading a popular revolt, however, the Cossacks were crossing over from their own recognized turf (the wild country of the steppe) to join peasant insurgents in state-controlled territory from which they had previously fled.

The relation of the 'apiru to peasant rebellion would appear to have ben similar to that of the Cossacks, only on a far smaller scale in the sort of terrain which prevails in Palestine and Syria. As already noted, the 'apiru appear to have been semi-independent bands or communities with their own territory on the fringes of the Canaanite city-states. Because of the rugged terrain, the mountains and valleys which provided natural barriers and divisions between the small city-states and petty principalities of Canaan, however, 'apiru bands were in much closer physical proximity to peasant villages than were the Cossack communities. They may well have been 'apiru serving as mercenary forces for city-states in the coastal plain. But as Chaney points out, it was only in the remoter areas, particularly the mountainous terrain, where the chariot forces of the city-states could not operate effectively, that 'apiru bands could form in the first place and that more ambitious rebellions by peasants or 'apiru could occur.

The *second* relationship Hobsbawm discerns is that, "at times when mass unrest grips the peasantry, banditry merges with these larger movements, and notable increases in banditry may indeed prepare and announce them."[81] Insofar as Cossacks or Haiduks are another variant form of social banditry (the escape valve or social form which peasant protest takes when conditions are intolerable), increased flight of peasants to join Cossacks on the frontier, like the increase in banditry, may well be the precursor of widespread peasant revolt. For

---

[80]Hobsbawm, "Social Banditry," 146.
[81]Hobsbawm, "Social Banditry," 146.

example, there was extensive famine and social upheaval in Muscovy during the "Time of Troubles" under Boris Gudunov, at the very beginning of the seventeenth century. "Many landlords were unable or unwilling to feed their peasants, and yet these peasants were no longer allowed to move to other lords who might provide for them. Boyars began to sack their retainers and, inevitably, crowds of destitutes took to the roads looking for subsistence. Many turned to brigandage, and many sought refuge with the Cossacks of the frontier."[82] There ensued several years of devil war and extensive popular uprisings led by Cossacks.[83] Again at mid-century, during the decades preceding the revolt led by the Cossacks under Stenka Razin, ten of thousands of peasants fled to the Cossack areas and not only swelled their ranks but produced a distinct stratum of Cossack poor known as "the naked ones."[84] In both these and other cases, the massive flight to the Cossack areas "prepared and announced" the revolts which were to come.

However, while the bandits studied by Hobsbawm merged with or were absorbed into larger movements of popular revolt, the Cossacks appear more to have led or even to have touched off massive peasant rebellions. During the "Time of Troubles," (1606) for example, Ivan Bolotnikov, at the head of a coalition of his own Cossack band, a large contingent of Don Cossacks, and a host of Zaporozhian Cossacks, rallied to the cause of the (spurious) Tsarevich Peter. Serfs and peasants by the thousands joined the revolt to place a "good" Tsar on the throne of Russia.[85] In another time of famine two generations later (1666), when Vasili Us and his 500 Cossacks marched northwards into the Russian province of Voronezh, hordes of hungry peasants joined the insurrection – and Us refused to surrender the peasants with him when the authorities attempted to buy off the Cossacks.[86] Then a few years later, Stenka Razin actively appealed to the peasants to join his rebellion against "the traitorous nobles and advisers," promising to bring "freedom to the poor."[87] Similarly in the Ukraine, rebellions such as that against the polish magnates i 1590 were actively and definitively led by Cossack bands and leaders such as Kristov Kosinsky.[88] The mass uprisings in the Ukraine aiming to subvert the feudal

---

[82]Longworth, 76.
[83]Longworth, 78.
[84]Longworth, 126-130. On the Cossack role in the seventeenth century Russian peasant uprisings in comparative perspective, see further M.O. Gately, A.L. Moote, and J.E. Wills, "Seventeenth-century Peasant 'Furies:' Some Problems in Comparative History," *Past and Present* 51 (1971). 68-80; and R. Mousnier, *Peasant Uprisings in Seventeenth-century France, Russia and China* (London: Allen & Unwin, 1971).
[85]Longworth, 78.
[86]Longworth, 129.
[87]Longworth, 140-148. Further illustration could be given from the revolt led by Pugachev in 1773-75; besides Longworth's chapter in *Cossacks,* see his "The Pugachev Revolt: The Last Great Cossack-Peasant Rising," in *Rural Protest* (see note 4, above), 194-256; and "Peasant Leadership and the Pugachev Revolt," *Journal of Peasant Studies* 2 (1974-75), 183-205.
[88]Gordon, 113-121.

system were provoked by the Cossacks, although the peasants and townspeople "used" the Cossacks for their own purposes as much as the Cossacks "used" the people for their own.[89]

The *'apiru* groups mentioned in the Amarna letters appear to have been more like the Cossacks than regular social bandits in their relation to broader peasant movements. They appear more to have helped provoke peasant uprisings than to have merged with broader popular movements. The kings or governors in Amarna Canaan such as Rib Adda of Byblos appear anxious that their peasants or towns have joined with the *'apiru* troops. *'Apiru* groups (and not simply the *'apiru* Abdi-Ashirta) are already active threats to the governors or kings, who are afraid that their own peasants will make common cause with the outlaw troops.[90] The *'apiru* similarity to the Cossacks can be thrown into relief with a parallel to Hobsbawm's social bandits from later Jewish history. It is clear from Josephus' histories that Jewish social banditry escalated to epidemic proportions in the 60s CE and *merged with* a widespread peasant revolt against Roman rule in Palestine, both in the battles against Cestius Gallus near Jerusalem and in the general uprising in Galilee.[91] Judging from the correspondence of the panicked governors in Armana Canaan, however, the *'apiru* groups inaugurated hostilities against their cities and provoked and then led the broader popular uprisings.

In the *third* relationship distinguished by Hobsbawm, "banditry may itself provide the model or cadre of certain kinds of primitive peasant insurrection or guerrilla activity."[92] Hobsbawm is somewhat vague in his delineation of this third relationship between social bandits and broader peasant movements. As Chaney correctly discerns, he apparently has in mind primarily "the systematic use of bandit tactics and experience for the technically very similar activities of guerrilla warfare."[93]

However, beyond this similarity of bandit tactics and guerrilla warfare – shared by social bandits and Cossacks alike, as well as by peasant revolts – the Cossacks provide a model or cadre for broader peasant insurrection. In his chapter on "Bandits and Revolution" Hobsbawm comments that "the Cossacks, who developed large and structured permanent communities of their own, and very substantial mobilizations for their raiding campaigns, provided only leaders and not models for the great peasant insurrections: It was as "people's tsars" and not as atamans that they mobilized these."[94] This is surely true of the overall

---

[89] Gordon, 151, 164, 181.
[90] See esp. the selections for which Chaney provides a vivid English translation, Chaney, 73-76.
[91] Horsley,"Ancient Jewish Banditry," esp. 426-432; Josephus, *Jewish War* 2.503-512, 541, 562-563; 4.84; *Life* 7, 77, 105-111. Cf. Hobsbawm, *Bandits,* 102: "Banditry is therefore more likely to come into peasant revolutions as one aspect of a multiple mobilization, and knowing itself to be a subordinate aspect ..."
[92] Hobsbawm, "Social Banditry," 147.
[93] Chaney, 82; Hobsbawm "Social Banditry," 147.
[94] Hobsbawm, *Bandits,* 101-102.

purpose of goal of the uprisings in the Cossacks' minds. However, the Cossacks did provide a "model" as well as a "cadre" for "certain kinds of primitive peasant insurrections" in Russian history. As Hobsbawm himself states, but perhaps fails to appreciate, the rebellious peasants often imitated the Cossacks, even declaring themselves to be Cossacks. In response to the campaign led by Cossacks under Bolotnikov in 1606, thousands of peasants "turned Cossacks" and "threw over their landlords and chose their own atamans."[95] Stenka Razin offered the peasants as well as deserting Tsarist soldiers the opportunity to "become free Cossacks."[96] Following up on his Joshua and Jericho-like conquest of Tsaritsyn, Razin grouped the responsive people "into tens and hundreds and told them to elect atamans."[97] In town after town, Razin and his forces fostered the establishment of a "Cossacks democracy." To those who came to swear loyalty to Razin himself, he insisted that he would not be their sovereign; rather, they must continue to serve the Tsar but govern themselves grouped in tens and hundreds and choosing their own atamans.[98]

The tendency of Russian peasants to "become Cossacks" and to adopt Cossack forms in the course of their rebellions provides a striking parallel to the relation of peasants and *'apiru* as described (by governors) in the Amarna letters. Not only do the peasants and townspeople "act like *'apiru*," driving out or assassinating their governors, and not only do they "join with the *'apiru*" or "desert to the *'apiru*." There are even slaves who "become *'apiru*." The passages from the Amarna letters provided by Chaney in translation at the beginning of his Excursus ("The *'Apiru* and Social Unrest ...") offer some vivid parallels to the Cossack-led peasant rebellions especially that headed by Stenka Razin. Most striking of all are the communications from Abdu-Heba of Jerusalem and Milkilu of Gezer:

> ... but now *'apiru* hold the cities of the king. There is not one "governor" (left) to the king, my lord – all are lost! Behold, Turbazu has been slain in the (very) gate of Sile, (yet) the king is negligent. Behold, (as for) Zimrida of Lachish, servants who had become *'apiru* smote him.[99]

> ... Let the king, my lord, know that the hostility against me and against Shuwardata is powerful. So let the king, my lord, deliver his land from the hand of the *'apiru*. If not let the king, my lord, send chariots to fetch us, that our servants not slay us.[100]

Like the Cossacks in Russia and the Ukraine, so the *'apiru* in Amarna Canaan provided aggressive leadership and provocation for wider popular rebellion. The

---

[95]Longworth, 78.
[96]Longworth, 132-138.
[97]Longworth, 142-143.
[98]Longworth, 144-146.
[99]*EA* 288:36-43, cited from Chaney, 74.
[100]*EA* 271:9-21, cited from Chaney, 74.

peasantry in response deserted to the *'apiru,* joined the *'apiru* in attacking their kings/governors, and even became *'apiru,* as they broke away from our overthrew the ruling class of the city-states. The *'apiru,* like the Cossacks, appear to have provided a model for the peasants at least at the beginning stages of widespread popular revolt.

Finally, because of their size and relative independence, the Cossacks and *'apiru* groups had yet a *fourth* relationship to broader peasant rebellion, one not shared by the typical social banditry in Hobsbawm's analysis. As Gordon points out in connection with Cossacks-led rebellions in the Ukraine,

> Through ability to maintain their autonomous space, military prowess and assertiveness in demanding liberties, the Cossacks frequently created dual power situations, to use the classic terms of history of revolutions. In other words, the Cossacks, consciously or not, periodically created alternative power centers to that of the central government.[101]

Combined with the weakness of local and central governments, the alternative power base of a large semi-independent community of warriors made possible the frequent and temporarily successful widespread popular insurrections touched off and led by Cossacks in the Ukraine and Russia. The large and semi-independent *'apiru* bands in Amarna Canaan would appear to have had a similar relation to the rebellions of their subjects spoken of by the kings and governors in the diplomatic correspondence of the Armana archives.

Revolutionary?

However much they provoked and led peasant rebellions, the Cossacks and the ancient *'apiru* were ultimately no more revolutionary in the political sense than were the bandits analyzed by Hobsbawm. Socially as well as geographically their communities were more cut off from the peasantry than were social bandits, who remained in close contact with and proximity to their villages of origin. The Cossacks' and *'apiru's* very mercenary status meant that they were semi-dependent on the system. If they were in the employ of or allied with one local ruler/magnate, they did not hesitate to plunder the villagers under the authority of another principality.

As semi-independent communities of free men, the Cossacks made virtually no attempt to extend their privileges of self-government and certain rights to their peasant sympathizers or townspeople.[102] They were concerned primarily with their own independence. They often stopped fighting in a given rebellion when they had regained that independence or recognition of their traditional special rights and privileges. They had virtually no long-term offensive goals, no universalized social ideals, no broad-ranging critical analysis of the social

---

[101]Gordon, 210.
[102]Gordon, 85.

system on the fringes of which they operated, no revolutionary program beyond getting rid of particular forms of oppression.[103] Peasants were often far more revolutionary in their goals or social program, having in mind at least the structural change in the system of abolishing serfdom. Even in the midst of widespread peasant rebellions the Cossacks had no sense of their potential power as peasant leaders or of the potential power of alliance between Cossack communities and the peasantry.[104]

The principal times during which the Cossacks thought of the possibility of extending their privileges and freedom to others was in the midst of revolts they had touched off. But they could apparently conceptualize this only in terms of peasants or townspeople or former soldiers *becoming Cossacks* and/or organizing their villages or towns like Cossack bands. But Cossack communities did not provide an adequate model for constructing a new social order. The Cossack brotherhood was indeed a social form capable of expansion. As noted already, it was a network of connections and loyalties in between kinship and nation. As bands of professional raiders or mercenary fighters "settled down" they included part-time fighter peasants with families who worked the land or raised some livestock. There thus appeared "whole communities which reproduced themselves, making Cossackness hereditary, one of the requirements of nationality. The snowballing of the Cossack groups in times of rebellion, and their spreading reputation even in peace time, provided a point of identity for people who were neither kin nor neighbors." Moreover, the "brotherhood developed a rough model or self-government ... and mechanisms for collective decision-making."[105] Yet the Cossacks' continuing self-identification as a military brotherhood with a military organization, with the corresponding lack of a sense of responsibility for any broader social whole, arrested their developing into a model for a new agrarian society, a new order for a whole people. In one of the ironies of history, in Russia at least, Cossack fighters of the nineteenth and twentieth centuries ended up as some of the last defenders of the very autocratic and hierarchical social order which their original ancestors had desperately fled, repeatedly opposed, and periodically rebelled against.

Similarly, as Gottwald points out, the *'apiru* in Amarna Canaan did not constitute "an egalitarian social movement that directly challenged" the established social-economic system. Insofar as early Israel was a evolutionary break with the established order, it cannot simply have evolved gradually out of *'apiru* communities expanding as they absorbed more and more of the peasants withdrawing from the Canaanite city-states. Indeed, in the course of his qualification of his main point about the prerevolutionary character of the *'apiru*, Gottwald appears to overstate their role and effect as "nuclei" for a new social order. He suggests that "*'apiru* of longer standing provided fugitive peasants

---

[103] Gordon, 117-118, 140, 212; Hobsbawm, *Bandits,* 101-102.
[104] Gordon, 212-213.
[105] Gordon, 211.

with "adaptive organization."[106] Actually, Gottwald implicitly corrects his own overstatement of the case a few paragraphs later: As local and central governments control weakened, "'*Apiru*, no longer receiving regular supplies from a dynasty, would tend to settle and cultivate land as their own. Villagers, openly or covertly resistant to the authorities, would tend to develop local defense measures."[107] In other words, far from the *'apiru* communities providing any sort of model for the new social order, they provided primarily the fighting experience. They may also have provided the military organization, but certainly not the models of social and economic organization. As local city-state power crumbled or fell to popular rebellion, the *'apiru* groups necessarily would have ceased operations as mercenaries of these governments. If any new social order was to emerge, they also had to cease operations as raiders, at least on the villagers with whom they were now allied or even leading in resistance to the city-state rulers.

The social and economic model for the new order was provided not by the *'apiru* but by the peasant village communes which may have been crumbling under the heavy exactions of the ruling class, but which were still very much alive in the minds of the peasants now becoming free of their (former) overlords. The *'apiru* bands surely provided a refuge and a military organization for fugitive Canaanite peasants. But if a new social order was to emerge to supplant the old one, in which *'apiru* were social-economic dependents and parasites, the model had to come from outside the *'apiru* experience. The very example chosen by Gottwald to illustrate how *'apiru* bands functioned as a model can be extended to illustrate how the *'apiru* community and experience were inadequate for any truly revolutionary result. The destitute out of Israel gathered to join David as a band of freebooters (1 Sam 22:1-2; 27:8-12). But of course they then became mercenaries in the hire of Philistine overlords (1 Sam 27:1-7). Finally, when David and his large band of *'apiru* became leaders of the Israelite rebellion against Philistine hegemony, the result was an imitation of the old established ancient Near Eastern social-economic order and a subversion of the more revolutionary order with which the Israelites had been experimenting for several generations before David.

Indeed, it may be primarily because of the emergence of early Israel that we even raise the question of the possible revolutionary character or effect of *'apiru* groups. Nevertheless, outside of Biblical and other evidence related to Israel, there is one other major set of evidence of *'apiru* activity resulting in a widespread revolt and the successful establishment of a new social-political entity. It is evident from the Amarna letters that a new "state" was emerging around the leadership of Abdi-Ashirta and his sons in middle Syria (Amurru). It is difficult to determine from the ambiguous word-usage of the Amarna letters

---

[106]Gottwald, 407.
[107]Gottwald, 408.

whether Abdi-Ashirta and his followers actually got their start as a band of *'apiru*. It seems clear, however, both that he used *'apiru* groups in expanding his sphere of influence and control and that he provoked the peasants of other states to rebel against their governments and to act like *'apiru*.[108] The result, however, was that the "state" brought into existence by Abdi-Ashirta and his sons was subject to Egyptian overlordship and that eventually the Hittite empire took control of his territory (Amurru). The parallel to the Ukrainian "state" or people brought together under the leadership of Bogdan Khmelnitsky only to come under the rule of the Muscovite Tsar is striking. In any case, the career of Abdi-Ashirta and his sons may provide another example of how *'apiru* groups provoked and headed widespread peasant insurrections, but could not or did not lead toward, or provide a model for any serious revolutionary change in the social-economic-political system.

Neither the Cossacks nor the *'apiru* played a genuinely revolutionary historical role. Both may have been protorevolutionary. Comparative analysis indicates that both had a passion for freedom. Having themselves originated as fugitives, both apparently received further peasant refugees into their ranks. Moreover, apparently *'apiru* as well as Cossacks provided both leadership and a model for discontented peasants as social unrest turned to outright revolt. Hence the Cossacks and the *'apiru* both displayed a certain revolutionary potential. In order for genuine social as well as political revolutions to occur, however, conceptions of different social orders and new social forms were necessary. In Russian history such a combination of factors did not come about until early in the twentieth century – and by then, ironically, the Cossacks, having long since been co-opted by the Tsar, fought against the revolution. In the ancient Near East, on the other hand, bands of *'apiru* joined with other forces to form a new people, which succeeded in establishing an alternative social order in the hill country of Palestine. Nevertheless, while *'apiru* bands provided fighting experience and leadership, the concept of a new social order came from elsewhere, and the *'apiru*, until David at least, apparently became part of the independent peasant society of premonarchic Israel.

---

[108] Chaney, 73, 82; Liverani, "Social Implications ...," (see note 27, above), 18-20.

Chapter Two

Ancient Israel's Scripture and Its Religion: The Achievement of Helmer Ringgren

Ernest S. Frerichs
Brown University

The twentieth anniversary of the English translation of Helmer Ringgren's study of Israelite religion provides a desirable basis for renewing the life of this work for the English reader. This Scandinavian scholar, successor to Ivan Engnell at the University of Upsala, contended successfully with certain tendencies of his age in the approach to ancient Israelite religion, and offered a distinctive Scandinavian flavor to comparable studies of the 1950s and 1960s.

The entire notion that one could study the religion of ancient Israel as a discrete field, distinct from the religion of the Bible, and justified on grounds independent of its contribution to the formative stages of Judaism and Christianity, is itself a very modern view. Born in the eighteenth century, this view would experience several revolutions before Ringgren's study. Perhaps the most far-reaching of these changes was that effected by the decipherment of several Near Eastern languages in the nineteenth century and later, a change which opened to students and scholars the vast estate of life in ancient Egypt and the world of Sumeria, Assyria and Babylonia.

The public exposure of the ancient Near East, within which ancient Israel stood as a small state to be likened and contrasted, was a new era for the study of Near Eastern antiquity. The last century and a half has seen the development of a series of new fields – Sumerology, Egyptology, Assyriology – and the continuing exploration of all aspects of those cultures and civilizations, including their religious life. Those changes altered forever the way in which ancient Israel would be studied. Never again would it be so simple to subsume ancient Israel entirely within Judaism and Christianity and to use the perspectives of those religions as the way to view the religious phenomena of ancient Israel. The Bible would emerge as a library of ancient Near Eastern religious life and practice, not just the basis for early Jewish and Christian faith and ritual.

The changes inaugurated in the nineteenth century would place Israel in a context of other religions of the ancient Near East, an entry in that catalogue which would encourage approaches from other contemporary religious traditions. This shift would lead Ringgren to affirm that the main issues of "Israel's Place among the Religions of the Ancient Near East" (*Supplements to Vetus Testamentum* XXIII [1972], 1) is the issue of "similarity and difference."

Professor Ringgren's *Israelite Religion* gives serious attention to the question of similarity and difference. On the one side, he rejects the "parallelomania" which is fueled by the search for parallels by traditions which share commonalities in language, or time, or place. Ringgren's study confronts the assertion of parallels with a series of questions. Does the identified parallel have the same place in the life of its community, does it fulfill the same function in its own culture? The quest here for Ringgren is the quest for the *sitz im leben,* the situation in the life of the communities when the identification of parallels is proclaimed.

If the study of comparative religion was a major outcome of decipherment breakthroughs, Ringgren shows serious concern for understanding what it was that was being compared.

As comparative religion spawned an approach labeled "history of religions," the tendency toward absorbing Israel totally within the ancient Near East continued and grew. Interest in any nexus between ancient Israel and subsequent Judaism and Christianity declined. The Mesopotamian and Egyptian domination of the ancient Near East led to a minor role for Israel viewed as the cultural pariah of the mighty empires of its time. Assyriology and Egyptology grew, informed by a view of their own cultural superiority in the ancient Near East and understanding Israel as little more than a minor state within which the cultural traditions of the ancient Near Eastern empires would find expression. Israel was a melting pot of cultural droppings from the giant empires of its time. The rise of Palestinian archaeology at the end of the nineteenth century did little more than to underscore the dependence of Israel upon its larger neighbors in terms of all the arts of civilization. The forms, styles, architecture and cultic practice of Israelite religion were presumed to be understood best as borrowings from developments elsewhere in the major centers of ancient Near Eastern life.

There was a predictable response to this direction in the period before and after the Second World War. Various scholars, Christian and Jewish, strove to regain a distinctive role for Israel among the nations of the ancient Near East. This reaction took several forms. One was to deny that Israel bore any resemblance to the environment of its time, more closely in Canaan, more distantly in Mesopotamia and Egypt.

A particular form of this protest was to inveigh against parallels and to cry out for a distinctive Israelite expression which was not only original, but indeed unique. The late G. Ernest Wright's work, *The Old Testament and Its Environment* (1950), was a rallying center for those who wished to preserve

Israel from the pollution of popular ancient Near Eastern religion. Such an effort sought not only to demonstrate the distinctive character of Israelite religion, but indeed to portray an Israel superior in religious understanding to the other religious expressions of the ancient Near East (Patrick D. Miller, "Israelite Religion," Douglas A. Knight and Gene M. Tucker, eds., *The Hebrew Bible and its Modern Interpreters* [1985], 201-237).

The drive of Wright's work was to focus on the "faith" of ancient Israel and to argue for a certain theological uniqueness in the Israelite tradition. Assertions were made about the unique Israelite understanding of history as the particular arena of God's revelation.

If the revolt of Christian scholarship against the history-of-religions approach is exemplified in the work of G. Ernest Wright, a parallel rejection by Jewish scholarship was occurring in the extensive *History of Israelite Religion* by Yehezkel Kaufmann. Kaufmann's work stressed the historical elements in Israelite religion and the rejection of those assertions of comparative religionists who stressed the common ancient Near Eastern background with emphases on nature and mythology. Paganism was to be rejected and with it all attempts to portray Israelite religion as characterized by borrowed polytheism or idolatry.

Into such a world came the distinctive work of Helmer Ringgren. The theological reaction to the comparativists and the dominance of views such as those of Wright and Kaufmann were chronicled in 1957 by W. A. Irwin ("The Study of Israel's Religion," *Vetus Testamentum* 7 [1957], 113-126). Irwin states the concern of many in 1957 in the face of a "biblical theology" appropriation of the religion of ancient Israel. Such an approach has little serious interest in that which is not focused on the major traditions of Judaism and Christianity. In addition, the emphasis against which Irwin spoke is that which stresses the contemporaneity of the biblical tradition. His cry of alarm is directed both to those who fall to the aridity of archaism as well as to those who fail to see the curse of contemporaneity.

Ringgren was very aware of these dangers and wrote *Israelite Religion* as a guide to the better directions of the study of Israelite religion for the future and a rejection of several obvious trends of his time. He wished neither to succumb to the perils of parallels nor to surrender to a theological perspective which took its guidelines from the concerns of formative Judaism or Christianity. Ringgren was clear that the tradition of Israel bore the marks of many Near Eastern traditions; it was not the product of an "isolated vacuum" (H. Ringgren, "The Impact of the Ancient Near East on Israelite Tradition," D. Knight, ed., *Tradition and Theology in the Old Testament* [1977], 31-46). Ringgren's concern was to demonstrate that when borrowing occurred, the borrowing was adapted to suit the environment of ancient Israel.

Ringgren himself is a modifier of more radical emphases in his own time. No more striking example of this can be offered than his view of kingship, an area of central concern to Old Testament scholars of Scandinavia. "Divine kingship" is not a helpful term to Ringgren, who prefers to speak of "sacral kingship." He is restrained in his approach to notions of any particular Israelite royal ideology. There is a frank recognition of important differences between conceptions of sacral kingship in Israel, differences which include both opposition and acceptance of sacral kingship. We are made aware of differences pre-Davidic and post-Davidic, southern kingdom and northern kingdom, biblical texts which favor and those which oppose. Claims of royal divinity are viewed with great caution, especially in the light of a varied tradition which can view the king as the son of God, the anointed of the Lord, or the servant of the Lord. Despite this restraint, Ringgren will still affirm an Israelite king who has sacral duties and functions.

The more radical statements, especially from Scandinavian scholarship, of kingship-patternism decline in the third quarter of the twentieth century. A major figure in the modification of those radical statements is Helmer Ringgren (W. Zimmerli, "The History of Israelite Religion," G.W. Anderson, ed., *Tradition and Interpretation* [1979], 351-384).

The approach of Ringgren to the history of Israelite religion is clear in the structures of his book which show the centrality of the monarchy in his conception. The first part of Israel's history through the Judges is described as "pre-Davidic." The heart of the book, chapter II, is dedicated to "The Religion in the Period of the Monarchy" and the final section of the book is devoted to "The Exilic and Postexilic Period (Judaism)." The centrality of kingship, and of Davidic kingship, is clear. The importance of "the Davidic Covenant," however, is to serve as a symbol for introducing the idea of kingship as a blanket for earlier terminology. The national hopes of Israel can be carried forward by the use of language such as phrases describing the king as the monarch of the world.

Ringgren is a moderating, modifying scholar who makes his way among the positions of scholarly extremity in his day. He himself is clear about the degree to which the student of Israelite religion can "easily lose his way in a jungle of diverse opinions and dogmatically conditioned judgments."

The merit of his study is to have modified the view of his own age in attractive ways and to have interpreted with fair accuracy the direction of the succeeding phases in the study of Israelite religion. In straight-forward terms he invites the reader to find in his study "a history of the Israelite religion, with primary emphasis on a descriptive presentation of the religion during the period of the monarchy." His invitation is accurate and the reader of twenty years later will find the book a commendable introduction to the history of Israelite religion.

Chapter Three

The Present State of Research on Joseph and Aseneth

Christoph Burchard
University of Heidelberg

In 1952 G.D. Kilpatrick published a note on the Last Supper because he felt he had discovered through the romance of Joseph and Aseneth (JosAs) an alternative to the Passover meal as a possible background of Jesus' last meal.[1] In a quick rejoinder J. Jeremias tried to show that Kilpatrick's argument was ill-founded but he underscored the importance of JosAs as a historical source for ancient Judaism and hence the *Umwelt* of the New Testament. This was how modern research on JosAs was born. Up to that time the book had been a dark horse, and particularly to those who ought to have been most interested, viz. the students of the Bible and of Judaism in the Greco-Roman world. JosAs was available in various languages, both ancient and modern, and standard reference works such as E. Schürer referred to it. It is true that the Greek text published by P. Batiffol in 1889-90 was hard to find. Moreover, as Schürer reported, Batiffol had presented JosAs as a Byzantine work of the 5th century which was based on a short Jewish legend of the 4th. Although it was soon discovered that the book must be Jewish and is no later than A.D. 100, few scholars stopped to look it up. Kilpatrick and Jeremias made the tide turn, and the boom of Biblical and Jewish studies beginning in the sixties of this century gave it fresh momentum, particularly by way of the new Pseudepigrapha collections which are sprouting all over the scholarly world. JosAs has been re-edited, translated, commented upon, exploited, and viewed with an interested eye generally in a diversity of quarters. It is not too early for an assessment of what has been achieved and what remains to be done.[2]

---

[1] Bibliographical references are given in the bibliography at the end. I wish to thank Mrs. Helga Wolf for typing and correcting the manuscript.
[2] A careful survey of research up to 1978 is by D. Sänger, *Antikes Judentum und die Mysterien*. For a general introduction one may consult the newer translations or one of the recent handbooks on ancient Jewish literature, e.g. by J.H. Charlesworth, A.-M. Denis or G. Nickelsburg.

1. The Text

JosAs is no better off than ancient literature in general. The autograph, if there ever was one, is lost. Reconstructing it, after a thorough analysis of the tradition which emanated from it, is the prime task incumbent on scholarship. It is by no means completed.

JosAs is extant today in 16 Greek manuscripts dating from the 10th to the 19th centuries, and in 7 ancient or early modern translations dating from the 6th to the 17th centuries and representing so many more Greek manuscripts. An Ethiopic version once existed but appears to have left but a handful of reminiscences (see below). Little of that kind of secondary tradition is known in any other language except Latin, and what we have is of no avail to recover the original form of JosAs. This makes a total of 23 witnesses. They fall into at least four groups:[3]

- **a:** 6 Greek mss., the most important being Vatican Library, Vatican Greek 803 (11-12th cent.). This was printed by Batiffol.
- **b:** 4 Greek mss., namely Mt. Athos, Vatopedi, 600 (15th cent.); Virginia Beach, Va., private property of Mrs. Helen Greeley, formerly owned by D. McK. McKell, Chillicothe, Ohio (ca. A.D. 1580); Bucharest, Library of the Academy of the Socialist Republic of Rumania, Greek 966 (17th cent.); Mt. Sinai, St. Catherine, Greek 1976 (17th cent.), and 6 versions, namely Syriac (6th cent.), Armenian (6-7th cent.?), Latin I (prior to A.D. 1200), Latin II (prior to A.D. 1200), Modern Greek (16th cent.), and Rumanian (17th cent.). The Greek mss. were never published as such, the versions are available in printed editions except Latin II.
- **c:** 3 Greek mss., the oldest and most important being Jerusalem, Greek Orthodox Patriarchate, Panhagios Taphos 73 (17th cent.). None has ever been published as such.
- **d:** 2 Greek mss., namely Vatican Library, Palatine Greek 17 (11th cent.), and Oxford, Bodleian Library, Baroccio Greek 147 (15th cent.), and the Serbo-Slavonic version (15th cent. at the latest). A critical edition of **d** is by M. Philonenko.

Most scholars would agree that **a, b, c,** and **d** are families deriving from four different ancestors, α, β, ζ, and δ, and that there is a common archetype, ω, back of them all. Moreover, there is no doubt that α was a revision, no later than the 10th century, aiming at improving the biblicized Greek of JosAs to make it pleasant reading to Middle Byzantine eyes and ears. This means that Batiffol's edition is antiquated, and so are E.W. Brooks' and P. Rießler's translations which are based on it.[4] Batiffol anyway was no more than a mediocre transcription of Vatican Greek 803 with a faulty apparatus from some other witnesses. However, he gives a fair idea of what α was like because the Vatican codex is very good. Brooks is still useful since he was a meticulous translator and included some important passages from **b** and **d** not contained in α. Rießler is unreliable throughout, but he will be remembered because he

---

[3] Full inventory in *Untersuchungen*, pp. 4-17; *ANRW*, ch. iii.
[4] D. Cook first quoted the translation, if it is one, by M. Brodrick. I have not seen it.

broke JosAs down into verses which are still in use, although they are often too long (chapters are by Batiffol).

To replace Batiffol, two different attempts to unravel the textual history of JosAs have been developed. Philonenko opines that δ comes closest to ω. It is about one third shorter than α and even more than the other two families. 11:1x-18, most of chs. 18 and 19, 21:10-21 (read by some **b** witnesses only), 22:6b-9a and a series of verses and clauses extending over the whole range of the narrative are lacking. A manuscript close to δ was reworked and expanded into β at an early date, a **b** witness was then edited to yield ζ and last of all, a **c** manuscript became the *Vorlage* of α. Consequently, Philonenko proceeded to reconstruct a critical text on the base of δ touching it up now and then with the aid of other witnesses, mainly of the **b** group. The outcome is not quite what it might have been. Philonenko ought to have made more of the Serbo-Slavonic which he himself admits is often superior to the two Greek manuscripts. Furthermore, if the **b** group is an offshoot of δ or a related text which branched off very early it should have been taken into account in a systematical way, after some effort to determine the original β and its *Vorlage*. Finally, whereas Philonenko registers all variants from the **d** group he is eclectic as to the rest. Most of the excess matter from β, ζ, and α over against δ does not appear in the apparatus. So his reconstruction cannot be judged on his edition alone. Nevertheless, with the extensive introduction, a good French translation accompanied by suggestive footnotes and a Greek word list, Philonenko's is the most comprehensive work on JosAs as yet published. No wonder that A. Suski, M. de Goeij, R. Martínez Fernandez, A. Piñero, and D. Cook translated his text instead of Batiffol's. Incidentally, Philonenko devised a new system of versification to suit the shorter text; it was retained by his translators.

I myself have worked on a different line. It seems to me that δ is a shortened text, abbreviation being a common thing to happen to tales like JosAs. It originated no later than the 11th century. Since δ is much closer to α where they overlap than to β or ζ, including some manifest common mistakes e.g., in ch. 6, I suspect that they share a common ancestor αδ. α has preserved the length but altered the working, δ preserved the wording but reduced the bulk. It remains to be seen how old α, δ, and αδ were. A possible approach is to find out whether they were written in uncials or in a minuscule hand. Chances are that the three of them were produced during the Macedonian Renaissance in Byzantium (9th-10th centuries), which took pains to transcribe the literary heritage hitherto transmitted in uncials, and often edited it in the process. As to β, I would agree with Philonenko that it is very old. Its readings are often superior to those of αδ on inner grounds but not always, suggesting that the two are independent from each other. Finally, ζ is a late medieval or early modern product and probably never existed beyond 16:17a (it then goes on to summarize the story down to 21:9 in modern Greek). It cannot have been at the bottom of α or αδ, nor can it be an offshoot of those two because it is closer to, though not dependent upon, β. So I think that the idea that β, αδ, and ζ evolved in a straight line has to be abandoned altogether. This makes it harder for an editor in search of ω. He will have to constitute an eclectic text on the base of β, never reconstructed in itself so far, with help from αδ and ζ. I had a stab at it, not too wholeheartedly, by establishing a preliminary text because I needed one to translate for *JSHRZ* and *OTP*, and Batiffol or Philonenko would not do. The text provides just the raw words, but footnotes exhibiting the main differences between the groups are included in the translations.

The trouble with this text is that in piecing it together I have come to realize that the existence of β is far from being proven. **b** is a very variegated group in which several subgroups are discernible. My conclusion that they form a family with a common ancestor may have been precipitated by the discovery that they do not belong to either **a, c**, or **d**, but that is not enough. Further research into **b** is in order and of course, if **b** happens to disintegrate in the process, into the relationship of the ancestors of such new groups as may appear and the established ones, αδ and ζ. Attention ought to focus on the threesome, Syriac, Armenian, and Latin II. They have much in common and their readings are sometimes superior to their rivals on internal grounds, the Greek evidence included. Since Latin II has never been published and the Armenian only in a rather poor way (the most important manuscript, Erevan, Matenadaran, 1500, ca. A.D. 1282/83, is virtually unexploited), critical editions of those two are imperative.

That leaves us with a problem which exists no matter how the textual history of JosAs (and that of most other Pseudepigrapha, too) is conceived, but is aggravated if the Syriac, Armenian, and Latin II are major witnesses to its oldest form. Our Greek manuscripts are Middle or even Late Byzantine. Whatever variant is judged to be original, how can we be sure about the original Greek wording? If **b** readings are preferred the case is particularly difficult because the oldest Greek manuscript is 15th century. And what if a good reading from the older versions is not represented among the Greek **b** manuscripts but only by αδ or ζ, not to mention the need of retranslation if readings from the versions are not found in Greek at all? Fortunately many of these problems will not affect a translation.

A major critical edition will therefore not be produced before long, and not without help and advice from other scholars. To this end a minor edition presenting the textual evidence as fully as possible might be useful. I am thinking of republishing the preliminary text with a full apparatus from α, δ, ζ, and the major witnesses of the **b** group in some distant future.

If and when we know what ω was like, next comes the question of how it relates to the original JosAs. Philonenko feels that his text may be considered as the original for all practical purposes, and most scholars relying on Batiffol have handled his text in the same way. However, ω may not be that old. JosAs comes right after a piece ascribed to Ephraem Syrus (A.D. 306-377) and conveniently called *Life of Joseph* in a number of witnesses from all groups save c. The two works were seemingly coupled to make a complete dossier of the patriarch. There is a good chance that this goes back to ω or even a predecessor. If that is so, ω cannot be older than Ephraem, and it may be younger because the authenticity of the *Life* is disputed. In either case we have no textual evidence showing what happened to JosAs when it was engaged as a sequel to the *Life* and in the three or more centuries before that. We must allow at least for the ordinary run of scribal errors, but interpolations (cf. T. Holtz) and other forms of editing are not excluded *a priori*. So when ω is established, literary criticism, grammatical analysis, vocabulary statistics (then hopefully aided by A.-M. Denis' Concordance) and other means of literary detection will have to carry on where manuscript criticism stopped.

Most recently J. Schwartz has argued that JosAs started out as a short romantic piece which was composed in the Egyptian Diaspora prior to the revolt under Traian (ca. A.D. 115-117) and involved but the nucleus of the love story in chs. 1-21 and possibility the plot of chs. 22-29. It is lost. The extant forms of JosAs Schwartz feels are the outcome of a complicated process of rewriting most of which occurred in early Byzantine times in the context of Christian hagiography, with no such thing as an archetype discernible (an idea also suggested by Philonenko, but his textual reconstruction runs counter to it). So far Schwartz' analysis is restricted to isolated passages and therefore is more convincing to him than it is to me. But it is a welcome reminder that the existence of ω must not be taken for granted and that a period of darkness separates it from the original JosAs.

To close this section upon a conciliatory note: the original JosAs was a Greek work. Translation from Hebrew has been argued in the early days of JosAs research. But the idea seems to have been abandoned, and rightly so.

2. Literary Character and Genesis

The structure of JosAs is simple. It falls into two parts of unequal length with two different episodes told, chs. 1-21 and 22-29. Part I is laid out between two allusions to the biblical story of Joseph, Gen 41:46-49 and 41:50-52 respectively. So we are to understand from the outset that chs. 1-21 are an extended footnote to the Old Testament. They combine two plots, a story of sudden love and marriage engaging Aseneth and Joseph in chs. 3-9 and 19-21, and a conversion story involving Aseneth and the Prince of the Angels in chs. 10-18. Aseneth is the main character, being nearly always on the scene. The entire developments take place in the house of Aseneth's father Pentephres in Heliopolis on a Sunday when Joseph arrived there to collect grain, including the following night, and a week later when Joseph came back from more grain collecting. Aseneth's repenting in sackcloth and ashes in between is stated but not described. Only the wedding occurs some indefinite span of time later at Pharaoh's court. Part II opens with a reminiscence of Gen 41:53f.; 45:26-46:7;

47:27. So another supplement to the biblical narrative is announced. It is a tale of abduction and revolution, taking place eight years later. Pharaoh's firstborn son, never given a name, who had gone on record in 1:7-9 as wanting Aseneth's hand in marriage, attempts to kidnap her, aided and abeted by some of Joseph's brothers, slay Joseph and his father and become king over Egypt. He is thwarted by the joint efforts of Benjamin, Simeon, Levi, and the other brothers. Pharaoh's son loses his life in the affair, Pharaoh himself dies from sorrow, and Joseph becomes viceroy in Egypt for 40 years until the younger son of Pharaoh is ready to take over, but this is just stated, not narrated, by way of conclusion. The story involves Pharaoh's firstborn and the two groups of Joseph's brothers; Aseneth appears only in chs. 22 and 26-28. The main dealings take place on two successive days, first at an ill-defined place in Pharaoh's residence, possibly the chambers of his firstborn son, and then in some wadi, location unspecified, where Aseneth has been caught in an ambush.

The two parts can be read independently. 1:7-9 sets the stage for Part II, otherwise there is nothing in I to suggest that II is to follow. Part II refers back to I in a few places (23:3, 27:10), but is intelligible all by itself.

If summarized this way JosAs promises to make exciting reading, but it does not live up to the promise. Much space is devoted to describe Aseneth's luxurious penthouse and garden, people's looks, clothes, and emotions. The wedding in Part I and the military entanglements in II are treated very curtly. The rest is mostly dialogues with some long monologues thrown in, especially in chs. 11-13 where Aseneth confesses profusely to the sin of arrogance and implores God to receive her, and in ch. 21 where she recounts her conversion in a psalm. The chronological and geographical framework of the book is vague. Pentephres and his daughter are introduced at some length, the rest of the cast pop up as though the reader was acquainted with them. So indeed he or she must have been. Obviously JosAs was to be read as a companion to the book of Genesis or perhaps, an idea never explored, to some parallel account such as the Book of Jubilees or Pseudo-Philo's Biblical Antiquities.

So the literary merits of the book are questionable. Nevertheless it has a right to be appreciated as a piece of literature. G. Delling has done so in a way a man of his generation would. As far as I know no one versed in the newer techniques of structural analysis or literary criticism has ever touched the book.

By contrast there has been some dispute about the genre. The word generally used today is novel or romance. The problem is whether JosAs can be associated with any possible subdivision of this heterogeneous group of ancient writing. The book has been classed with Ruth, Esther, Jona, Judith, Tobit, by Kilpatrick; with the erotic Greek novels including *Cupid and Psyche* as narrated in Apuleius' *Golden Ass,* iv, 28 – vi, 24, by Philonenko and S. West; with certain apocryphal Acts, notably *Paul and Thecla,* by T. Szepessy. R.I. Pervo argued that JosAs updates the older form of what he calls "Sapiental novel" such as Ahiqar, Tobit, Dan 1-6 by integrating elements from the erotic variety. With full acknowledgment of the merits that all these approaches have it must be observed that neither of them does full justice to the three main features combined in JosAs, love, conversion, and dangerous adventure. Recently, H.C. Kee tackled the problem afresh by redefining the paradigm of the hellenistic novel thus:

> The work serves as propaganda for a cult.
>
> It depicts a conversion experience.
>
> Conversion leads to a sacred marriage.
>
> The literary style shifts between narrative and poetical or liturgical forms.
>
> The plot is moved along by inner and external conflicts of the hero or heroine, with deliverance accomplished by divine action.
>
> The climax of the story involves the death and rebirth of the hero or heroine, a theophany, and the self-dedication of the hero or heroine to the god.

He goes on, "Not all of these features are present in every romance, but all are found in J&A" ("Socio-Cultural Setting," p. 398).

Are they really? I am not yet convinced that JosAs is a work of propaganda, and certainly Aseneth's conversion is not the climax of the story, but only of chs. 1-21. Moreover, if not all of the six features are present in every romance, how many must be there for a work to share the genre of JosAs? Nonetheless strong affinities are there, and perhaps that is all we need. Pervo may be right after all that the romance "is probably the most formless of all ancient genres" (p. 172), being an excuse for literary syncretism rather than a defined form which developed along its own lines. As Kee rightly stressed what a novel looked like was heavily dependent upon the particular setting in which it functioned. So we had better not search too hard for twins or doubles of Aseneth among the ancient novels but acknowledge affinities wherever they present themselves, especially such as may be interpreted as genetical ties, and then judge the genre of JosAs on its own merits.

Next comes the question of sources. If the word means what the Gospel of Mark is to Matthew, none has been unearthed so far for JosAs or parts of it. If source is extended to include what *Pygmalion* is to *My Fair Lady,* we are still at a loss. A third form of source is involved if JosAs, or at least the conversion part of it, transcribes ritual into narrative. This has been argued in different ways by Philonenko, W.-D. Berner, S. Anandakumara,[5] and D. Sänger. To my mind neither of them has coped with the general methodological problem of retranslating narrative into ritual or rites which may underlie it. If it were

---

[5] Some information on these unpublished theses is contained in *ANRW*, ch. vi.

solved, JosAs would give access to a facet of Ancient Judaism of which we are virtually ignorant.

Another aspect is the problem of models which may have suggested or influenced the composition of JosAs without contributing much to its narrative content. Many writings named above come up for reconsideration at this point. An author who had read Judith or Esther would doubtless be more inclined to busy himself with a figure from Israel's past than one who had not. Once he had settled upon Aseneth the biblical story about her husband would naturally attract his attention, or was it the other way round? If he knew that the hellenistic world around him cherished erotic novels he may have decided to adapt some of their techniques so that his book could compete and maybe diminish the attraction the pagan variety might hold for Jewish readers. Last but not least the conversion element in JosAs invites comparison with Jewish and Christian texts narrating repentance or conversion, especially if they concern an important historical person and contain visions such as TJob 2-5; ApAb 1ff.; Dan 4, especially v. 33a-34 in the LXX version; Lk 7:36-50; Mt 16: 16-18; Acts 9:1-19 and parallels. As K. Berger and others have shown JosAs seems to follow a pattern of how conversion to Judaism ought to be presented. On the pagan side, Apuleius' Isis book (*Golden Ass*, xi) deserves special attention, as Kee has underscored.[6]

Tracing the origin of details is easier. Many of them are drawn directly from the Old Testament, and others can be shown to be traditional by comparing Jewish and Early Christian literature. The general framework, the cast of characters, and many individual features clearly come from Gen 37-50, except Pharaoh's firstborn who may be modeled upon Shechem (Gen 34). The visit of the Prince of the Angels in JosAs 14-17 recalls Judg 13. Benjamin's bravery in chs. 27 and 29 re-enacts David's slaying of Goliath in 1 Sam 17. Aseneth's prayers in chs. 11-13 and 27:10 reflect traditional and possibly contemporary forms. Indubitably JosAs also has many clichés in common with contemporary pagan writing, especially the romances. For example, the introduction of Pentephres and his daughter in 1:3-10 reads much like a biblicized version of the beginning of Chariton i,1:f., Xenophon of Ephesus i, 1:1-3, or Cupid and Psyche (Apuleius, iv, 22:1-24:4). As to the Jewish tradition, a host of references and interpretative suggestions is contained in the copious footnotes which invariably accompany the works of Berger. For the erotic novels one may consult Philonenko and West. So there is a wealth of material awaiting further inspection. A thorough analysis of JosAs, or parts of it, in terms of form-criticism and tradition history would be most welcome.

Just a modicum of attention has been wasted on the *realia* of the story such as landscape, seasons, calendar, agricultural products, architecture, clothing, and the like. It remains to be determined whether they have come with the sources

---

[6]Cf. also the synopsis drawn up in *Zeuge*, pp. 66-81.

or traditions that were used, or reflect what the author saw around him, or what he thought they were like way back in the age of the patriarchs. Closer investigation would not only help to understand JosAs better but also go a long way towards ascertaining its date and place of origin.

As to language and style, the fact that JosAs is written in a simple *koine* with a marked "Semitic," i.e., Hebrew and/or Aramaic, flavor at a leisurely pace with a lot of redundance and repetition, has escaped nobody's notice. Specifically, the vocabulary, syntax, idioms, and narrative techniques have a strong Biblical ring, the author's Bible being the Septuagint (there is no evidence that he read Hebrew or Aramaic). However, borrowings from individual passages are scarce, although they do occur (cf. 12:7; 15:7; 17:8, 20:5, 22:7, 27:1-5; 29,2). What stamped the language of JosAs in this respect is probably not so much the Book itself but an established literary style designed to fit holy subjects. It was nourished by the Septuagint, synagogal parlance (in itself influenced by the Greek Bible and possibly vice versa), and maybe conversional Greek as spoken among Jews in the diaspora. Kilpatrick, Philonenko, and G. Delling have done a lot to elucidate the "Semitic" element in JosAs' language (Delling finds that the influence of Genesis and the Psalms is most marked). There are of course many parallels in early Christian literature, too. A handy tool to investigate those, with profit to both sides, is the list of parallels to JosAs 1-21 (Batiffol's text) drawn up by E.W. Smith in his thesis. What is still lacking is an assessment of the features which are Greek rather than "Semitic," for such do exist. In fact, recent research into the language of contemporary works such as the Gospel of Mark by M. Reiser, or Chariton by A. Papanikolaou, suggests that phenomena conventionally regarded as "Semitic" like the protracted use of parataxis or the inverted order of subject and verb were common enough in certain strands of *koine* literature.

3. Provenance

JosAs does not say when and where and by whom it was written. External evidence is lacking. The book is certainly Jewish.[7] The way it depicts Aseneth as a model proselyte and the mother of many proselytes suggests that proselytism was a lively prospect in the author's day, with no trace of the Christian Church as a competitor visible. In other words, JosAs antedates the Second Jewish Revolt under Hadrian (A.D. 132-135) and more precisely the revolt under Traian referred to above, if the book is Egyptian as it seems to be. Local alternatives such as Palestine or Syria have been proposed but never argued properly. Egypt is the most likely birthplace of a tale extolling the conversion of an Egyptian chief priest's daughter and showing the children of Israel involved in local political strife.

---

[7]P. Hofrichter apparently would like to connect it with Johannine christianity, but I have not seen his study.

At the far end of possibilities, the earliest conceivable date of JosAs is less obvious. The book presupposes the Septuagint, probably all of it. Its conversion theology is well developed. That Pharaoh's firstborn son is engaged to the daughter of the king of Moab (1:9) may reflect the political status which the Nabateans had achieved around 100 B.C. All things considered it is probably safe to say that JosAs hardly antedates the late second century B.C.

Attempts to narrow down the date have never been vigorous nor, to my mind, successful because they relied too much on a general impression or on isolated observations. Most recently, however, D. Sänger developed a suggestion of Kilpatrick's into a new approach. He regards the different characters in the story as representing social groups which existed in the author's world and analyzes their relationships. Joseph, Asenath, Levi and the rest of Joseph's good brothers represent the main body of the Egyptian Jews, Proselytes included, who are, or would like to be, friendly with the Egyptians. Pharaoh and Pentephres, the heads of the ruling class, are sympathizers or even God-fearers. Pharaoh's firstborn son impersonates the local anti-Judaism desirous to intercept the growing friendship between the crown and the Jews by force, if necessary. Joseph's bad brothers are a Jewish faction ready to conspire with the former group for opportunity's sake. Sänger then goes on to fit this pattern into what we know about Jewish-Egyptian relations from 100 B.C. to A.D. 100, and comes up with the pogrom in Alexandria under Caligula in A.D. 38 as a good setting for JosAs.[8] This is probably not yet the last word. Pharaoh's firstborn son wants to do away with Joseph because he is married to Aseneth, now a Jewish proselyte, not because he is a Jew. I do not see anti-Jewish feelings mirrored anywhere in JosAs (unless it were argued that the very absence is motivated by wishful thinking). If they were, I wonder whether Caligula is really the only option. We may not know enough about the Jews in Egypt to exclude similar clashes before that date. Nonetheless Sänger's method looks promising, especially if its scope were broadened to include the *realia* inherent in the story (see above) and the milieu which is back of it.

To be sure, the milieu is a problem in itself. There seems to be a growing consensus that JosAs does not come from any known organized group such as the Essenes or the Therapeutae (*pace* Rießler and K.G. Kuhn), nor from an unknown one. The book advocates Judaism, not some particular denomination as opposed to others or to vulgar Judaism at large. The opposition is idolatrous heathendom. The authors and his readers belonged to what is conventionally termed "the Synagogue." However, much like today, synagogues in antiquity were apt to differ from one another according to the place where their members lived, to the social class or classes which they encompassed, and to the special

---

[8]The date itself is not new. It was proposed, e.g., by Anandakumara, p. 86, and tentatively by Kee, "Socio-Religious Setting," p. 190. On p. 199, n. 5, Sänger reports a letter from M. Hengel pleading for a date toward the end of the Ptolemean era, i.e., around the middle of the first century B.C.

religious outlook which they favored. Internal pluralism was possible if they were large. In this sense we may continue to speak of, and look for, a group which is responsible for JosAs.

Philonenko had opted for a village or small town where the local Jews were on friendly terms with their pagan neighbors. Untouched by the exclusive philosophical monotheism which reigned in Philo's Alexandria they had absorbed enough of Egyptian religion to turn their faith into a regular mystery cult with rituals to match (see above). Both their situation and their religious outlook inspired the hope that conversion of their heathen fellow men was under way. As Philonenko himself put it he had discovered a rural variant of the mystic Judaism described at length by E.R. Goodenough. Philonenko's interpretation of JosAs as the narrative rendering of a full-blown initiation into a Jewish mystery has been criticized by Sänger in his thesis, and probably rightly so. Furthermore, one wonders whether countryside and the high degree of literary and religious sophistication which Philonenko detects in JosAs after all, are not mutually exclusive. An urban upper class milieu as suggested e.g. by Kee seems to be more appropriate, and why not Alexandria, although it may impose itself too readily because we know a lot about it and too little about the Jews elsewhere in Lower Egypt.

That is not to say that the case for a mystic orientation of JosAs, as opposed to a legalistic, quasi-philosophical, or sapiental one, has been kicked out of court. It is the main thrust of Kee's contributions to have reopened it in a much more cogent way than Philonenko did. By pointing out affinities with the Isis cult as represented e.g. by Apuleius on the one hand and with Jewish Merkavah Mysticism on the other, Kee arrives at the idea that JosAs comes from an esoteric Jewish milieu that cherished as its highest value personal, revelatory experience which mediated insights into the mysteries of the divine world leading to rebirth and a new life governed and protected by spirit power from above. Aseneth is the prototype of a person living by such experience. I would like to submit by way of a demurrer that the heavenly things revealed to Aseneth in JosAs 14-17, the paradisiac manna which she is given to eat in ch. 16, and the corporeal transformation which she undergoes in ch. 18, may not be meant to be everybody's experience. Doubtless they will be after death, in the "place of rest" in heaven. But it seems to me that Aseneth is supposed to be the only person to have experienced them in full while still on earth. To use St. Paul's language, she is a "firstborn from the dead" (1 Cor 15:20; Col 1:18, cf. Acts 26:23) whose fate is indicative, and maybe causative, of the fate of all people if they will cross over to Judaism. But just as those who are "in Christ" are not yet like Christ, who lives as a "life-giving spirit" in heaven (1Cor 15:45) by virtue of his resurrection (Rom 1:4), those who are "in" Aseneth, the City of Refuge (JosAs 15:7; 16:16, 19:8), are not yet like her. Moreover, the "ineffable mysteries of the Most High" revealed to Aseneth (16:14) seem to be less profound than Kee thinks. They relate to the heavenly origin of the manna which embodies the spirit of life, i.e. they reveal not the heavenly order in general but the secret of how to attain eternal life (cf. WisSol 2:22, the whole chapter merits closer comparison with JosAs on several accounts).

If that is so, the quest for the milieu which produced JosAs is still open.

4. Theology

Several points have been touched upon in the preceding sections. The most important study to have appeared in recent years is Kee's. As to the rest I can be brief. The formula which J.H. Charlesworth developed for *OTP* called for a rather extensive treatment of the key ideas of each book received into the collection. It was carried over into *JSHRZ* in an expanded form. Moreover, much interpretative work on JosAs has been done in connection with research into the New Testament, and I have summarized that part elsewhere (except a neglected study by R. Scroggs and two recent ones by E. Stegemann and G. Sellin). This includes some fresh remarks on the problem once raised by Kilpatrick only to become the most widely debated individual aspect of JosAs, viz. the so-called meal formula in 8:5 ("It is not fitting for a man who worships God, who will bless with his mouth the living God and eat blessed bread of life and drink a blessed cup of immortality and anoint himself with blessed ointment of incorruptibility to kiss a strange woman ...") etc., and its bearing on the Lord's Supper, notably Jn 6 and 1Cor 10 and 11 (add K.-G. Sandelin to the dossier).

A neglected field is the ethics of JosAs. It has been duly considered whenever the occasion called for it, e.g., by J. Piper in his book on love of enemy, but it was never studied in itself. Such study would have to include not only the maxims professed by various persons at various places, above all those beginning, "It is not fitting for a man (or woman) who worships (the one and true) God," in 8:5,7; 21:1; 23:9,12; 29:3, cf. 28:5,14, but also the morality that is implicit in the portrayal of the characters and their actions.

As a general impression I would like to add that JosAs has too often been used as a quarry, without first giving it the benefit of that good old-fashioned exegesis which has become a must in Biblical studies, let alone of the methodological innovations that have accrued in recent years.

5. Pictures

The combination *Life of Joseph* – JosAs is accompanied by illustrations in three Greek manuscripts, all very recent. Most important is the McKell codex, both by the number and the artistic elegance of the pictures. It was done by the noted Rumanian bishop and calligrapher, Luke the Cypriot, around A.D. 1580. Then there are two lesser lights in modern Greek, Mt. Athos, Koutloumousiou 100, a local production of the 16th century, and Oxford, Bodleian Library, Roe 5, executed by some Georgios of Ainos near Constantinople in A.D. 1614.

Nobody cared for the illustrations until the discovery of McKell by J. and O. Pächt, and they concentrated on the *Life* in that manuscript. The full cycles in the whole lot – 63 images for the *Life* and 17 for JosAs in McKell, 21/3 and 28/19 (plus two empty frames) in the other two – were investigated in extenso by G. Vikan in his thesis. Excellent reproductions of Koutloumousiou 100 are by Pelekanidis et al.

Vikan thinks that the three sets of pictures go back to a common archetype, though not directly. McKell is derived from a Late Byzantine model which may have originated in the *Hodegon* monastery in Constantinople in the 14th century, and the other two from a Turkish-Byzantine ancestor produced on Mt. Athos in the 16th. The pictorial archetype of them all Vikan assumes was contrived in Constantinople, a rather unusual thing to happen to literature of this type. Excluding the overlaps 75 images for the *Life* and 35 (maybe 34, see *ANRW*, ch. v,1) for JosAs have survived. The original cycle may have held more, because just like text, images have a tendency to evanesce in the process of transmission; we cannot be sure, on the other hand, that all those preserved really come from the original. Vikan feels that no earlier traces of the cycle are discernible, contrary to the pioneer suggestion of the Pächts that the prototype of the McKell series was close to the famous Vienna Genesis (6th century, Syria).

Most of this is in the province of book painting, and I am no judge of that. From my point of view, further research seems possible, and indeed promising, as to the relationship of image and text. The illustrations often reflect older and sometimes fuller forms of the text which they are now employed to illustrate. Vikan of course covered this angle but he had only the editions and translations printed up to 1975 to go on. A more detailed correlation of the pictures and the manuscript tradition, particularly of the **b** group, will help to determine and to date pictorial elements with more precision, and by the same token throw more light on the textual history of JosAs. It remains to be seen whether Vikan's archetype can be characterized textually. Chances are that it belonged to the **b** group, subject to the qualifications stated above.

For more Aseneth pictures in other contexts, see *ANRW*, ch. v,1.

6. Cultural Importance

Ever since Batiffol first edited the Greek JosAs attention has been paid to the broad trail which the book has left as it made its way through time and space. Because it never achieved the rank of a standard work of reference, an academic textbook, or a devotional classic, it did not make history in the proper sense of the word. Nevertheless Aseneth has left a goodly number of fingerprints in different parts of the Christian world, and some of them are closely enough related to allow some of her doings to be reconstructed with a measure of coherence.

Most of what we know is due to chance finds by scholars who happened to have an interest in the afterlife of the books of the Bible or had their attention drawn to JosAs. To name just two of them, the renowned Cambridge historian and cataloguer, M.R. James, discovered Latin I and presented it to Batiffol to publish along with the Greek text. In our day we owe most of the Ethiopian material regarding Aseneth to G. Haile, at present cataloguer of Ethiopian manuscripts at Hill Monastic Manuscript Library, Collegeville, Minnesota (published in *ANRW*, ch. iii, 5). Further results might be gained by exploring systematically the exegetical literature on Genesis, the Joseph lore, the Aseneth iconography outside JosAs, the use of Aseneth as a proper name, and hagiography and liturgy generally. That is a tremendously large order, and one wonders whether the outcome would be worth the effort. In the meantime, what has been observed so far is collected in *ANRW*, with the highlights exposed in *OTP*, pp. 195-199, awaiting further digestion. Here I just offer a few comments.

Although there is no positive evidence Aseneth must have been christened at an early date, when the Church was still fighting idolatry. Chances are that it happened in Egypt. The reason may be gleaned from Athanasius' famous 39th Paschal Letter of A.D. 367. The Alexandrian bishop states that the Wisdom of Solomon, Ben Sira, Esther, Judith, Tobit, the Didache, and Hermas were aggregated to the Scriptures because "the Fathers ordained them to be read by those who want to accede and to be instructed in the rules of piety." JosAs would have served the purpose nicely. As in similar cases, the adoption of JosAs by the Church, if nothing else, probably caused the Jews to abandon the book. All traces of it are Christian except perhaps the identification of Pentephres' and Aseneth's houses in Heliopolis reported by Egeria around A.D. 380. The Jewish Aseneth lore as digested by V. Aptowitzer and L. Ginzberg shows no influence of JosAs.

How did JosAs progress from Egypt? If pieced together on the assumption that the book was not read in a given place a long time before we know that it was, the evidence suggests that it did not radiate freely into all directions but followed a trajectory through the Near East to Byzantium and then to Northwestern Europe, with sidelines branching off the main course now and then. JosAs first migrated to Syria to arrive in time to influence, e.g. the Passion of St. Irene in the 5th century, maybe earlier. Ties between Egypt and Syria have always been close (from both sides: the best of the two Syriac manuscripts of JosAs was found in a monastery in the Nitrian valley, not in Syria). A natural place for Aseneth to go from Syria was Armenia where JosAs was translated in the 6th or 7th century. While the Syriac churches did not take to JosAs much, the Armenians valued it highly at least from the 11th century onwards. They even received it into their Bible, though not as a canonical book. Doubtless this accounts for the fact that more copies are preserved in Armenian than in all other languages thrown together. Forty-five manuscripts are on record to date, with more yet to be discovered. Surprisingly enough JosAs made no headway from Armenia; no Georgian version is known.

On the main line, JosAs appeared in Byzantium and/or Greece around the 9th century, perhaps from Syria after the Macedonian dynasty (A.D. 867-1056) had reconquered large parts of the East. αδ, α and δ were produced early in that period. JosAs enjoyed a measure of success right through the 11th century and maybe into the 12th, the most important witness being the illuminated de luxe edition referred to above. The two Latin translations, both made prior to A.D. 1200, are likely to have been prompted by this happy period in Aseneth's afterlife. There is no evidence that their *Vorlagen* were imported from the Greek world around the Aegean Sea, and if so when, but we have the Testaments of the Twelve Patriarchs for a good, if slightly later, parallel. The manuscript which Robert Grosseteste, bishop of Lincoln (A.D. 1170-1253) had translated into Latin in 1242, now Cambridge University Library, Ff 1.24, was brought over from Athens a few years before. H.J. de Jonge has shown that its existence had been signalled as early as *ca.* A.D. 1200. It is a 10th century copy of excellent quality. The *Vorlage* of Latin II may well have been of the same calibre. By contrast, Latin I goes back to a Greek text which was marred by itacisms, errors, and lacunae. It may have been a fresh copy made to the order of someone who wished to carry it home.

Latin II itself is of uncertain provenance, possibly Northern France, and is attested in Sweden and Austria down to the 15th century. No further influence is known. Latin I appears to have been made in England, probably Canterbury, and may well be the first piece of Greek ever translated in Britain. The last known copy is 14th century, but the book was still read at the beginning of the 15th, witness the Middle English verse translation which was printed by H.N. MacCracken. Few copies of Latin I seem to have found their way across the Channel into France. But one of them was condensed into a form soon to become a hit (see below).

Back to the Greek world, we know or suspect that JosAs was never quite forgotten in and around Constantinople. We also find it on Mt. Athos since the 15th century. The modern Greek version, actually a paraphrase, was made and illuminated there in the 16th. It was from there and/or from Constantinople that Aseneth travelled North. JosAs skimmed the world of the Slavs by way of the Serbo-Slavonic version no later than the 15th century, but got no farther than that. It was more of a success in Rumania. The McKell codex was made there around 1580, the Bucharest manuscript copied or imported in the 17th century, and the Rumanian version, rather a digest, translated from a manuscript much like the Bucharest one no later than the 18th.

Finally, or maybe not, a 10th century manuscript of the **a** group found its way to Mt. Sinai, unknown when. St. Catherine's also houses another copy of the same group of the 15th or 16th century, possibly a local product, and another one of the 17th which is very close to the Bucharest manuscript. So Aseneth may have made the pilgrimage to Mt. Sinai more than once. From the 17th century on there is the **c** group in Palestine. ζ may have been redacted there, but there is no way of telling how long the *Vorlage* had been there and where it came from.

Last question, who read JosAs and for what? We know nothing about the reception of the original. Even the purpose is in dispute. Many have regarded JosAs as a missionary tract enticing non-Jews to convert, and perhaps Jews to make it easy for them to cross over, with a defense of exogamy (if the non-Jewish partner is willing to turn Jewish) as a secondary motive. A modification of this view is Kee's idea that the work was to propagate the special kind of mystical experience which he feels is extolled in it. I have been more inclined to think that JosAs was meant to explain to Jews, proselytes, and maybe God-fearer, what privileges they possessed as compared with their pagan environment.

As a Christian book, JosAs appears to have been copied, translated, and handed on way up into the Middle Ages by monks and clerics to be read by their likes in ecclesiastical libraries, refectories, or cells. They may have communicated its contents to a more general public, but there is little evidence of that. To note a few exceptions: The miniature cycle is likely to have been executed for a rich layman, and McKell certainly was, maybe for the reigning voevod of Wallachia, Mishnea II. The Middle English verses were written for a noble lady, though again by a clergyman who may have been her chaplain. Armenian bibles including JosAs were commissioned by well-to-do people in the 17th century.

Things became different in medieval Europe after Vincent of Beauvais had included a condensation of Latin I into his *Speculum historiale*, i, 118-124 (ca. A.D. 1244/50), a world history which soon became a standard work.[9] It was widely copied and translated into French and Dutch. The JosAs digest was copied separately and/or welded into other works, mostly devotional, and influenced still others. Thus JosAs became public property and was eventually to be read in Czech, Dutch, English, French, German, Polish, Russian, and Scandinavian including Icelandic, first in handwritten form and then, after Gutenberg's invention caught on, in print. The oddest offshoot of this line of tradition is *Los desposorios de Joseph,* a one-act verse play based on JosAs 1-21, which was performed in Sevilla in 1575 and in Madrid on Corpus Christi Day, 1608. It was printed by L. Rouanet.[10]

So the main purpose to read JosAs was at all times devotion and moral education. To be sure the erotic element did not hurt its acceptance. Probably most readers were convinced that JosAs was a true story, but some thought more of it. The Syriac version was soon incorporated into a large historical

---

[9]No critical text exists. The last edition is Douai, 1624, reprinted Graz: 1965. Cf. Guzman.

[10]I have not been able to follow up the references to Aseneth in other Spanish plays, vol. iv, p. 182. Also I do not know whether anyone paid attention to the play since Rouanet.

compilation of the 6th century, later attributed to one Zacharias Rhetor. It is in this form only that it has survived. Vincent, too, must have deemed JosAs a historically reliable account. The last to have used it as a historical source was Philipp von Zesen, the famous baroque writer. He published in 1670 a historical novel about Joseph calling it *Assenat,* because among other things, he had been able to lay his hands on a German or Dutch version of Vincent's abridgement and had integrated large bits of it into his narration. Yet another motive was operative in the Rumanian translation. While its first aim certainly was moral, its wider context was the emergence of a national Rumanian culture. So it came to be considered as part of the national heritage. It is the only version ever printed for the general reading public, witness the edition of chs. 1-21 by C. Bobulescu in a series called "People's Library."

To close the survey, I suspect that the most exotic development that JosAs is supposed to have undergone never took place. Batiffol advanced the idea, to be developed at some length by Philonenko, that JosAs influenced *Yussuf and Zuleikha,* one of the classical themes of Islamic literature. Basically, it is the story of Joseph and Putiphar's wife, following the Bible and Jewish haggadah for what they offer on the subject but adding as a happy end that the two got a pair after the treacherous woman had spent years in repentance. The topic has been treated time and again by various authors in different languages including Persian, Turkish, and Urdu, notably by the renowned Persian poets, Firduzi (A.D. 939-1020) and Djami (A.D. 1414-1492) in 1009/20 and 1483 respectively. Closer inspection suggests that parallels of Zuleikha and Aseneth are not so close after all, and that they appear more in the later forms of the Islamic story than in the earlier ones, suggesting that they are due to internal development, not external influence. Definite judgment must be withheld until we know the evolution of *Yussuf and Zuleikha* better than we do, and that requires the hand of a specialist.

This is a good point at which to stop. Aseneth has received more attention lately than most of her likes, and we have come to know her well in many respects. Further progress will depend in no small measure upon the cooperation of scholars from all fields concerned.

7. Bibliography

Only the works quoted in this survey are listed. Further bibliographies are to be found under the titles marked, "Bib." Those designated by an asterisk do not refer to JosAs.

a) Texts, Translations, and Concordance

Batiffol, Pierre, "Le Livre de la Prière d'Aseneth," in Batiffol, *Studia Patristica. Études d'ancienne littérature chrétienne* (Paris: 1889-90), pp. 1-115.

Bobulescu, Constantin, *Istoria frumosului Iosif si a prea frumoasei Asineta. Dupa un manuscris din 1753* (Bucharest: 1922).

Brodrick, M., *The Life and Confession of Asenath the Daughter of Pentephres of Heliopolis, Narrating How the All-Beautiful Joseph Took Her to Wife*. Prepared by M. Brodrick, from Notes supplied by the late Sir Peter Le Page Renou (London: 1900).

Brooks, Ernest W., *Joseph and Asenath. The Confession and Prayer of Asenath Daughter of Pentephres the Priest* (London: 1918).

Burchard, Christoph, "Ein vorläufiger griechischer Text von Joseph und Aseneth," *Dielheimer Blätter zum Alten Testament* 14 (October 1979), pp. 2-53 (Corrections ibid. 16, December 1982, pp. 37-39).

———, "Joseph und Aseneth," in *Jüdische Schriften aus hellenistisch-römischer Zeit*, ed. by Werner Georg Kümmel, vol. ii, fasc. 4 (Gütersloh: 1983) (quoted, *JSHRZ*) (Bib.).

———, "Joseph and Aseneth," in *The Old Testament Pseudepigrapha*, ed. by James H. Charlesworth, vol. ii (Garden City, NY: 1985), pp. 177-247 (quoted, *OTP*).

Cook, D., "Joseph and Aseneth," in *The Apocryphal Old Testament*, ed. by H.F.D. Sparks (Oxford: 1984), pp. 465-503.

Denis, Albert-Marie, and Schumacher, Jean, *Concordance des Pseudépigraphes grecs d'Ancien Testament* (Lourvain-la-Neuve: in the press).

Goeij, M. de, *Jozef en Aseneth. Apokalyps van Baruch* (Kampen: 1981).

MacCracken, Henry N., "The Storie of Asneth. An Unknown Middle English Translation of a Lost Latin Version," *The Journal of English and Germanic Philology* 9 (1910), pp. 224-264.

Martínez Fernandez, Ramon, and Piñero, Antonio, "José y Asenet," in *Apócrifos del Antiguo Testamento*, ed. by A. Díez Macho (Madrid: 1983), pp. 191-238.

Philonenko, Marc, *Joseph et Aséneth. Introduction, texte critique, traduction et notes* (Leiden: 1968) (Bib.).

Rießler, Paul, "Joseph und Asenath," in Rießler, *Altjüdisches Schrifttum außerhalb der Bibel* (Augsburg: 1928; 2nd ed., Heidelberg: 1966).

Suski, Andrzej, "Józef i Asenet. wstp, przekład z greckiego, komentarz," *Studia Theologica Varsaviensia* 16 (1978), pp. 199-240.

b) Pictures

Pächt, Jeanne and Otto, "An Unknown Cycle of Illustrations of the Life of Joseph," *Cahiers Archéologiques* 7 (1954), pp. 35-49, pl. xii-xvi.

Pelekanidis, Stylianos M., Christou, P., Tsioumis, Ch., and Kadas, S., *The Treasures of Mount Athos. Illuminated Manuscripts. Miniatures – Headpieces – Initial Letters*, vol. i (Athens: 1974), pp. 456, 458f., ill. 339-341.

Vikan, Gary K., *Illustrated Manuscripts of Pseudo-Ephraem's Life of Joseph and the Romance of Joseph and Aseneth*, 3 vols. (Ph.D. thesis, Princeton University: 1976).

———, "Illustrated Manuscripts of the Romance of Joseph and Aseneth," in *SBL 1976 Seminar Papers*, ed. by George MacRae (Missoula, MT: 1976), pp. 193-208, 15 ills.

c) Studies

Anandakumara, Sunanda, *The Gentile Reactions to the Christ-Kerygma – The Problems Involved in the Reception of the Christ-Kerygma in the Young Gentile Christianity in the New Testament* (Dr. theol. thesis, Hamburg: 1975), pp. 29-91, 316-335.

Aptowitzer, Victor, "Asenath, the Wife of Joseph. A Haggadic Literary-Historical Study," *Hebrew Union College Annual* 1 (1924), pp. 239-306.

Beckwith, R.T., "The Solar Calendar of Joseph and Aseneth: A Suggestion," *Journal for the Study of Judaism* 15 (1984), pp. 90-111.

Berger, Klaus, *Die Gesetzesauslegung Jesu. Ihr historischer Hintergrund im Judentum und im Alten Testament, I: Markus und Parallelen* (Neukirchen-Vluyn: 1972).

———, "Jüdisch-hellenistische Missionsliteratur und apokryphe Apostelakten," *Kairos* 17 (1975), pp. 232-248.

———, *Die Auferstehung des Propheten und die Erhöhung des Menschensohnes. Traditionsgeschichtlitche Untersuchungen zur Deutung des Geschickes Jesu in frühchristlichen Texten* (Göttingen: 1976).

Berner, Wolf Dietrich, *Initiationsriten in Mysterienreligionen, im Gnostizismus und im antiken Judentum* (Dr. theol. thesis, Göttingen: 1972), pp. 156-172.

Burchard, Christoph, *Untersuchungen zu Joseph und Aseneth. Überlieferung-Ortsbestimmung* (Tübingen: 1965) (Bib.).

———, *Der dreizehnte Zeuge. Traditions – und kompositionsgeschichtliche Untersuchungen zu Lunkas Darstellung der Frühzeit des Paulus* (Göttingen: 1970).

———, "Der jüdische Asenethroman und seine Nachwirkung. Von Egeria zu Anna Katharina Emmerick oder von Moses aus Aggel zu Karl Kerényi," in *Aufstieg und Niedergang der römatischen Welt*, ed. by Hildegard Temporini and Wolfgang Haase, vol. ii, 20 (Berlin-New York: 1987), pp. 543-667 (quoted, *ANRW*; Bib.).

———, "The Importance of Joseph and Aseneth for the Study of the New Testament," *New Testament Studies* 33 (1987), pp. 102-134 (Bib.).

Charlesworth, James H., assisted by Patricia Dykers, *The Pseudepigrapha and Modern Research* (Missoula, MT: 1976; 2nd ed., 1980).

Delling, Gerhard, "Einwirkungen der Sprache der Septuaginta in 'Joseph und Aseneth,'" *Journal for the Study of Judaism* 9 (1978), pp. 29-56.

———, "Die Kunst des Gestaltens in 'Joseph und Aseneth,'" *Novum Testamentum* 26 (1984), pp. 1-40.

Denis, Albert-Marie, *Introduction aux Pseudépigraphes grecs d'Ancien Testament* (Leyde: 1970), pp. 40-48.

Ginzberg,Louis, *The Legends of the Jews,* 7 vols. (Philadelphia, PA: 1909-38).

*Guzman, Gregory G., "A Growing Tabulation of Vincent of Beauvais' *Speculum historiale* Manuscripts," *Scriptorium* 29 (1975), pp. 122-125.

Hengel, Martin, "Anonymität, Pseudepigraphie und 'Literarische Fälschung' in der jüdisch-hellenistischen Literatur," in *Pseudepigrapha,* vol. i (Vanœuvres-Geneva: 1972), pp. 229-329.

Hofrichter, Peter, "Johanneische Thesen," *Bibel und Liturgie* 54 (1981), pp. 212-216.

Holtz, Traugott, "Christliche Interpolationen in 'Joseph und Aseneth,'" *New Testament Studies* 14 (1967/68), pp. 482-497.

Jeremias, Joachim, "The Last Supper," *Expository Times* 64 (1952/53), pp. 91f.

*Jonge, Henk J. de, "La bibliothèque de Michel Choniatès et la tradition occidentale des Testaments des XII Patriarches," in *Studies on the Testaments of the Twelve Patriarchs. Text and Interpretation,* ed. by Marinus de Jonge (Leyde: 1975), pp. 97-106.

Kee, Howard C., "The Socio-Religious Setting and Aims of 'Joseph and Asenath,'" in *SBL 1976 Seminar Papers,* ed. by George MacRae (Missoula, MT: 1976), pp. 183-192.

———, "The Socio-Cultural Setting of Joseph and Aseneth," *New Testament Studies* 29 (1983), pp. 394-413.

Kilpatrick, George D., "The Last Supper," *Expository Times* 64 (1952/53), pp. 4-8.

———, Review of Burchard, *Untersuchungen,* and Philonenko, *Joseph et Aséneth, Novum Testamentum* 12 (1970), pp. 233-236.

Kuhn, Karl Georg, "The Lord's Supper and the Communal Meal at Qumran," in *The Scrolls and the New Testament,* ed. by Krister Stendahl (New York: 1957; London: 1958), pp. 65-93, 259-265.

Nickelsburg, George W., Jr., *Jewish Literature between the Bible and the Mishnah. A Historical and Literary Introduction* (Philadelphia, PA: 1981), pp. 258-263, 271f., 274f.

———, "Stories of Biblical and Early Post-Biblical Times," in *Jewish Writings of the Second Temple Period,* ed. by Michael E. Stone (Assen-Philadelphia, PA: 1984), pp. 33-87.

*Papanikolaou, Antonios D., *Chariton-Studien. Untersuchungen zur Sprache und Chronologie der griechischen Romane* (Göttingen: 1973).

Pervo, Richard I., "Joseph and Asenath and the Greek Novel," in *SBL 1976 Seminar Papers*, ed. by George MacRae (Missoula, MT: 1976), pp. 171-181.

Philonenko, Marc, "Joseph et Aséneth," in *La Bible. Écrits intertestamentaires* (Bibliothèque de la Pléiade), ed. by André Dupont-Sommer and Marc Philonenko (Paris: 1987), pp. cxxii-cxxv, 1559-1601.

Piper, John, *"Love your enemies." Jesus' Love Command in the Synoptic Gospels and in the Early Christian Paraenesis. A History of the Tradition and Interpretation of Its Uses* (Cambridge: 1979).

*Reiser, Marius, *Syntax und Stil des Markusevangeliums im Licht der hellenistischen Volksliteratur* (Tübingen: 1984).

Rouanet, Léo, *Coleccion de Autos, Farsas, y Coloquios del siglo XVI*, 4 vols. (Barcelona-Madrid: 1901), vol. i, pp. 331-357 (text); vol. iv, pp. 179-182 (notes).

Sänger, Dieter, *Antikes Judentum und die Mysterien. Religionsgeschichtliche Untersuchungen zu Joseph und Aseneth* (Tübingen: 1980) (Bib.).

———, "Erwägungen zur historischen Einordnung und zur Datierung von 'Joseph und Aseneth,'" *Zeitschrift für die neutestamentliche Wissenschaft* 76 (1985), pp. 86-106.

Sandelin, Karl-Gustav, "Måltidens symboliska betydelse i den alexandrinska judedomen. Ett bidrag till frågan om den kristna eukaristins bakgrund," in *Meddelanden från Stiftelsens för Åbo Akademi Forskningsinstitut* 56 (Åbo: 1980), pp. 128-134.

Schürer, Emil, *Geschichte des jüdische Volkes im Zeitalter Jesu Christi*, vol. iii (4th ed., Leipzig: 1909; reprinted, Hildesheim: 1964), pp. 399-402.

———, *The History of the Jewish People in the Age of Jesus Christ 175 B.C.-A.D. 135). A New English Version Revised and Edited by Geza Vermes, Fergus Millar, and Martin Goodman*, vol. iii, part i (Edinburgh: 1986), pp. 546-552.

Schwartz, Jacques, "Recherches sur l'évolution du roman de Joseph et Aséneth," *Revue des études juives* 143 (July-December 1984), pp. 273-285.

Scroggs, Robin, "Paul and the Eschatological Woman: Revisited," *Journal of the American Academy of Religion* 42 (1974), pp. 532-537.

Sellin, Gerhard, *Der Streit um die Auferstehung der Toten* (Göttingen: 1986).

Smith, Edgar W., Jr., *Joseph and Asenath and Early Christian Literature: A Contribution to the Corpus Hellenisticum Novi Testamenti* (Ph.D. thesis, Claremont Graduate School, Claremont, California: 1975).

Stegemann, Ekkehard, "'Das Gesetz ist nicht wider die Verheiβungen!' Thesen zu Galater 3,15-29," in *Theologische Brosamen für Lothar Steiger zu seinem fünfzigsten Geburtstag* gesammelt von Gerhard Freund und Ekkehard Stegemann (Heidelberg: 1985), pp. 389-395.

Szepessy, Tibor, "L'Histoire de Joseph et d'Aseneth et le roman antique," *Acta Classica Universitatis Scientiarum Debreceniensis* 10-11 (1974-75), pp. 121-131.

West, S., "Joseph and Asenath: A Neglected Greek Romance," *The Classical Quarterly* 24 (1974), pp. 70-81.

Zesen, Philipp von, *Assenat*, 1670, ed. by Volker Meid (Tübingen: 1967).

Chapter Four

The Dawning of a New Epoch in Research on Christian Origins
The New English Pseudepigrapha

James H. Charlesworth
George L. Collord Professor of New Testament Language and Literature
Princeton Theological Seminary

It is a real personal pleasure to dedicate this paper to Howard Kee, one of the most careful and cooperative members of the research team that produced the two-volumed *The Old Testament Pseudepigrapha*. Kee is one of the very few distinguished scholars who has contributed to so many divergent areas of research into Christian Origins, as placarded by his numerous books on such topics as Mark, miracle, magic, sociological approaches to earliest Christianity, and his many articles on Early Judaism, especially the model contributions on the Testaments of the Twelve Patriarchs. His depth and breadth of intellectual abilities include music; he has even authored a musical drama that was featured at a national biblical meeting. Above all, Howard has been a warm engaging colleague; he rarely criticizes others, but has frequently supplied those crutches that have helped me on the way.

Primary Sources Phenomenally Increased

The Nag Hammadi Codices, the Qumran Scrolls, and the Old Testament Pseudepigrapha have revolutionized the study of Early Judaism and Christian Origins. We have entered a new era of research.

In the early nineteenth century the Tübingen School dominated the scientific approach to Christian Origins. From the mid-nineteenth century to the beginning of World War I attention was intermittently drawn to the study of texts, new editions, often an *editio princeps,* lexicons, and concordances because of the phenomenal recovery of manuscripts, like Ethiopic Enoch, the Didache, and most importantly the two sensational discoveries in St. Catherine's Monastery, namely Codex Sinaiticus, by Tischendorf, and Syrus Sinaiticus, by Lewis. From the 1920s to the 1960s the Bultmannian School dictated the concerns and methods of many New Testament specialists. Now ancient documents have once again become central to our craft, thanks primarily to the unexpected rich discoveries near Nag Hammadi, in the Judean wilderness and Jordan rift, and the rediscovery of Syrus Sinaiticus through space-age photographic technologies and computer enhancement.

An age has ended. It was the period when theological abstraction and literary analysis, with their twin-offspring Form Criticism and Redaction Criticism, defined the subject and approach. Now, by utilizing the best from these methodologies and sensitivities and by adhering to philology and a refined understanding of historical criticism, scholars – throughout the world, and especially here in the U.S.A. – have been forced to take seriously the increased literary data before them. And they have prosecuted their research with a new appreciation of the social setting and historical matrix behind the documents.

A new era is inaugurated.[1] It is characterized by an expanded, more inclusive perspective – including Iran, Egypt, and Syria as well as Rome, Greece, and Palestine.[2] In the *centrum* are ancient documents, hundreds of them, all somewhat contemporaneous with and in various ways significant for understanding both Early Judaism and Early Christianity.

New Skills and Paradigms

To focus upon the ancient documents means to develop new skills and paradigms. Scholars are no longer preoccupied by comparing Bultmann with Barth, or Conzelmann with Cullmann; instead, they are juxtaposing 4 Ezra with 2 Baruch, and these two with the Revelation of John. The alteration has been therapeutic for our discipline; we have been forced out of the twentieth-century halls of academia into the ambience and swirling world-culture of Early Judaism and Early Christianity.

Complexity as Much as Quantity

The influx of more data is not merely like a shot-in-the-arm; it is more like an avalanche of voluminous documents. A mere three decades ago New Testament scholars worked primarily with 27 documents, which are so brief that Lee Keck labels them mere "pamphlets."[3] In light of the gigantic volumes – like Jubilees and 1 (Ethiopic) Enoch – now before us, the New Testament writings appear diminutive. The Nag Hammadi Codices and the Qumran Scrolls provide us with well over 100 works that were unknown before the '40s. In

---

[1] See my introductory article in the volume on the Old Testament Pseudepigrapha to be published in Wege der Forschung and edited by me and H. Lichtenberger. The following footnotes are highly selective, in order to clarify the essential points.

[2] See my "Greek, Persian, Roman, Syrian and Egyptian Influences in Early Judaism: A Study of the History of the Rechabites," in *Judaica et Hellenica (Festschrift for Valentin Nikiprowetzky)*, in press.

[3] L.E. Keck, "Is the New Testament a Field of Study? or, From Outler to Overbeck and Back," *The Second Century* 1 (1981), 19-35.

Charles' edition of The Old Testament Pseudepigrapha only 17 documents were included; the new edition by Doubleday amasses 52 documents, plus 13 other compositions in a supplement. And some of these documents are over 70 chapters long (viz. 1En, 2En, 2Bar), whereas some New Testament writings have only one chapter (viz. Philemon, 2Jn, 3Jn, Jude).

Such comparisons reveal even more disparity than a contrast in quantity. The complexity of the Pseudepigrapha exceeds that of the New Testament documents. First, they are extant in numerous languages: Greek, Hebrew, Syriac, Aramaic, Coptic, Ethiopic, Armenian, Arabic, Karshuni, Latin, and Slavonic. Second, the extant manuscript or manuscripts may be translated from a lost Greek text, which itself derives from a Semitic original.

The New Testament writings are preserved in Greek and derive from Greek originals (based in places on lost Semitic sources). The Slavic Pseudepigrapha preserved in Cyrillic texts, by contrast, evolved from old Slavonic manuscripts in Glagolitic script, which are lost, and which not only translated but redacted Greek texts, which are both now lost and were in turn translated from Semitic manuscripts, which themselves – often through redactions – evolved from Semitic originals. St. Cyril himself, who created the Slavonic alphabet (*slo'zi pismena*) in order to translate the Greek Gospels into Slavonic, was a gifted linguist (one of the reasons the Emperor Michael III chose him), who knew Hebrew and Samaritan (see *Vita Constantini,* ed. P.A. Lavrov and F. Pastrnek).[4] To publish elegant, idiomatic English translations of such extant texts is unscholarly, because it falsifies the lost and distant original.

Even a greater problem confronts those who study the Pseudepigrapha. Many of the writings in the Old Testament Pseudepigrapha are redacted and interpolated by later authors; some redactors were Jewish, others Christian. Some documents – perhaps the Testaments of the Twelve Patriarchs, the Ascension of Isaiah, and the Hellenistic Synagogal Prayers – probably were written by Jews, later redacted by other Jews, and finally redacted by Christians. The final product may even have been interpolated by post-Nicene Christians. The task of separating tradition from redaction is notoriously difficult, as a perusal of recent research on the Testaments of the Twelve Patriarchs discloses.[5]

---

[4]For a succinct summary of St. Cyril, who changed his name from Constantine, see R. Auty, *Texts and Glossary* (Handbook of Old Church Slavonic, Part II) (London: 1960, reprinted 1968).

[5]See the discussion on redaction and interpolation that took place at Duke University during the SNTS conference of 1976, published in Charlesworth, *The Old Testament Pseudepigrapha and the New Testament* (SNTS Monograph Series 54) (Cambridge: 1985), pp. 99-102. Also, see M. de Jonge (editor), *Studies on the Testaments of the Twelve Patriarchs: Text and Interpretation* (Studia in Veteris Testamenti Pseudepigrapha 3) (Leiden: 1975).

In summation, the quantity of new documents in the Pseudepigrapha intimate the disparity between these writings and the New Testament documents. This contrast is heightened by the complexity of the data.[6]

The Old Testament Pseudepigrapha is Not a Canon

Unique problems confound the study of the Old Testament Pseudepigrapha. The collection is not a canon, as unfortunately some non-specialists have surmised. It is not produced by developments in confessing communities, as was the case with the Old Testament and the New Testament. It is a modern collection that defies definition and can only be described; and that means primarily by what is within the corpus.[7] Obviously, once the edition is published a document is either in or out; this choice was sometimes difficult, but it was always facilitated by international dialogues over criteria and definition.[8]

Likewise, the Old Testament Pseudepigrapha is unlike the Nag Hammadi Codices and the Qumran Scrolls, because it does not constitute a library tied to a particular locale. It is a modern collection of ancient, Jewish and Christian documents, that are usually related to the Old Testament writings, many of them are even pseudonymously attributed to figures in the Old Testament.[9]

The New Edition

The preliminary observations distinguish present research from past endeavors and spawn a myriad of questions: How did the project that produced the new English edition of the Old Testament Pseudepigrapha begin? Who served on the Board of Advisors? How were contributors chosen? Who organized the format for each contribution? By what criteria were documents chosen for inclusion? How did each contribution move from first draft to galleys? How was the project funded?

---

[6] The purpose of the present discussion is to draw attention to disparities between the Old Testament Pseudepigrapha and the New Testament. A discussion of similarities is found in other publications, notably see my "The Jewish Roots of Christology: The Discovery of the Hypostatic Voice," in *Scottish Journal of Theology* 39 (1986) 19-41; and "The Background and Foreground of Christian Origins," in *Proceedings of the Irish Biblical Association* 10 (1986), in press.

[7] See the discussion "Definition of Pseudepigrapha" in *The Old Testament Pseudepigrapha*, vol. 1, pp. xxiv-xxv.

[8] Deep appreciations are here tendered to the many scholars who have helped me understand the complex problems involved in any definition. I am especially grateful to my colleagues in the SBL Pseudepigrapha Group and in the SNTS Pseudepigrapha Seminar.

[9] In addition to the "Definition of Pseudepigrapha" noted earlier, see my "Pseudepigrapha," in *Harper's Bible Dictionary*, edited by P.J. Achtemeir (San Francisco: 1985), pp. 836-40; "The Old Testament Apocrypha and Pseudepigrapha," in *The Encyclopedia of Religion*, edited by M. Eliade, in press.

Initial Phases

The project began in November 1972 with a letter to James H. Charlesworth from John J. Delaney, the editor at Doubleday & Co., Inc., New York. The first paragraph of his letter of November 6, 1972, reads as follows:

> For some time I have been studying the possibility of a new translation with commentary of the Pseudepigrapha of the Old Testament and perhaps the Apocrypha of the New Testament. While discussing the possibility of such a project with Fr. Raymond E. Brown last week, he told me you had been working in this field and suggested that I get in touch with you as he felt that perhaps much of the work you have been doing would fall within the scope of the project I mentioned above. In such a case, he felt most strongly that you were the man to undertake such a project.

Over six months later, after lengthy discussions with scholars, administrators, and lawyers, Delaney and I reached an agreement to publish a new English edition of the Old Testament Pseudepigrapha. During this long period of reflection I learned much from revered colleagues and administrators at Duke University, notably Professor W.D. Davies, Chairman Bill Poteat, Dean Tom Langford, and President Terry Sanford. As the project grew to include over 50 scholars in more than 11 countries, and as deadlines and even guidelines were often broken, I lamented for approximately 10 years of having assumed the responsibilities as editor of the new edition of the Old Testament Pseudepigrapha. A project that was to take three years consumed five, then twelve years of exhaustive and lengthy work. The project often threatened to become chaotically cumbersome and unwieldingly complex. For the beautiful product, unimagined on the way, I wish to salute my colleagues at Doubleday, namely Robert T. Heller, Executive Editor, Religion Department; Theresa M. D'Orsogna, general editor; and Harold Grabau, head of the copy editors. As numerous reviews have stated, Doubleday has established a standard by which other works will be judged.

The Board of Advisors

Senior colleagues who were specialists in the Old Testament Pseudepigrapha and who were experienced in somewhat similar projects were chosen. I wish now to acknowledge that the high quality of the final product is due to conversations with and advice received from the Board: Ray Brown, W.D. Davies, Walter Harrelson, Bruce Metzger, Roland Murphy, and John Strugnell.

Choosing Contributors

Contributors were chosen according to two criteria. First, the scholar must be able to write good English, and have demonstrated the ability to translate ancient languages into meaningful and reliable English. He or she must have demonstrated the ability to treat the texts as authoritative, and not as drafts to be improved.

Second, he or she must be recognized as an expert who has already contributed – either directly or indirectly – to our understanding of the document being considered. The procedure was to choose the documents first and then to discern who was best qualified to introduce and translate each of them. The ideal situation was to invite an English-speaking revered expert who had just completed a critical edition of the document. The ideal was elusive; but *The Old Testament Pseudepigrapha*, 2 vols. (Garden City, NY: Doubleday, 1983-1985) should provide the stimulus and basis for a complete set of critical editions.

The Format

After long sessions with experts here and abroad, and after discussing the focus and needs of the project with the authorities at Doubleday and with the Board, I – as editor – drafted a format that was to be followed, *mutatis mutandis*, by each contributor. The format was approved, and sent to each contributor. It is outlined in *The Old Testament Pseudepigrapha*, vol. 1, pp. xv-xvi. Since the project was to include the public as well as scholars, the editor informed each contributor that scholarly jargon was to be avoided, and that the contribution was to be addressed to the average intelligent reader.

Composing the Corpus

Documents were chosen for inclusion according to criteria now explained in *The Old Testament Pseudepigrapha*, vol. 1, pp. xxi-xxix, and in *The Pseudepigrapha and Modern Research With a Supplement* (SBL SCS Series 7S; Chico, CA: 1981; pp. 15-25). First, some documents were obvious choices; these included works like 1 (Ethiopic) Enoch, 2 Baruch, the Psalms of Solomon, 4 Ezra, Jubilees, Joseph and Aseneth, Life of Adam and Eve, the Testament of Moses, 3 Baruch, 3 and 4 Maccabees, and the Letter of Aristeas.

Second, documents were included that were similar to this core group, but which are extant only in later, perhaps heavily edited manuscripts. This group includes especially the Slavic Pseudepigrapha, which were probably shaped by the Bogomiles.[10] Within this distinct group are, for example, 2 Enoch, the Apocalypse of Abraham, and the Ladder of Jacob.

Third, writings in the Pseudepigrapha are exceptional in contrast to other Jewish writings like those in the Old Testament, in the Old Testament Apocrypha, in the Qumran libraries, and in the Philonic corpus. Many of them were preserved only by Christians and only in interpolated, even considerably expanded, forms. The consensus was strong and clear that such writings should

---

[10]See the discussion on "Slavic Pseudepigrapha," in *The Old Testament Pseudepigrapha and the New Testament*, pp. 32-36.

be included in the Old Testament Pseudepigrapha; and it is now recognized by experts here and abroad that these documents must be presented in their *full* form. Within this category are such works as the Testaments of the Twelve Patriarchs, the Ascension of Isaiah, the Sibylline Oracles, the Hellenistic Synagogal Prayers, and the Fourth Book of Ezra (which is the name that Metzger and I have given to the extant Christianized form of the Jewish work called 4 Ezra).

Fourth, there are other documents which should be included within the Old Testament Pseudepigrapha for a variety of different reasons. Some are difficult to date or categorize, but appear to contain early Jewish traditions or even portions of otherwise lost Jewish documents. A few are placed within the Pseudepigrapha because all other collections are closed. With this *alia* category we enter the greying limits of the Old Testament Pseudepigrapha.

This consensus today is that *far more* documents must be placed under the category, the Old Testament Pseudepigrapha, than were included in the brief selections published by Kautzsch and Charles. Hence, the question uppermost in our critique should be: How many other documents should be added to the collection? Surely we would do well to consider including some Qumran fragments, such as the Prayer of Nabonidus, and the apocalyptic pseudo-Danielic compositions. In my judgment, these works should be included only when we are certain that they were not composed by the Qumran covenanters, and that the integrity of the category, the Dead Sea Scrolls or the Qumran Scrolls, is not jeopardized.

The Production

Contributors began their tasks in dialogue with the editor. When a final draft was ready for submission it was sent to the editor, who read it, checked the translation for accuracy and clarity, corrected it, and then handed it to a research assistant who checked references, assured consistency according to a notebook of guidelines, and drew attention to areas for improvement. The editor then met with the assistants and discussed the edited contribution. The contribution was then sent to an outside reader who was uniquely qualified to assess the work. The draft was then returned to the contributor with a list of suggested improvements (*corrigenda* and *addenda*). Photocopies of relevant, but uncited, publications were also shipped to the contributor.

In the second phase of production the corrected and improved contribution was resubmitted. The same process was again followed; and sometimes the editor returned the contribution or portions of it for further improvement. Finally, the work was submitted to Theresa M. D'Orsogna who drew attention to other areas for improvement. After these were incorporated, with the approval of the contributors, the work was given to the copy editors. Numerous inconsistencies in punctuations, spellings, capitals, and abbreviations were corrected at this stage. The contribution was returned with pages of queries to the editor. Working with his assistants and in dialogue with the contributor the work was finally resubmitted to Doubleday.

In the third phase the contribution – with corrections in pencil, and in blue, red, and green ink – was sent to the printer. Subsequently a photocopy of the contribution and one set of galleys were sent to the contributor. The original typescript with the master galleys were sent to the editor. The contributor corrected the galleys and sent only them to the editor. The editor studied the corrections, checking the typescript, sometimes rechecking the text, and transferred the corrections with others to the master galleys. These were then sent back to Doubleday with the typescript. Final correspondence tightened up loose ends and moved the production through to its completion.

The above procedure might appear cumbersome to many, but it insured that the introduction, translation, and notes were as authoritative and impeccable as humanly possible. Indeed, the process was far more complex than outlined above. Not one but 65 documents went through this process. The final typescript delivered to Doubleday was mountainous. It exceeded 6,000 pages; and that total amounts to 30 publications of 200 typescripts each.

The edited typescript stacked to the right of my desk, waiting to be taken to Heller and D'Orsogna at Doubleday, rose to over five feet in height. Obviously it had been necessary, for efficient and accurate editing in my office and in the full editorial process at Doubleday to transport the bulk of the entire work to Heller's office at one time. This procedure demanded, of course, that the deadlines for contributions be staggered over at least five years. Some translations were submitted, edited, and polished before the SNTS conference at Duke in 1976. Such was the case for the contributions on 1 Enoch and the Testaments of the Twelve Patriarchs.

It is disappointing to read some reviews that incorrectly assume the preparation of *The Old Testament Pseudepigrapha* was analogous to the publication of an ordinary research book. The editorial process at Doubleday encompassed five years, after the submission of the 6,000 and more pages, and it cost approximately $250,000.

To criticize Professors Isaac and Kee for not utilizing Milik's volume on the Qumran Aramaic fragments or M. de Jonge's *editio maior* on the Greek of the Testaments of the Twelve Patriarchs is to expose one's own ignorance. Both of those fine and important works postdate the completion of the contributions on 1 Enoch and the Testaments of the Twelve Patriarchs. I, as editor, saw the significance of these books and added in brackets a reference to them in the bibliography of each introduction. Isaac added in the notes to his translation the important variants in the Aramaic (for examples see *OTP*, vol. 1, pp. 24-27).

The international community of scholars had ample opportunity to learn about the pioneering and superb work by Kee and Isaac. Kee presented a major paper in the SNTS Pseudepigrapha Seminar, at Duke in 1976; it was summarized in the seminar report,[11] and was published in *New Testament Studies*.[12] Isaac read a major paper on 1 Enoch at the SNTS Pseudepigrapha Seminar, at Tübingen in 1977, drawing the attention of Enoch specialists, like Black, Knibb, Nickelsburg, Andersen, and others, to the existence of the earliest, and least corrupt, manuscript of 1 Enoch, namely Kebran 9/II. Isaac's research was summarized in the published seminar report.[13] Knibb subsequently added an appendix to his edition of 1 Enoch, drawing attention to Kebran 9/II.[14] It is absurd to claim that Isaac should have consulted Knibb's work; Knibb's publication was subsequent to and influenced by Isaac's research. Knibb's "Preface" is dated "December 1977," clearly postdating the Tübingen conference in August 1977.

Fortunately, almost all reviewers avoided such unprofessional and embarrassingly uninformed attacks on sensitive and dedicated scholars. The accolades poured on me must be shared with the research team and with the unparalleled excellence of the Doubleday team.

It is now opportune to congratulate all contributors and express my appreciation for model collegiality and cooperation. The shocking abuses received from some colleagues and the burdens placed upon me by developments crescending from a letter received one cold November day were borne along with the pains and problems endured by many. An entire book could be written about the sacrifices and dedication of the contributors; some members of the project died before the first volume appeared, others endured severe illnesses or divorces, more than one was in bed for months because of an automobile accident. Fortunately each contributor helped the venture to succeed, and we can state now that the fates (for once) did not find a way.[15]

Funding

The massive project was funded by grants from the Duke University Research Council, and from many other sources, especially the Phillips Investment Corporation, and the Mary Duke Biddle Foundation. A large advance, against royalties, from Doubleday insured that no individual would profit unduly from the venture; the advance underwrote only the expenses of the

---

[11] Charlesworth, "Reflections on the *SNTS* Pseudepigrapha Seminar at Duke on the Testaments of the Twelve Patriarchs," *New Testament Studies* 23 (1977), 296-304.
[12] H.C. Kee, "The Ethical Dimensions of the Testaments of the XII as a Clue to Provenance," *New Testament Studies* 24 (1978), 259-70.
[13] Charlesworth, "The *SNTS* Pseudepigrapha Seminars at Tübingen and Paris on the Books of Enoch," *New Testament Studies* 25 (1979), 315-23.
[14] M.A. Knibb, "Appendix," *The Ethiopic Book of Enoch: A New Edition in the Light of the Aramaic Dead Sea Fragments*, in consultation with E. Ullendorff (Oxford: 1978), pp. 425-28.
[15] For more reflections, see my "The Significance of the New Edition of the Old Testament Pseudepigrapha," in *La littérature intertestamentaire*, edited by M. Philonenko (Paris: 1985), pp. 11-28.

initial phase of the project. These grants and gifts have made it possible to market the volumes at an amazingly low price in today's business world.

Significance

It is not easy to glimpse the significance of the new edition of the Old Testament Pseudepigrapha. On the one hand our published research must be representative of the whole world of Early Judaism and Early Christianity; we must endeavor to understand *all* the literary *and* archaeological evidence. It would be unwise to stress that the Pseudepigrapha is the most important collection of ancient Jewish and Christian writings. As my introductions to each section in this corpus clarifies, the documents help solidify the importance of Philo, Josephus, the Old Testament Apocrypha, the Qumran Scrolls, and Jewish Magical Papyri,[16] and – of course – the Old Testament[17] and the New Testament.[18]

We must acknowledge that something momentous has been accomplished by an international and interconfessional team of experts. It is simply unperceptive to dismiss the new edition with the comment, "Well, there is little new here, I read the Pseudepigrapha in a seminary course 30 years ago." Much has transpired over the last few decades, it simply is not possible to return to the imagined "good old days."

We have entered a new epoch. Now, for the first time we have a collection of the Pseudepigrapha, and not merely a selection of them. Now we have all the Jewish apocalypses and apocalyptic literature in one volume, with reliable translations and notes, and with introductions that stress the *status quo* regarding our search for manuscripts, and the original language, date, and provenance of each document.

Now we have conveniently before us the evaluations of an international team of experts. Their voice is clear and commanding. These once neglected and discarded writings reveal an unexpected brilliance, sophistication, and erudition in Early Judaism.[19] Early Jews not only memorized ancient Israelite lore and

---

[16]See H.D. Betz (editor), *The Greek Magical Papyri in Translation, Including the Demotic Spells* (Chicago, London: 1986).

[17]For more discussion, see my "The Pseudepigrapha as Biblical Exegesis," in the Brownlee Festschrift, in press.

[18]See my *The Old Testament Pseudepigrapha and the New Testament*.

[19]M.E. Stone writes about the rapidly emerging "new picture of Judaism in the period of the Second Temple" (p. 10), which has been surprising and revolutionary to him, causing him "to change my view of what Judaism looked like then, of what it was, and how it developed (p. viii)." Some of the ideas now clearly representative of Early Judaism "are totally unexpected" (p. 35). See Stone's personal, idiosyncratic, but brilliant reflections in *Scriptures, Sects and Visions: A Profile of Judaism from Ezra to the Jewish Revolts* (Philadelphia: 1980).

tradition, they also mastered the best scientific advancements in Egypt, Iran, Greece, and Rome.[20]

The witnesses of scholars is challenging: Early Judaism was not a cold legalistic religion; it was a lively organism receiving insights from a world drawn closer together. Long before the destruction of Jerusalem in seventy, Jews produced literary masterpieces.[21] They created impressively faithful and deeply pious poetic treasures, especially prayers and liturgies like the Hodayoth and the Prayer of Manasseh.[22]

In summation, the new collection of the Old Testament Pseudepigrapha draws us away from our insular offices and classrooms, and away from preoccupations with secondary discussions. We are again drawn *ad fontes*. It is obvious that the sources for Judaism and Christianity are neither conflicting and contradictory nor antagonistic and antipodean.

As Kee has endeavored to show, through his teaching and writing, Early Judaism and Early Christianity shared so much that it is often impossible to distinguish an early Jew who "followed" Jesus from one who did not. Christianity "arose out of Judaism," and the early Christian group "like the Dead Sea sect, considered itself to be the true heir of the new covenant."[23]

---

[20]In addition to the publications cited earlier, see my "Folklore, Humor, Inscribed Seals and Reflections on the Origin of Jewish Apocalyptic Literature," in the Fischel Festschrift, in press. The Samaritan Papyri, about to be published by F.M. Cross, prove that Greek influence in Palestine obviously antedates the conquests by Alexander the Great: They are early fourth-century papyri, and they contain seals bearing Greek mythological figures. It is impressive how recent research and discoveries are proving M. Hengel's thesis about the interpenetration of Hellenism, and other cultures, deep within early Jewish culture. See Hengel's masterful *Judaism and Hellenism: Studies in Their Encounter in Palestine During the Early Hellenistic Period*, 2 vols., translated by J. Bowden (Philadelphia: 1974). This work was advanced in Hengel's *Jews, Greeks and Barbarians: Aspects of the Hellenization of Judaism in the Pre-Christian Period*, translated by J. Bowden (Philadelphia: 1980).

[21]As G. Nickelsburg rightly judges, the early Jewish sages, "transcended the apocalyptic eschatology of Third Isaiah in qualitative and significant fashion" (p. 95). See his *Jewish Literature Between the Bible and the Mishnah: A Historical and Literary Introduction* (Philadelphia: 1981). I fully agree with him that the "seedbed of the church was first century Judaism" (p. 2).

[22]See Sh. Talmon, "The Emergence of Institutionalized Prayer in Israel in the Light of the Qumran Literature," in *Qumrân: Sa piété, sa théologie et son milieu*, edited by M. Delcor (Paris: 1978), pp. 265-84. Also, see "Prayers, Psalms, and Odes," in *The Old Testament Pseudepigrapha*, vol. 2, pp. 607-771; Charlesworth, "A Prolegomenon to a New Study of the Jewish Background of the Hymns and Prayers in the New Testament," *Journal of Jewish Studies* 33 (1982), 265-85 [the Yadin Festschrift edited by J. Neusner and G. Vermes]; and D. Flusser, "Psalms, Hymns and Prayers," in *Jewish Writings of the Second Temple Period*, edited by M.E. Stone (Compendia Rerum Iudaicarum ad Novum Testamentum, 2, II) (Assen, Philadelphia: 1984), pp. 551-77.

[23]Kee, *Understanding the New Testament*, fourth edition (Englewood Cliffs, NJ: 1983), p. 66.

FORMATIVE CHRISTIANITY

Chapter Five

Jesus of Galilee and Judas the Maccabee: Hero Worship or Messianic Machinations?

John T. Greene
Michigan State University, East Lansing, Michigan

I

The early movement which grew up around the figure of Jesus attracted members from a cross-section of the Palestinian population. I maintain that a Maccabee-Hasmonean messianic faction with interest in Jesus as one who followed the career of the Maccabee-Hasmoneans closely and which understood him to have been working toward the restoration and continuation of the Maccabee-Hasmonean line of priest-king messiahs, was a part of this cross-section. I maintain further that this view is mirrored most clearly in the Fourth Gospel, especially in 1) its use of the Temple cleansing episode, 2) the specific mention of Hanukkah (Feast of Dedication), 3) Jesus observing the feast, 4) questions being directed at Jesus concerning his messiahship while he is observing the feast, plus 5) the light motif which pervades the work. To be sure, this Maccabee-Hasmonean interest has been overlaid with later interests and foci which have produced the Fourth Gospel as we presently have it. Enough remains, however, to suggest provocatively that an earlier stratum of what ultimately became this Gospel at least reflects the early interests of a Maccabee-Hasmonean faction among the early Jesus movement in Palestine. Both Jewish history and early Christian history (especially where these two overlap and become the same) would contain an unfortunate and damaging *lacuna* if a Maccabee-Hasmonean messianic hope of restoration were not present in the canonical Gospels or was left unacknowledged in the history of the messianic idea.

What one did, or what was later claimed that one did, determined which view of the messiah(s) was held for that person. Because Jesus was viewed by the evangelists as fulfilling so many different offices concurrently that had been held by separate individuals at one time or other in ancient Israel, it is clear that some held him to have been all things to all people; a sort of Moses for all seasons. It is obvious that one of these offices was believed to have been that of messiah.

Of the various "proofs" offered by the evangelists that Jesus was a messiah, only two, his entry into Jerusalem riding on an ass amid shouts of Hosanna! from the throng, and the so-called cleansing of the Temple episode involve what the majority of contemporaneous Palestinian Jews would have expected of a messiah.[1]

II

The famous prophecy of Nathan at 2 Samuel 7 – especially 7:12b-16 – carried with it the expectation that a messiah (=anointed ruler in Jerusalem, offspring of the House of David) would rule in perpetuity. With the notable exception of King Athaliah (ca. 842-837 B.C./E.) from ca. 966-587/6 B.C./E. a Davidide had indeed served as messiah. Such a long tenure caused the adherents of the "divinely appointed kingship theology-ideology" to believe that David's throne and successors would continue endlessly. The first major challenge to this theology came in 587/6 B.C./E. when the Davidic successor, Zedekiah (Mattaniah), was deported in chains to Babylonia. The ignominious end of this messiah and his potential successors is summed up in 2 Kings 25:6-7. When a messiah sat on the throne in Jerusalem again in 104 B.C./E. the royal kingship theology-ideology received its second major challenge.[2] From Messiah David to Messiah Zedekiah two offices had been held concurrently by one individual. These messiahs had been priest-kings.[3] In 104 B.C./E. another priest-king began to rule again in Jerusalem, but he was neither of the Davidic line, nor House of Judah. Instead, Aristobulus I was of levitical lineage.[4] The idealists who had expected the eventual reestablishment of the Davidic messiahship must have recoiled in horror; this went against Nathan's prophecy (=Yahweh's word)! However, the more pragmatic observers and interpreters of the times accepted the existential situation as a *fait accompli*, and adjusted accordingly to the messiahs of the Hasmonean Dynasty.[5]

---

[1]The Davidic genealogical tables contained in According to Matthew and According to Luke as "proofs" are discussed below.

[2]Sources both ancient and modern are undecided on the issue of who was actually acknowledged as priest-king and who functioned as "high priest-first citizen." Josephus and the authors of I and II Maccabees are cautious in assigning titles. Gottwald, *A Light to the Nations* (New York: Harper, 1959), p. 502 assigns titles more liberally in his table. Most agree, however, that Aristobulus I enjoyed the title priest-king officially.

[3]David's bringing of the ark to Jerusalem dressed in the priestly ephod, Solomon's serving in a priestly capacity at the dedication of the new Temple of YHWH, and Josiah's reforming efforts all mirror the designation found in the Psalter (Ps. 110:4).

[4]We learn that the Maccabee/Hasmoneans were Levite priests from the *Testament of the 12 Patriarchs, Book of Jubilees, Book of Covenant of Damascus*, etc., which respond to their tenure.

[5]These pragmatists are listed below in Part III's pro-levitical messiah sources.

III

Messiahs in Israel might have been expected to ride asses (i.e., the royal mount), but from where did the concept of a Temple-cleansing messiah derive?

Judah the Maccabee, by succeeding in cleansing, rededicating, and re-establishing the Temple and its cult, launched speculation concerning a new messianic age and messianic office. It is not difficult to understand how Judah could have been thought of as a messiah, both immediately and in retrospect.[6] In fact, the messianic age, dated ca. 200 B.C./E. to 200 A.D./C.E. rounds out the initial and final acts of this period – Judah 165 B.C./E. to Simon bar Kochba 135 A.D./C.E. Such an event brought on by Judah would not have been forgotten by subsequent Jews. That Hanukkah which commemorates Judah's feat(s) was being observed during the time of Jesus is attested by According to John 10:22. We are aware, however, that a claim for messiahship on the part of Judah or his immediate successors would not have been looked upon favorably at first by the majority of Judeans. A review of the main reasons why is in order. His successors, and consequently Judah himself, eventually did come to be viewed as legitimate messiahs, however.

Reactions pro and con to the ascent of the Jewish priest-king-messiah Aristobulus I and his immediate successor, Jannaus Alexander are contained in the Testaments of Judah (con); Reuben 6:7-12; Levi 2:11; 18; Dan 5:10-13; Naphtali 8:2-3; Gad 8:1 and Joseph 19:11 of the *Testament of the Twelve Patriarchs,* and the *Book of the Covenant of Damascus* (8:1-21 as well as IQS 9:9-11 and 4Q Testim. 14-20) (all pros). These works of the pro group hold that the messiah is from the house of Levi. A somewhat middle of the road attitude is adopted by the writer of the Midrash-Aggadah-Halakhah, the *Book of Jubilees* (31:13-17; 31:13-20; 32:9, etc.), where Jacob jointly blesses Judah *and* Levi as "princes" over the people. What this literature makes evident is that more than one specific type of messianic hope thrived during the Hasmonean period 167-63 B.C./E.[7] Some clung to the hope that a Davidide would again sit on the throne and continue the line which had been interrupted by divine punishment (Test. of Judah). Others believed God's will for a messianic lineage had been realized in the present priest-kings of Jerusalem (Test. of Levi, etc.). Still others could accept the legitimacy of messiahs from both camps (Jubilees). It would appear that either, or a combination of any of the above messianic hopes – and these are only a small sampling – could be justified and defended on the basis of fact, sentiment and, above all, contemporaneous scriptural hermeneutics. Messianic hope hermeneutics became a mature exercise reaching fever pitch during the

---

[6] For the history conscious among Jews during the Maccabean period, it was obvious, in retrospect, that Judah's leadership and success had inaugurated a new and significant era not witnessed since the fall of the House of David in 587.

[7] See the lively discussion in the Critical Notes by Bruce V. Malchow, "The Messenger of the Covenant in Mal. 3:1" *JBL* 103, 2 (June, 1984): 252-255.

period from Judas the Maccabee to Jesus of Galilee;[8] and beyond to Simon bar Kochba.

Works such as those produced by Ringgren and Mowinckel provide a job description of the messiah in ancient Israel, while the *opus* of Klausner, for example, traces the history and development of the messianic idea through literature covering a twelve hundred year period. Schürer's work covers the crucial period from 175 B.C./E. to 135 A.D./C.E. Placing Jesus and those messianic claims made for him by his followers (contemporaneous and surviving) into the historical scheme presented by the foregoing works and others is a difficult but necessary task. With regard to messianic claims *for* Jesus, one camp holds that little or nothing contained in the Gospels pointed to messianic machinations on the part of Jesus.[9] Another camp infers from "glimpses" gained by peering through the "cracks" of theological and apologetical overlays provided by the evangelists that Jesus manifested many of the important requirements of the messiah's job description; one simply had to read between the lines.[10]

IV

The Gospels are repositories for many messianic hopes, either single or composite.[11] Jesus is viewed as being the point of confluence for most of these hopes. One hope which the historian would expect to find included appears to be conspicuously absent, that of the Hasmonean messiah. But is it? The Fourth Gospel has a decidedly different messianic view (or views). There is an emphasis on the Temple cleansing occurring at the beginning of Jesus' Jerusalem-based activities. A light-dark theme pervades the work which does not depend on the Synoptics for gospel pattern.[12] And an event which resulted in the Hasmonean Dynasty being created is celebrated by Jesus in this Gospel and no other. Moreover, this celebration itself has as one of its themes supernatural light. These would point to an inclusion of the Hasmonean messianic hope. I contend that it would be odd indeed if it were not present in some form in one of these canonical Gospels. The anniversary of the fall of the House of Hasmon was in

---

[8]See H. Ringgren, *The Messiah in the Old Testament* (London: SCM Press, Ltd., 1967, c. 1956), S. Mowinckel, *He That Cometh* (Nashville: Abingdon, 1954, c. 1951), and J. Klausner, *The Messianic Idea in Israel* (New York: Macmillan, 1955), and the penetrating work of Emil Schürer, *A History of the Jewish People in the Time of Jesus* (New York: Schocken, 1971, c. 1961).

[9]Geza Vermes, *Jesus the Jew* (New York: Macmillan, 1973), pp. 86-99 wherein Vermes holds that Jesus himself appears to have preferred the title "prophet" to all of the possible titles attributed to him.

[10]S.G.F. Brandon, *Jesus and the Zealots* (New York: Scribner, 1967), pp. 330-334, *et passim*.

[11]Within the canonical Gospels one can discern the Davidic, Son of Man, Suffering Servant, Humble Messiah, the Prophet (like Moses), and (as this essay is in the process of arguing) the Levitic messianic hopes.

[12]This motif is found at 1:4; 5; 7; 8; 9; 8:12; 9:32's man born blind (darkness) and being made to see (light) must also be understood within this motif, *et passim*.

its approximate 93rd year whereas the anniversary of the fall of the House of David was in its approximate 617th year at the time of Jesus' Jerusalem based activities. The former, having occurred less than a century before, would certainly be basis for an active restoration-messianic hope hermeneutics as well.

Hanukkah celebrated the cleansing and rededication of the Jerusalem Temple by Judah, a levite priest. The Fourth Gospel places Jesus in Jerusalem early in his activities performing a symbolic act reputed to be directed at a later defiling of the same Temple. The cleansing by Judah became viewed by some as having inaugurated a new messianic era and the establishment of what eventually became a messianic kingdom. The cleansing by Jesus (as viewed by the Fourth Gospel) signalled the beginning of a reestablishment of this messianic kingdom. A supernatural light is associated with the launching of this Maccabean/Hasmonean era, light burning in a Temple lamp which is said to have burned for eight days, but containing only enough oil to burn but one day. This "light" motif is also present in the Fourth Gospel with the supernatural (Jesus) Christ being considered the light. The Gospel's use of the term light is radically different from its use by any other evangelist. Judah's cleansing launched the celebrating or observance of the Feast of Dedication, the site where it all began.[13] Again, only the Fourth Gospel contains this information, especially the notation that it was in the winter time when this occurred (25 Kislev). The most telling piece of information for my thesis, however, is the conversation which ensues in this Gospel after we are told Jesus' location on this date. It is a conversation with "the (nebulous) Jews" concerning *messianic activity!*[14] Jesus is asked whether he will own up to being the messiah at this time. But just as quickly as we are given this glimpse of messianic oriented material, it is wrenched from us and replaced or "watered down" once more by one of the numerous reproving discourses placed in the mouth of "Jesus" and aimed at "the (nebulous) Jews." Messianic discourse has been replaced by polemics. If messianic expectation is the subject of the brief glimpse and the date is 25 Kislev, and the place is the Temple, one cannot be accused of forcing the issue that a Hasmonean messiah is the subject under discussion here. Of course, one would have to hold many preconceptions about Jesus the Davidic messiah in abeyance, and be open to the possibility of a Jesus the Hasmonean candidate for messiah, or wisher for such a messiah.

V

"Jesus" of the Gospels often "speaks" the theology of the post-Easter Church; a theology which often proceeds from the "mouth of Jesus" according to the needs and beliefs of the four evangelists as well as other anonymous contributors to these works. In this regard, what "Jesus" says or does must be

---

[13] According to John 10:22.
[14] According to John 10:24.

subjected to multidisciplinary scrutiny to ascertain as far as possible whether a given action attributed to "him" could plausibly have been performed by, as well as have been of relevance to, the first century A.D./C.E. Palestinian Jew Jesus.[15]

Two of the four canonical Gospels produce genealogies which attempt to show that Jesus had Davidic pedigree.[16] Although both genealogies fail to convince the careful reader, the attempt to establish Jesus in the Davidic royal succession points to a faction making *specific* claims *for* Jesus; that he was a legitimate heir to *Davidic* messiahship. It does not matter that the faction's claims are untenable when viewed under the light of close scrutiny. The material reflects the purpose and view of a faction. Other messianic expectations are also found in these two Gospels including Son of Man as a savior figure, but not messianic, and the humble messiah of Zechariah 9:9. In fact, the *Davidic* claims for Jesus in these two Gospel's genealogies appear to be later additions, perhaps in response to some other messianic claim for Jesus made by a rival group. At any rate, the Davidic claims are secondary, not the primary argument for the messiahship(s) of Jesus as viewed in the Gospels.

Two Gospels do not contain genealogies. It is reasoned that According to Mark, as the first written Gospel which served as the basis for the versions of Matthew and Luke, was not concerned with Davidic messiahship apologetics. The absence of a genealogy in According to John is explained as being due to "In the beginning was the *logos*..." setting the tone for Jesus Christ's beginnings, thus rendering an infancy narrative or genealogy unnecessary. The first (Mark) was too primitive and the fourth was too superior and spiritual, many argued, to need genealogies. But this argument, especially with regard to the Fourth Gospel, rests on the assumption that it was written toward the end of the first century A.D./C.E. and this after the Synoptics had already been written. This argument does not explain why the schema of Jesus' life and activities differ in the Synoptics versus the Fourth Gospel. Besides, the jury is still out concerning the date, provenance and destination of the Fourth Gospel.[17]

Otto Piper called attention to what he held was the origin of the gospel pattern and argued that this pattern was shaped by the *kerygma*.[18] Far from producing a "primitive gospel" that would have formed the basis of the written Gospels, this gospel pattern "left room for diversity in the arrangements of the materials available as well as for their selection."[19] We already know that at

---

[15]This includes the discipline which views the canonical Gospels as aretalogies. See Moses Hadas and Morton Smith, *Heroes and Gods: Spiritual Biographies in Antiquity* (London: Routledge and Kegan Paul, 1965).

[16]According to Matthew 1:1-17 and According to Luke 3:23-38.

[17]See especially the arguments forwarded by J.A.T. Robinson, *Redating the New Testament*, (Philadelphia: Westminster, 1976), pp. 254-311. Although Robinson's argument (Note 1) is strong and well argued, it is not considered the *ipsissima verba* on this issue, but merely good, necessary input to a complex problem of dating portions of the New Testament.

[18]Otto Piper, "The Origin of the Gospel Pattern," *JBL* LXXVIII (June 1959) Part II: 115-124.

[19]Ibid., p. 124.

some point in its development, the gospel pattern which took the form of According to Matthew and According to Luke responded to a challenge to justify the messianic pedigree of Jesus as being specifically Davidic. Here the problem begins. Matthew 1:16's "...and Mary, of whom Jesus was born..." is brilliantly nebulous and depends on *Gestalt*. Mary, the mother of Jesus, is Elizabeth's kinswoman in Luke 1:36. Elizabeth and Zechariah are of priestly stock and point strongly to Mary's priestly familial pedigree also. Thus, where Matthew is nebulous on the subject, Luke provides enough material to show that whereas Joseph might have been of Davidic lineage, Mary, and thereby Jesus on his mother's side, was more than likely of *priestly* descent. Zecharias being designated a priest of the division of Abijah does not sufficiently narrow down the *type* of priest, i.e., Zadokite, Levite, etc., he was.[20] Again, the lack of unimpeachable evidence in this issue of the royal versus the priestly pedigree is not the important factor. What is important to note is that out of the two Gospels which contain infancy narratives and genealogies, one, Matthew, attempts to establish a Davidic pedigree of Jesus, whereas the other, Luke, reflects the possibility of two different pedigrees being held out for Jesus, one Davidic through Joseph and one priestly through Mary. At this time one hears of only Zadokite and Levite priests of various orders. Luke's account makes smooth reading without the addition of 1:27's "betrothed to a man whose name was Joseph, of the house of David." If this view is tenable, an earlier stratum in the development of According to Luke appears to have presented the case for an exclusively *(Levitical?)* priestly pedigree for Jesus. This, too, is important and must not be overlooked.

VI

Let us consider the "Temple cleansing" attributed to "Jesus." The Gospels treat the Temple-cleansing incident differently. The so-called Synoptics show it as belonging to the *final* public activities of Jesus in Jerusalem before his arrest. The Fourth Gospel has it taking place *early* in the Jerusalem activities of Jesus. The Fourth Gospel, however, is the only Gospel which connects the observance of the Maccabean revolt and especially Judah's Temple cleansing with Jesus' observance of the festival (feast) commemorating it.[21] I regard this as purposive and significant for those who regarded the Maccabee-Hasmoneans as heros.

Scholarly views abound concerning the Temple cleansing of Jesus. These views concern the nature and purpose, but do not question the historicity, of the event. An unquestioning historical view suggests that the "cleansing" was part of a two-pronged attack by zealot and allied forces (including those of Jesus)

---

[20]Scholars concerned with the Hebrew, Israelite and Jewish priestly factions acknowledge three main groups, 1) Zadokite, 2) Levite and 3) Abiatharite. Several subgroups are also acknowledged.

[21]According to John 10:22.

designed to wrench back Jerusalem from the Romans and their collaborators.[22] That the "cleansing" may have been a timely *statement of warning* to dishonest Temple entrepreneurs (witnessed even by the acquiescing authorities) has also been advanced.[23] Yet another view within the framework of contemporaneous banking holds that the "cleansing" was an unfocused, unfortunate incident which netted its perpetrator an unfortunate execution at the behest of those whose economic world had been threatened.[24] Winter states that the incident amounted to nothing more than a brawl in a mid-eastern Bazaar.[25] It has also been suggested that the "cleansing" was a necessary preparation for the Kingdom of God.[26] No harmony of these views appears to be forthcoming. None of these views, however, suggests a connection with the cleansing under Judas the Maccabee, especially as this cleansing is used in the Fourth Gospel.

VII

I suggest that on the specific issues of 1) what type of messiah Jesus was thought to have been, or 2) with which messianic movement he was associated, or 3) even which messianic movement(s) saw him as *their* type of messiah, According to Luke and According to John have a connection generally not acknowledged. Both put priest and messiah together as key ingredients of a messianic hope hermeneutics. The temple cleansing incident is the point where priest and messiah would meet in the form of a priestly messiah.

Why would a priestly messiah have been of such importance during the first century A.D./C.E. in Palestine? We readily acknowledge the hopes of the idealists who expected the eventual reestablishment of the Davidic messiahship. This hope asserted itself more strongly and for a longer period than any other messianic hope. We also acknowledge no denial that other messianic hopes did not survive. The second strongest hope would have been help by the heirs of those who were thoroughly impressed that Judah and his successors were a legitimate dynasty. 2 Kings 25:6-7 chronicled the end of the Davidic messianic dynasty, Josephus' *Antiquities* chronicled the end of the Hasmonean messianic dynasty. Having been replaced by the House of Antipater-led, Roman-client government, the late Hasmonean Dynasty would have had its mourners just as the late Davidic Dynasty would have had (and indeed did) its. Messianic hopes grew up as a result of the unexpected and untimely demise of both dynasties.

---

[22]Brandon, *Jesus and the Zealots*.
[23]Haim Cohn, *The Trial and Death of Jesus* (New York: Harper, 1967), pp. 53-59.
[24]Neil Q. Hamilton, "Temple Cleansing and Temple Bank," *JBL* LXXXIII (Dec. 1964), Pt. IV: 365-372.
[25]Paul Winter, *On the Trial of Jesus* (Berlin: De Gruyter, 1961), p. 143.
[26]Richard H. Hiers, "Purification of the Temple: Preparation for the Kingdom of God," *JBL* XC (March 1971), Part I: 82-90.

VIII

When placed in historical perspective, a Hasmonean messianic claim is not really farfetched. Galilee and the Hasmoneans have a connection which goes back to John Hyrcanus, a Maccabee-Hasmonean.[27] It was he who expanded the Hasmonean kingdom and settled numerous Jews in the frontier region (i.e., Galilee of the north).[28] The Galileans would have had cause to keep a hope alive that the Hasmonean type of messiah would again reassert himself. We know that the House of Antipater was not looked upon favorably, by Galileans especially.[29] We know of a Galilean family whose activities and energies were associated with messianism and who were active both in Galilee and Judah.[30] Their activity began soon after the fall of the House of Hasmon. Brandon deals with this family at length in his two works, but even he assumes that their activity is carried out under the canopy of *Davidic* messianic hopes.[31] Josephus, commander of the northern defense forces in the war against the Romans, claimed Hasmonean priestly descent. Thus, a Hasmonean descendant is involved in an attempt to rid Palestine of Roman presence and influence long after the time of Jesus.

Jesus' activities as recorded in the Fourth Gospel reflect a whole new way that a certain special interest group of his day or shortly thereafter either viewed his messiahship, or attempted to include their view of Jesus' messianic legitimacy into the other legitimizing messianic views concerning him. This group appears to have brought certain interpretations of Jesus and his movement with them when they joined the Jesus movement. These interpretations were informed by the group's pro-Hasmonean messianic stand. It is worth stating, however, that I make these remarks about the Maccabee-Hasmoneans being

---

[27]Schürer states in Op. cit. "...for it was one of the first acts of the Maccabee brothers...to bring help to their brethren in the faith in Galilee...who had been oppressed by the heathen..." (p. 16). Also "But after Simon had defeated the heathen in Galilee, he led all the Jews away out of Galilee...into Judea, in order that there he might keep them in safety" (p. 16) (I Macc. 5:23).

[28]Flavius Josephus, himself a Hasmonean descendant, was the commanding officer in charge of the defense of the Galilee at the beginning of the Jewish war against the Romans in A.D./C.E. 66. The assignment was not without import.

[29]In ca. 44 B.C./E. Ezekias, a Galilean dissident, took up arms against the regime of Antipater. Antipater's son, Herod, captured and executed Ezekias as an outlaw (much to the chagrin of the Sanhedrin which brought Herod up on charges).

[30]Several of Ezekias' kinsmen, including a son, Judas, and a grandson, Menahem, also engaged in anti-"House of Antipater" activity. Note, too, the words of the Galilean Jesus in According to Luke 13:32, and this after the execution of John the Baptizer at the order of Herod Antipas, tetrarch of Galilee and Perea. Also of special note is the description of the inhabitants of the Galilee by Vermes, *Jesus the Jew*, pp. 42-57.

[31]Brandon, *Jesus and the Zealots* and *The Trial of Jesus of Nazareth* (New York: Stein and Day, 1968). Although he has ample opportunity to make such a case, Brandon either focuses on the possible dynasty building attempts of the family of Ezekias or their attempts to rid the country of Romans and their collaborators. Other than alluding to this being a family tradition, he does not evaluate their "messianic" machinations in light of all of the contemporaneous hopes. In this respect his two works are cliffhangers unnecessarily.

looked upon as heros with some necessary reservations. These reservations do no violence to my thesis. Therefore, I present them with no fear and trembling. One must surely ask: "Why would the Hasmonean Dynasty have been missed?" Surely it is known that the Hasmoneans cultivated Hellenism assiduously and mocked many Jewish practices and sensibilities. In doing so, how could any Jews remotely see them as messiahs?" "Why would Jews find a hero in a man like Alexander Jannaeus who gave orders that numerous Jews who opposed his policies were to be put to death?" The questions could be multiplied.

One need merely read the accounts of David's successors, holding up such figures as Manasseh, Ahaz and Jehoiakim in relief, to see that all that glittered during the Davidic Dynasty, too, was not gold. Yet the hope of messianic restoration was advanced, honed, furbished and polished by successive generations. It was the renewal of the dynasty as an ideational concept, not the fact that one or more of those who comprised it went askew, which stoked the fires of that hope.

The Maccabee-Hasmonean heros of the Galileans were on reflection Judas through Aristobulus I, with John Hyrcanus and Aristobulus taking the lime light. We have no specific reaction on the part of a single Galilean to the slaughter of Jews under Jannaeus in the "nation of the Jews" which had Jerusalem as its center.[32] We are well aware of antipathy between Galileans and those of the "nation." This would explain some of the silence on the part of the Galileans but not all. Certainly Judah, Jonathan and Simon were remembered warmly and Hyrcanus I and Aristobulus I were viewed as patrons, protectors and heros by them. The Maccabee-Hasmonean block so understood is more than suffcient reason why Galileans would have wanted to see it restored and would have fought for its restoration. It is no accident that a Galilean named Jesus is depicted in the Fourth Gospel, albeit viewed through the nebulous literary patchwork of this Gospel, paying homage to the freedom-giving activities of Judas son of Mattathias on 25 Kislev.

There are hundreds of reasons why a Galilean, Jesus, would have admired the Maccabee-Hasmoneans and five of them in particular. It is understandable why some who knew him or heard of him would have had cause either to see him as one whose Temple-cleansing activity either showed him to be one attempting to put into motion a series of events geared to restore their dynasty or see him as one who attempted to repeat one of the famous and unforgettable acts of heroism in Jewish history to that time.

---

[32]Elias Bickerman, *From Ezra to the Last of the Maccabees: Foundations of Post-Biblical Judaism* (New York: Schocken Books, 1962), p. 57.

Chapter Six

Der biblische Hintergrund der paulinischen Gnadengaben

Otto Betz
University of Tübingen

1. Das Problem des Begriffs χαρις, χαρισματα.

1.1 Die neutestamentlichen Exegeten haben sich, wie es scheint, ganz damit abgefunden, dass es für den Begriff und die Sache der paulinischen Gnadengaben (χαρισματα) keine alttestamentliche Wurzel gibt; ja, auch der Begriff "Gnade" (χαρις) habe "keine Vorgeschichte."[1] Vielmehr sei Damaskus, wo Paulus "Gnade und Apostelamt" empfing (Röm 1,5), der Ort, an dem das Wort χαρις gleichsam aus der Taufe gehoben wurde und von da an nicht nur die an Paulus selbst erwiesene gnädige Tat Gottes, sondern auch dessen Heilshandeln allgemein bezeichnete und theologisch begründete.

In der Tat wurde die Berufung zum Apostel von Paulus als eine ganz unverdiente Zuwendung Gottes empfunden und mit einer formelhaften Wendung gerühmt als "Gnade, die mir gegeben wurde" (Röm 12,3; 15,15; 1. Kor. 3,10; Gal 2,9).[2] Darüberhinaus geschieht die Rechtfertigung des Sünders und die Rettung aller Menschen "aus Gnaden" (Gal 1,6; Röm 3,24f); die Liebe Gottes (Röm 5,8) und die Liebe Christi (Gal 2,20f) werden dabei offenbar. Die Gnade ist demnach nicht nur Motiv oder Weise des göttlichen Handelns, sondern auch dessen Ergebnis. Besonders wirkt sie in der Kirche als dem Leibe Christi in der Form verschiedener Gnadengaben (χαρισματα); dabei wird einem jeden eine besondere Gabe geschenkt, so dass sich auch hier die persönliche Zuwendung Gottes erweist (Röm 12,3-6; 1. Kor 12,4ff; Eph 4,7ff).

---

[1] J. Jeremias, Der Schlüssel zur Theologie des Apostels Paulus. SUNT 2, Göttingen 1963, S. 22f; G. Hasenhüttl, Charisma, Ordnungsprinzip der Kirche, Freiburg 1969; K. Haacker, Die Bekehrung des Verfolgers und die Rechtfertigung des Gottlosen, in : Theol. Beiträge 6 (1975) S. 12; H. Conzelmann, Art. χαρις in ThWNT Bd. IX. Vgl. dazu S. Kim, The Origin of Paul's Christology, Tübingen 1984, S. 296.

[2] Vgl. dazu A. Satake, Apostolat und Gnade bei Paulus, in: NTS 15 (1968/9), S. 96-103.

1.2 Bei den Griechen war χαρις weder ein zentraler religiöser noch ein für die Philosophie bedeutsamer Begriff.[3] Die Septuaginta verwenden χαρις vor allem für das hebräische hen, das "Huld, Angesehenheit, Demut, Liebreiz, Wohlgefälligkeit" bedeutet und wie das paulinische χαρις mit der Verbum "geben" (natan) verbunden werden kann (Gen 39,21; Ex3,21 ua.).[4] Hen wird also vielfach für den menschlich-äesthetischen Bereich verwendet; zudem besitzt es keine Pluralform und konnte deshalb nicht zur Bezeichnung von Gnadengaben dienen. Dagegen bildet häsäd, ein hen nahestehender, aber viel häufiger verwendeter Begriff, einen Plural; dieser kann die rettenden Taten und gnädigen Gaben Gottes bezeichnen, während häsäd im Singular vor allem die "Bundeshuld" als Eigenschaft Gottes meint. Aber häsäd wird in der Septuaginta durch ελεος = "Erbarmen" wiedergegeben; eben darauf gründet sich das Urteil, es gebe keine alttestamentlich-jüdische Vorgeschichte des paulinischen χαρις – χαρισμα – Begriffs.[5] Ausserdem tritt auch ελεος nur im Singular auf. Paulus war demnach gezwungen, für die "Gnadengaben" etwas Neues, gleichsam extra legem, zu schaffen; das gelang ihm mit dem Begriff χαρισμα(τα), der sonst nur spät und selten verwendet wird.[6] Auch das Wirkungsfeld dieser Gnadengaben, nämlich die ekklesiologische Grösse des Leibes Christi, ist ja spezifisch paulinisch; alles spricht also für eine sprachlich-theologische Novität.

Ich möchte die schöpferische Kraft des Theologen Paulus nicht bezweifeln. Aber schon angesichts der grossen Bedeutung der Begriffe χαρις und χαρισματα für die Rechtfertigungslehre und das Leben der Kirche ist es kaum denkbar, dass Paulus ohne einen Bezug zum Alten Testament auskam. Wie lässt sich ein solcher aber nachweisen? Wo ist der Ort, an dem Paulus diese Steine für den Bau seiner Ekklesiologie gefunden hat?

2. Die Gnadengaben im Alten Testament.

2.1 Wir setzen methodisch bei den Charismen ein, da sie für Paulus besonders charakteristisch sind und sich ausserhalb des Corpus Paulinum (1. und 2. Korintherbrief, Römerbrief, Epheser, Pastoralbriefe) nur in 1. Peter 4,10 finden. Eine der wenigen Stellen, an denen die Gnadengaben bei den Apostolischen Vätern erwähnt sind, stellt ausdrücklich den Bezug zur jüdischen Tradition her. Justin behauptet gegenüber Tryphon: Die prophetischen Gnadengaben (προφητικα χαρισματα) haben früher bei den Juden existiert, sind aber jetzt nur bei den Christen zu finden, gleichsam zu diesen übergegangen (Dial. c. Tr. 82,5).[7] Er meint damit die alttestamentliche Prophetie, die mit falschen Propheten zu ringen hatte, so wie jetzt die charismatischen Christen von

---

[3] H. Conzelmann a.a.O. S. 364f.
[4] W. Zimmerli, Art. χαρις ThWNT Bd. IX, S. 368ff.
[5] H. Conzelmann a.a.O. S. 382: "Häsäd führt nicht weiter, da es auf ελεος hinführt."
[6] Bei Philo Leg Alleg III, 78 gibt es den Plural χαρισματα.
[7] οτι τα παλαι εν τω γενει υμων οντα εις ημας μετετεθη.

Irrlehrern bedroht seien. Die Prophetie ist aber nur eines unter den verschiedenen Charismen der paulinischen Gemeinden und zudem anders geartet als etwa die klassische Prophetie (vgl. aber 1. Tim 4,14). Deshalb kann letztere nicht der alleinige Ausgangspunkt für das Phänomen der paulinischen Charismen sein. Immerhin musste für den jüdischen Gesprächspartner Justins die klassische Prophetie im Alten Israel als eine "Geistesgabe", ja als das einzige Charisma, gelten, da der Heilige Geist im rabbinischen Judentum ausschliesslich als Geist der Prophetie verstanden wurde.

2.2 Von Justin her kommend, möchte ich im Neuen Testament mit einer Stelle beginnen, an der Paulus den Begriff χαρισματα nicht speziell auf die Gnadengaben der Kirche, sondern auf die Vorzüge des Volkes Israel bezieht: "Denn unverbrüchlich (αμεταμελητα) sind die Gnadengaben (χαρισματα) und die Erwählung Gottes" (Röm 11,29). Wo werden in der Schrift solche von Gott fest zugesagten und darum unverbrüchlichen Gnadengaben für Israel erwähnt? Im Kontext hatte der Apostel die Verheissung Jes 59,20f als Garantie Gottes für die endzeitliche Rettung von ganz Israel zitiert (Röm 11,26f). Im Unterschied zu Justin, nach welchem die Christen Erben der jüdischen Gnadengaben geworden sind, spricht Paulus von unkündbaren, unübertragbaren Gnadengaben für Israel; auf ihnen beruht die Erlösung des ganzen Gottesvolkes in der messianischen Zeit. Nun steht in der Nähe von Jes 59,20f die von Paulus in der Synagogenpredigt von Antiochien (Apg 13,34) zitierte Verheissung Jes 55,3: "Ich will mit euch einen ewigen Bund schliessen, (ich will euch) die verlässlichen Gnadengaben Davids (geben) (hasde david hanä' ämanim)." Gemeint sind nach Ps. 89,2 (vgl. 2. Chron 6,42) die zum Bund mit David gehörenden Gnadenerweise Gottes.[8] M.E. ist es diese Stelle (Jes 55,3), die zusammen mit ihrem Kontext eine Geschichte der paulinischen χαρισματα nachweisen und nachzeichnen lässt, zumal sie sich in der Jesusüberlieferung ebenfalls findet. Jes 55,3 geht die grosse Einladung Gottes vorauf, die Dürstenden möchten zum Wasser kommen, die Mittellosen sollten "ohne Preis" und "ohne Geld" Wein und Milch, Brot und Fett kaufen, um so ihre Kraft zum Leben aufzufrischen (Jes 55,1-2). Das ist bildliche Rede für das Angebot des Wortes Gottes, das die Seele leben lässt (V. 2), und für den ewigen Bund, in dem die "Gnadengaben Davids" verwirklicht werden. (V.3).

2.3 Nirgends im Alten Testament wird so konkret von der freien Gnade Gottes, der Gabe seines Wortes und der festen Zusage der messianischen Erlösung gesprochen wie in Jes 55,1-3.[9] Was sind aber die verlässlichen Gnadengaben Davids? Sie beruhen auf der Nathanweissagung 2. Sam 7,12-16,

---

[8]Vgl. Ps 106,7: Die wunderbaren Gnadentaten, die Gott an Israel in Ägypten getan hat.

[9]Justin zitiert Jes 55,3-5 in Dial. c. Tr. 12,1 als Beweis dafür, dass die Christen das wahre Bundesvolk, das geistliche Israel, darstellen. Die Juden hätten das Gesetz Gottes missachtet, durch das ihnen das Leben zugesichert war, und den Neuen Bund verworfen. Sie glauben, durch äusserliche Riten wie Beschneidung, Sabbat und Reinheitsvorschriften Gott zu gefallen, der durch das Opfer des Christus und die Erfüllung von Jes 55 das Heil für alle angeboten hat.

nämlich der feierlichen Zusage Gottes, er werde einen Sohn des Königs auf den Thron setzen, diesen wie einen Sohn behandeln und seine Gnade (hasdi V. 15) nie von ihm weichen lassen (VV. 2-16). Davids Haus solle fest sein (nä'äman) und sein Königtum für immer währen, sein Thron auf ewig stehen (V.16). In der Nathanweissagung werden somit die Sache und die wichtigen Begriffe von Jes 55,3 genannt; auch der "ewige Bund" (Jes 55,3) ist Kennzeichen der Davidszusage und der davidischen Dynastie. Aus der Verheissung 2. Sam 7,12-16 erwuchs die messianische Hoffnung des Alten Israel (vgl. Ps 89; 132); auf sie bezog sich auch die Erwartung eines Messias in Qumran (4 Q Florilegium). Ebenso hat die Nathanweissagung für David das messianische Sendungsbewusstsein Jesu (vgl. Mk 12,35-37; 14,58-62) und das urchristliche Credo entscheidend geprägt (vgl. Röm 1,3f). Diese Verheissung bot für Jes 55,3 nicht nur den Begriff häsäd und die Tatsache der Unverbrüchlichkeit der Gnade Gottes für das Haus David (2. Sam 7,15), sondern auch den Plural hasadim, wie die Frage Ps 89,50 zeigt: "Wo sind deine ersten Gnadengaben (hasadäkha harishonim), o Herr, die du dem David in deiner Treue (bä'ämunatäkha) zugeschworen hast?" Jes 55,3 gibt eine Antwort auf diese ungeduldige Frage, indem es die Nathanweissagung in einer komprimierten Fassung wiederholt und allen vor Augen stellt: Die David erwiesene Gnade soll in der Form von Gnadengaben ganz Israel zugute kommen. Ja, der Horizont wird ins Universale geweitet: Gott hat den David zu einem Zeugen, Fürsten und Gebieter für alle Nationen bestellt (V.4); bisher unbekannte Völker werden zu Israel kommen um Gottes willen, der sein Volk verherrlicht (V.5). Das sind endzeitliche Aussichten, die eine messianische Auslegung von Jes 55,1-5 gestatten.

2.4 Jes 55,3 ist die Stelle, an die Paulus im Röm 11,29 denkt, wenn er von den Gnadengaben Gottes für Israel spricht. Sie sind "unverbrüchlich," "fest" (αμεταμελητα = nä'ämanim), weil Gott sie in seiner "Treue" ('ämunah) dem David zugeschworen hat (Ps 89,50) und weil das Haus Davids "fest" (nä'äman) sein wird (2. Sam 7,16). Was hat Paulus konkret unter den χαρισματα für Israel verstanden, wie werden sie in der Endzeit für die Juden eingelöst? In Röm 11 verheisst Paulus die Rettung von ganz Israel (V. 26), die Erneuerung des Bundes, die auch Vergebung der Sünden einschliesst (V. 27). Das sind eher Gnadentaten als Gnadengaben im Sinne von Jes55,1-3. Auch in der frühjüdischen Auslegung steht der erste Aspekt im Vordergrund. Ps Sal 17 und 18 sind an 2. Sam 7,12-16 orientiert. Gott hat den David als König über Israel erwählt und ihm zugeschworen, sein Königtum werde nicht aufhören (17,4). Diese Zusage wird mit der Sendung des messianischen Davidssohns erfüllt (17,21ff), der auch über die Völker regieren wird; diese werden kommen, um seine Herrlichkeit zu sehen (17,30f, vgl. Jes 55,4f). Es wird somit auch an Jes 55 erinnert, aber die Gnadengaben für das Gottesvolk verblassen im Glanz der Messiasherrschaft.

In den Qumranschriften wird nicht nur die häsäd Gottes gerühmt, sondern auch – vor allem in den Gebeten – seiner hasadim gedacht.[10] Gott ist ein 'el ha-hasadim (1QM 14,8); der Beter stützt sich auf sie an jedem Tag (1 QS 10,17), ihre Verkündigung gehört zum Gottesdienst (1 QS 1,22; 2,4), sie retten den Wankenden (1 QS 11,11f). Die hasadim[11] stehen parallel zur Güte Gottes (1 QH 11,31f), zu seinem Erbarmen im Gericht (1 QH 6,9), zur Vergebung (1 QH 7,35). Sie sind keineswegs auf die Erfüllung messianischer Verheissungen bezogen, sondern werden im Leben des einzelnen Frommen und der Gemeinde erfahren. Aber sie sind keine Gnadengaben, charismatische Begabungen, sondern Handlungsweisen Gottes, Hulderweise.

3. Gottes Gnadenhandeln an Christus und die Gnadengabe des heiligen Geistes (Apostelgeschichte Kap 2 und 13).

3.1 In der Apostelgeschichte fehlt zwar der Begriff χαρισματα, aber Lukas erzählt, wie sich die Nathanweissagung an Jesus erfüllte und wie auch die Verheissung Jes 55,3 von Gott als verlässlich erwiesen wurde. Petrus und Paulus, die beiden grossen Verkündiger des Evangeliums, haben dies in ihren programmatischen Reden in Jerusalem (Apg 2) bzw. Antiochen (Apg 13) ausgeführt.

3.1.1 In der Rede des Petrus erscheint David selbst als ein "Charismatiker" im Sinne Justins (Dial. c. Tr. 82,1), als ein Prophet der messianischen Zeit und als Zeuge der Gnade Gottes für die Völker (Apg 2,30; vgl. 2,25-34). Er hat die Auferstehung Jesu vorausverkündigt und zwar als "Aufstellung" (2. Sam 7,12) in einem doppelten Sinn: a) als Auferstehung aus dem Totenreich in Ps 16,8-11 (Apg 2,25-31), b) als Inthronisation zur Rechten Gottes im Himmel in Ps 110,1 (Apg 2,32-36). David konnte deshalb die αναστασις des Messias vorausschauen und prophetisch ansagen, weil er aufgrund der Weissagung des Propheten Nathan "wusste" (ειδως) (Apg 2,30) dass Gott ihm einen ewig regierenden (d.h. messianischen) Thronfolger eidlich zugesagt hatte; 2. Sam 7,12-16 ist somit die Basis dieser davidischen Christusprophetie, mit welcher der König in der Tat zu einem Zeugen für die Völker wurde (vgl. Jes 55,4).

3.1.2 Der Messias erscheint hier wie in Ps Sal 17 zunächst als Gegenstand der Gnade Gottes;[12] die Nathanweissagung steht im Vordergrund. Aber daneben tritt nun auch eine Konkretisierung der dem Gottesvolk versprochenen Gnadengaben von Jes 55,3 ein, wobei der Messias zum Mittler der Gnade Gottes wird. Nach Apg 2,33 hat der erhöhte Christus vom Vater die "Verheissung" des

---

[10]Interessant ist das Nebeneinander von hasadim und hasidim im Weisheitspsalm 11 Q (ed. Sanders): "Gedenke der Gnadentaten deiner Propheten und die Werke deiner Frommen (hasidäkha) verherrliche" (Vgl. dazu M. Hengel, Judentum und Hellenismus, Tübingen 1969, S. 324.)

[11]Etwa in der Hälfte der 58 häsäd-Stellen in Qumran steht der Plural.

[12]Dadurch liess sich Ps 16,10, wo die Rettung des "Heiligen" Gottes (ο οσιος σου) verheissen wird, über eine Stichwortbrücke anschliessen.

heiligen Geistes empfangen und diesen an Pfingsten auf seine Jünger ausgegossen. Die Geistausgiessung auf das Gottesvolk sah Petrus zwar in Joel 3,1-5 vorhergesagt (Apg 2,17-21), aber die Tatsache, dass sie auf einer Verheissung beruht (επαγγελια, vgl. auch 2,38f; 13,32; Gal 3,14), konnte Jes 55,3 entnommen werden, wenn man zu den dort verheissenen Gnadengaben Davids vor allem den heiligen Geist zählte. Der König ist ja der mit dem Geist Gottes Gesalbte (vgl. 1. Sam 16; Jes 11,2). Der Messias als der Gesalbte kat exochen wird nun zum Mittler des Geistes und Erfüller von Jes 55,3 in demokratischem Sinn. Der Geist wurde an Pfingsten auf charismatische Weise manifest, nämlich durch ein Reden "in anderen Zungen" (Apg 2,3f.11) und durch prophetische Predigt (Apg 2,14ff); die Gabe des Geistes wird zur Begabung. An Jes 55,1-5 wird man auch da erinnert, wo Petrus seine jüdischen Hörer dazu einlädt, die "Gabe" (δωρεα) des heiligen Geistes zu empfangen (Apg 2,38), "denn euch und euren Kindern gehört die Verheissung, dazu auch all den Fernen, die Gott unser Herr berufen hat" (2,39). Wie in Röm 11,28 steht hier die Berufung neben den Gnadengaben, die dem Volk geschenkt werden sollen, das sich zum davidischen Messias bekennt.

3.1.3 Im Gegenstück zu Apg 2, nämlich in der Paulusrede Apg 13, wird Jes 55,3 ausdrücklich zitiert (V.34). Dieses steht dort an der Stelle, die in der Pfingstpredigt des Petrus (V.30) das Zitat 2. Sam 7,12 einnimmt, und fungiert als Verheissung der "Aufstellung" des endzeitlichen Davididen;[13] unmittelbar anschliessend wird auf den in Apg 2,17-21 ausführlich behandelten Auferstehungspsalm 16 hingewiesen (Ps 16,10 in Apg 13,35). Freilich bietet das dem Septuagintatext folgende Zitat von Jes 55,3 in Apg 13,34 die Wendung τα οσια Δαυιδ; vom Paulus der Briefe wäre die Wiedergabe von hasde Dawid durch τα χαρισματα Δ. zu erwarten. Auch die Gabe des heiligen Geistes wird in der Rede Apg 13 nicht erwähnt, obwohl Lukas das Verbum διδοναι in das Zitat Apg 13,34 eigens eingefügt und so den Gabecharakter der οσια Δαυιδ angezeigt hat. Vielleicht rechnete er zu ihnen die von Paulus seinen Hörern angebotene Sündenvergebung (Apg 13,38), die ja in Apg 2,38; Joh 20,22 zur Gabe des Geistes dazugehört; wie der Geist (Ez 36,26ff), so wird die Sündenvergebung (Jer 31,34) für den neuen Menschen im Neuen Bund gewährt.

3.2 Trotz dieses nicht sehr klaren und scheinbar unpaulinischen Gebrauchs von Jes 55,3 in Apg 13,34 ist anzunehmen, dass hinter dem neutestamentlichen und speziell paulinischen Begriff χαρις nicht etwa ein hebräisches hen, sondern das hoch-theologische häsäd[14] steht, das wie sedaqah auch einen Plural bilden und mit ihm die Akte bzw. Gaben der göttlichen Gnade bezeichnen kann.[15] Joh 1,17 beweist, dass häsäd das Äquivalent zu χαρις sein muss, da χαρις και αληθεια Wiedergabe der alttestamentlichen Wendung häsäd we'ämät darstellt. Da aber die

---

[13] Für den Aspekt der Erhöhung wird in Apg 13,33 die Stelle Ps 2,7 angeführt.
[14] 245 mal erscheint häsäd im Alten Testament und nur an 63 Stellen wird es profan gebraucht.
[15] 18 mal werden die Hulderweise Gottes (Taten oder Worte der Huld) erwähnt, vor allem im Psalter (21,8; 18,51; 89,50; 89,25.29 usw.).

Septuaginta häsäd durch das plurallose ελεος übersetzten, mussten sie den Plural hasadim fast zwangsläufig falsch wiedergeben;[16] τα οσια Δανιδ entspricht nicht hasde dawid, sondern setzt ein hebräisches hasidoth dawid voraus. Unglücklicherweise ist Lukas beim Zitieren von Jes 55,3 in Apg13,34 dieser Übertragung gefolgt, welche die "charismatische" Bedeutung dieses Jesajawortes nicht erkennen lässt. Deshalb war es für die neutestamentlichen Exegeten schwer, die grosse Bedeutung von Jes 55,3 für die Charismenlehre des Paulus zu erkennen und überhaupt die Beziehung zwischen den "Gnadengaben Davids" und der durch Christus eingelösten "Verheissung des heiligen Geistes" zu sehen. Paulus hatte eine glückliche Hand, wenn er zu dem seltenen Wort χαρισμα griff: Die von Gott zugesagten hasadim sind χαρισματα, Äusserungen der Gnade, unverdiente Gaben des grosszügigen und getreuen Gottes, der in Jes 55,3 und dessen Kontext zu Wort kommt. Die dort ausgesprochene Verheissung liess sich mit der messianischen Hoffnung verknüpfen, da in ihr das Heil als ewiger Bund mit unverbrüchlichen Gnadengaben bezeichnet wird.

4. Die Gnadengabe (χαρισμα) des ewigen Lebens (Röm 5,15f; 6,23)

4.1 In Röm 5,15f bezeichnet χαρισμα das gnädige, unserem Heil dienende Handeln Gottes durch Christus, vor allem dessen gehorsame Lebenshingabe um unserer Rettung und Rechtfertigung willen. Kennzeichnend für die paulinische Darstellung der Geschichte des Heils ist die universale Ausweitung des χαρισμα. Mit dem Christusgeschehen werden nicht nur die dem Abraham gegebenen Verheissungen erfüllt (so Röm 4; 15,8; Gal 3; 4), sondern auch die unverbrüchlichen Zusagen an David, die einen ewigen Bund garantieren (Jes 55,3) und damit auf die Endgeschichte weisen.[17] Von dort her führt Paulus das Wort χαρισμα in die Gegenüberstellung von Urgeschichte und Endgeschichte, Adam und Christus, in Röm 5, 12-21 ein: Die Übertretung (παραπτωμα) Adams wird durch das χαρισμα des Christusgeschehens aufgehoben (Röm 5,15). Was bedeutet hier χαρισμα? War die Übertretung Adams eine Tat, die über die Vielen den Tod brachte (V.15 a), so müsste analog dazu χαρισμα eine Gnadentat sein. Aber sie wird in V 15 b beschrieben als "Geschenk" (δωρεα), das durch die "Gnade" Gottes von dem einen Menschen Jesus Christus zustandegebracht und gegeben wurde. Und in V. 16 steht χαρισμα dem Begriff κατακριμα, der Verurteilung im Gericht, antithetisch gegenüber. Es müsste demnach den Gnadenakt Gottes meinen, der unsere Sünden erlässt. Aber auch hier erscheint als Gegengewicht zur Sünde Adams das "Geschenk" (δωρημα V. 16 a), so auch in

---

[16]Der Prophetentargum bleibt mit tabewat D. = "die Güte Davids" zu blass. Die hasadim sind eher den sideqot J., den Heilstaten Gottes, zu vergleichen. Tg Onqelos zu Ex 34,6 sagt zu häsäd we'ämät = lema'bed tabewan uqeshoth.

[17]Auch in Jes 55,4 ist eine weltweite Ausdehnung des ewigen Bundes und der fest zugesagten Gnadengaben Davids angedeutet. Aber David ist eher der gute Herrscher über die Völker als der Heilbringer für die Menschheit, den Paulus in Christus sieht.

V. 17, wo mit Tod und Leben die Früchte der Tat Adams bzw. Christi erwähnt sind: Die dank der Gnade erwirkte Gerechtigkeit ist eine Gabe (δωρεα). Die Erklärung des Geschenkcharakters des Heilsgeschehens in Christus bietet unzweideutig Röm 6,23: "Der Sold der Sünde Adams ist der Tod, die Gnadengabe Gottes das ewige Leben durch Jesus Christus, unseren Herrn." Im Gegensatz zum Sold ist hier das χαρισμα Gottes ein unverdientes Geschenk. Durch Röm 6,23 wird man kräftig an die Zusicherung des Lebens durch Gottes Gaben in Jes 55,1-3 erinnert, das von Paulus analog zum "ewigen Bund" in Röm 6,23 als "ewiges Leben" bezeichnet wird.

4.2 In Röm 5,15-17 rühmt der Apostel das Mehrgewicht der Gnadengabe gegenüber der Unheilsfolge des Sündenfalls. Schon im Alten Testament verbindet sich mit häsäd und hasadim die Vorstellung der "Menge" (rob) (vgl. Ex 34,6; Ps 103,8), und so erscheint auch in Eph 1,6 die Wendung "nach dem Reichtum (πλουτος) seiner Gnade." Nach Jes 55,7 ist Gott reich an Vergebung (jarbäh lisloah). Vor allem aber ist an Jes 53 zu denken: Mit dem "Leben," das der Gottesknecht "für die Vielen vergoss" (Jes 53,12), ist die Gnadengabe Gottes "auf die Vielen reichlich" vergossen worden (Röm 5,15).

5. Die Charismen als Geistesgaben in der Gemeinde

5.1 Erwähnt Paulus in Röm 5 und 6 die universale Geltung von χαρισμα als einer dem Heil der Menschheit dienenden Gnadentat, die als solche allen das ewige Leben schenkt, so meint bei ihm der Plural χαρισματα eher dem Einzelnen angepasste Begabungen, die im Leben der Gemeinde als dienstbare Geistesgaben wirksam werden sollen. Wie das χαρισμα (Röm 5,16), so sind auch die Charismen von Gottes Gnade verursacht, die sich naturgemäss mitteilen und den Menschen dienen will (Röm 12,6); in Eph 4,7 wird das dem Einzelnen nach dem Mass der Gabe Christi zuteil gewordene Charisma als χαρις bezeichnet. Zur Gabe wird die Gnade Gottes durch den heiligen Geist: Die χαρισματα in der Gemeinde sind alle Geistesgaben (πνευματικα, vgl. 1. Kor 12,4 mit 12,1; 14,1); ohne den Geist Gottes würden wir die uns geschenkten Gnadengaben (τα χαρισθεντα)[18] gar nicht als solche würdigen (1. Kor 2,13, vgl. 2, 10-12). So bleiben die Charismen, obwohl Begabungen der Gemeindeglieder, doch auch etwas Überpersönliches und Fremdes. Paulus kann zwar, gleichsam als Gastgeschenk, der Gemeinde in Rom eine "geistliche Gabe" (χαρισμα πνευματικον) versprechen (Röm 1,11). Aber er weiss, dass Gott selbst der Urheber aller geistlichen Gaben und die wirkende Kraft in der Gemeinde ist (1. Kor 12,6; vgl. 1. Petr 4,10), ferner dass der erhöhte Christus im Geist als

---

[18]Das Verbum χαριζομαι hat bei Paulus eine Wandlung gegenüber dem profan-griechischen Gebrauch erfahren. Dort meint es medial " sich gefällig erweisen" und im Passiv "angenehm sein," ist also auf zwischenmenschliche Verhaltensweisen bezogen (vgl. H. Conzelmann a.a.O. S. 365). Dagegen ist τα χαρισθεντα in 1. Kor 2,13 ein echtes Passiv (passivum divinum): Es meint das, was uns durch das Kreuz und die Auferstehung Jesu durch Gottes Gnade geschenkt worden ist.

ein Diener in der Kirche gegenwärtig ist (1. Kor 12,5). Im göttlichen Ursprung und christologischen Bezug liegt das harmonische Zusammenwirken und die Einheit der Geistesgaben – trotz ihrer Verschiedenartigkeit – begründet. Ein jeder hat eine eigene Gabe von Gott (1. Petr. 4,10), ja, die Gemeinde lebt dank der sich ergänzenden Verschiedenheit und reichen Vielfalt der Charismen.[19] Auch gibt es verschiedenwertige (z.B. "grössere") Charismen (1. Kor 12,31). Der Christ ist für sein Charisma verantwortlich, obwohl dieses ganz Gabe ist: Er soll ein höheres Charisma als etwa das der Zungenrede anstreben (1. Kor. 12,31) und die ihm zuteil gewordenen Gnadengaben nicht vernachlässigen (2. Tim 1,6).

Diese Verschiedenheit und auch die menschliche Verantwortung für die Charismen soll traditionsgeschichtlich untersucht werden. Wir wenden uns dabei zunächst der Verkündigung Jesu zu.

5.2 Jes 55 in der Verkündigung Jesu: Die gute Gabe des Geistes, die anvertrauten Talente, das Vermächtnis für die Jünger.

Jes 55 wird in den Evangelien nicht ausdrücklich erwähnt. Aber Jesus hat die Schrift weniger zitiert als vielmehr praktiziert. M.E. war für ihn das ganze Kap Jes 55 wichtig; ja, man kann sagen, er habe die paulinische Charismenlehre vorbereitet.

5.2.1 An die grosse Einladung Gottes in Jes 55,1f erinnert Jesus im Gleichnis vom Gastmahl des Gottesreichs (vgl. Mt 22,4), aber er hat sie auch durch seine Tischgemeinschaft und vor allem in den Speisungswundern antizipiert. Das wird an einzelnen Zügen dieser Berichte deutlich. Vor der Speisung der Fünftausend wollten die Jünger für 200 Denare Brot kaufen, um es den Volksmassen zu essen zu geben (Mk 6,37; vgl. Jes 55,1: "Kommt, kauft und esst!"). Aber Jesus liess die eigenen Brote und Fische verteilen (Mk 6,41) und bedeutete dadurch seinen Jüngern das "ohne Geld" (belo'käsäph) von Jes 55,1. Durch das Wunder der Brotvermehrung, d.h. durch den Reichtum der göttlichen Gnade (vgl. Mk 8,8 περισσευματα und Jes 55,2), wurden alle satt (Mk 6,42; Joh 6,7).

5.2.2 Das "Gratis," das nach Jes 55,1f die Gabe des Gotteswortes kennzeichnet (vgl. Jes 55,3 a), gilt nach der Weisung Jesu auch für den Dienst am Gottesreich, für die von Heilungswundern begleitete vollmächtige Verkündigung des Evangeliums: " Umsonst habt ihr empfangen, umsonst sollt ihr geben!" (Mt 10,8).

5.2.3 Ausserdem bietet der in Jes 55,10f angestellte Vergleich zwischen dem Regen, der die Erde feuchtet, den Samen sprossen lässt und so Nahrung schafft, und dem Gotteswort, das wirkt, was Er haben will und nicht leer zurückkommt, die Grundstruktur für die Saatgleichnisse Jesu: Was mit dem

---

[19]χαρισματα διαφορα Röm 12,6, vgl. διαιρεσεις χαρισματων 1. Kor 12,4. Nicht alle haben z.B. die Gabe, Heilungen zu vollziehen (1. Kor 12,30, vgl. V. 9.28).

ausgestreuten Samen geschieht, veranschaulicht das Wunder des Gottesreichs ("wie" – "so").

5.2.4 Die Aufforderung Jes 55,6: "Sucht den Herrn, solange er sich finden lässt, ruft ihn an, solange er nahe ist!" liegt dem Logion Lk 11,9/Mt 7,7 zugrunde: "Und ich sage euch: Bittet, so wird euch gegeben; suchet, so werdet ihr finden; klopfet an, so wird euch aufgetan!"[20] Auch die im Gebetskatechismus Lk 11 unmittelbar folgenden Verse 11-13 scheinen auf Jes 55 gegründet zu sein, und zwar speziell auf den für uns wichtigen V 3. Jesus preist dort die Güte Gottes, wobei er das Verhalten menschlicher Väter zu ihren Kindern in einen Analogieschluss (qal wachomer) einbezieht: "Wenn nun ihr, die ihr böse seid, euren Kindern gute Gaben zu geben versteht, wie viel mehr wird der himmlische Vater den heiligen Geist geben denen, die ihn bitten!" (Lk 11,13). Der Vergleich zwischen der natürlichen Güte eines Vaters zu seinen Kindern und der Güte Gottes zu uns Menschen ist von Ps 103,13, einem Vers aus dem Lieblingspsalm Jesu, inspiriert (vgl. auch Jes 55,7 b). Aber das Schenken gnädiger Gaben für Israel ist vor allem in Jes 55,1-3 belegt. Nach Mt 7,7 sprach Jesus dabei von "guten Gaben," und so hat der Targum die hasadim von Jes 55,3 übersetzt (tabwath dawid sing.); gute Gaben sind als endzeitliche Heilsgüter zu verstehen. Die in Lk 11,13 versprochene Gabe des heiligen Geistes stimmt mit der urchristlichen und paulinischen Deutung von Jes 55,3 überein: Was Gott durch den davidischen Messias schenken will, ist der heilige Geist als Kraft des Neuen Bundes.

5.2.5 Die Verantwortung für die uns von Gott anvertrauten Gaben macht Jesus vor allem im Gleichnis von den Talenten deutlich (Mt 25,14-30; Lk 19,12-27), das ohne die Beziehung zu Jes 55,3 recht blass bleibt: a) Jesus veranschaulicht in dieser Geschichte die tabwajetha = "die guten Gaben" Gottes durch $\tau\alpha\lambda\alpha\nu\tau\alpha$ = "Talente," mit denen gearbeitet werden soll; b) Sie verlangen deshalb einen "guten und getreuen Knecht" ($\alpha\gamma\alpha\theta\sigma\varsigma$ $\kappa\alpha\iota$ $\pi\iota\sigma\tau\sigma\varsigma$ Mt 25,21.33), weil sie ja selbst "gut" (Targum) und "getreu," d.h. verlässlich (nä'ämanim), sind (Jes 55,3); c) Die Notwendigkeit, mit solchen Gaben zu arbeiten, mit den Talenten zu wuchern, erklärt sich daher, dass sie – wie das Wort Gottes in Jes 55,10f – nicht leer zurückkommen, sondern das bewirken sollen, was ihr Urheber haben möchte (Mt 25,26); d) Das Lob für den treuen Knecht, der "in die Freude seines Herrn eingehen" soll, ist an Jes 55,12 orientiert: "In Freude werdet ihr hinausgehen und in Frieden geleitet sein!"; e) Schliesslich ist gerade von Jes 55 her die Kritik des faulen Knechtes an seinem Herrn und Geldgeber unberechtigt: Gott ist nur scheinbar ein harter Mann, der erntet, wo er nicht gesät hat, und einführt, wo er nicht ausgestreut hat (Mt 25,24.26); vielmehr erbarmt er sich des Bussfertigen (Jes 55,7). Auch bewirkt er durch Regen und Schnee, dass die Erde Samen hervorbringt und Speise gewährt (Jes 55,10), ja, sie kann geradezu eine

---

[20]W. Grimm, Weil ich dich liebe. Frankfurt-Bern 1976, S. 152-154. Vgl. auch Joh 16,23f mit Jes 55,1-3.6.

paradiesische Fülle schenken (Jes 55,12f). Gott sät zwar nicht, aber er gibt das Gedeihen für das Werk des Sämanns (Mk 4,26-29). Vor allem lässt er sein schöpferisches und rettendes Wort auf Erden wirksam sein (Jes 55,11).

5.2.6 Weil Gott so reichlich gibt, darum ist es auch die Aufgabe eines verantwortlichen Knechtes, seinen Mitarbeitern und Hausgenossen die Speise zur rechten Zeit zu geben (Mt 24,45; vgl. Ps 104,27). Egoismus und Gleichgültigkeit sind angesichts der Grosszügigkeit (Jes 55,1-2) und Treue (Jes 55,3) Gottes ein schweres Vergehen (Mt 24,48-51), genauso wie die Vernachlässigung anvertrauter Talente.

5.2.7 Schliesslich erinnert das Vermächtnis Jesu in Lk 22,29f an Jes 55,1-3. Dort wird den Jüngern verheissen: "Und ich vermache euch (die Herrschaft), wie mir mein Vater die Herrschaft vermacht hat (V. 30), damit ihr esst und trinkt an meinem Tisch in meinem Reich und auf Thronen sitzen und die zwölf Stämme Israels richten werdet."

Dieses Schlusswort der sogenannten Q-Quelle ist bei Lukas zu einem Testament Jesu ausgestaltet (V. 29-30a). Was wird den Jüngern vermacht? Die meisten Übersetzungen bieten die am Schluss von V. 29 erwähnte Herrschaft (βασιλειαν) als Objekt, was jedoch wegen der Stellung dieses Begriffs und wegen des Inhalts von V. 30 (εν τη βασιλεια μου) Schwierigkeiten macht. Man kann deshalb auch den ganzen V. 30 (Tischgemeinschaft und Mitregieren im Messiasreich) als Inhalt des Testaments ansehen (so die RSV), oder aber mit einigen Handschriften (A 579 u.a.) das Wort διαθηκην einfügen und als Gegenstand des διατιθεσθαι annehmen. Das Letztere liesse sich von Jes 55,3 her begründen, das eine ähnliche Diktion wie Lk 22,29 aufweist: και διαθησομαι υμιν διαθηκην αιωνιον. Dieser ewige Bund wird ja durch die Verheissung der verlässlichen Gnadengaben Davids konkretisiert. In Lk 22,29 ist deren Erfüllung der messianischen Zeit vorbehalten: Die Jünger werden im Reich Christi die Gäste dessen sein, der seine Güter und Speisen gratis gibt (Jes 55,1f), und als Mitregenten Jesu das neue Gottesvolk der Heiligen richten (vgl. Lk 12,32; 1. Kor 6,2), nachdem der Messias-Menschensohn die königliche Herrschaft von Gott empfangen hat (Dan 7,14). Von 2. Sam 7,12-14 her ist die Messiasherrschaft selbst die erste der Gnadengaben Davids in Jes 55,3; dem Plural hasadim wäre mit dem Regieren und der Mahlgemeinschaft der Jünger Rechnung getragen.[21]

5.3 Von Jesus zu Paulus

---

[21] προστασσων εθνων, vgl. Mt. 28,20: Die Jünger sollen die Völker all das lehren, was Jesus ihnen befohlen hat. Nach Apg 2,38f gilt die Verheissung allen, die Gott beruft, auch den Fernen. Die universale Mission ist durchaus im Sinne des irdischen Jesus. Denn dieser hat nicht nur das dem Volk Israel geltende Nathanorakel auf sich als Davidssohn und Gottessohn bezogen, sondern eben auch die auf diesem Orakel beruhende Verheissung Jes 55,1-5 mit der Basileia verknüpft. Darin wird Gott als der gnädige Vater sichtbar, der alle Menschen zu sich lädt und sie durch Israel mit seinen Gnadengaben beschenken will.

5.3.1 Beides, die Freigebigkeit Gottes und der Zeugendienst für Christus, sollen in der Zeit der anbrechenden Gottesherrschaft von den Aposteln praktiziert werden. Für diese Aufgabe werden sie mit dem heiligen Geist als der Kraft des Neuen Bundes und mit der Vollmacht, Sünden zu vergeben, begabt (Apg 1,8; Joh 20,22). Denn Gott, der die Gnadengaben Davids als Zeichen seiner Bundestreue schenkt (Jes 55,3), ist auch reich an Vergebung (Jes 55,7). Ihm entsprechend soll der Jünger handeln, der ausgesandt wird, wie Jesus gesandt worden war (Joh 20,21), und von ihm Frieden und Freude empfangen hat (Joh 20,19-21; vgl. Jes 55,12). Lukas zählte zu den Gnadengaben Davids vor allem den heiligen Geist, der als Geschenk Gottes allen bussfertigen Menschen frei angeboten wird (vgl. Apg 2,38f). Das "Gratis," "ohne Geld" der Geistesgabe hatte Simon Magus verkannt, als er den Aposteln Geld brachte, um so die Vollmacht der Geistverleihung zu erwerben (Apg 8,13f). In der Antwort des entrüsteten Petrus wird Jes 55,1-3 aktualisiert: "Dein Silber möge mit dir zusammen ins Verderben fahren, weil du wähntest, die Gabe Gottes (δωρεαν) durch Geld erwerben zu können!" (Apg 8,20). Es ist eine ins Verderben führende Sünde wider den heiligen Geist, wenn dieser als käuflich betrachtet wird; dagegen dient er als Kraft zum ewigen Leben, wo man ihn als Geschenk Gottes empfängt (Jes 55,1-3).

5.3.2 Weil der heilige Geist und die Vergebung der Sünden Gaben und Kennzeichen eines ewigen Bundes (Jes 55,3), d.h. des Neuen Bundes, sind (Ez 36,26ff; Jer 31,34, vgl. 1 QS 4,20-22), deshalb wurden sie nicht von David selbst, sondern erst vom davidischen Messias empfangen und den Menschen vermittelt. In der Pfingstpredigt des Petrus (Apg 2) werden die Gnadengaben Davids (Jes 55,3) gleichsam gegen ein Missverständnis geschützt. Nicht David war der Erbe des ewigen Bundes und Mittler der verheissenen Gnadengaben; denn er starb, wurde begraben und liegt noch immer im Grab (Apg 2,29). Was er von seiner Errettung aus dem Totenreich sagte, war deshalb auf den Davididen der Endzeit und ewig regierenden König (2. Sam 7,13) bezogene Prophetie (Apg 2,30f). David war auch nicht derjenige, der die Verheissung des Geistes hätte verwirklichen können; er ist ja nicht zum Himmel aufgestiegen (Apg 2,34). Vielmehr schaute er nach Ps 110,1 den zur Rechten Gottes erhöhten Herrn, der deshalb für die Erfüllung von Jes 55,3 sorgen konnte (Apg 2,33f).

5.3.3 Jes 55,3 wird, ähnlich wie von Jesus selbst, sowohl messianisch als auch charismatisch ausgelegt, mit Hilfe von 2. Sam 7 auf die "Aufstellung" des Christus bezogen und infolge der Geistausgiessung als verlässliche Zusage der Gnadengaben Gottes angesehen. Beides gehört zusammen; ja, die von den Juden erlebten Wirkungen des Geistes sollten ein klarer Erweis der bis dahin geleugneten Messianität Jesu sein: "So soll nun das ganze Haus Israel mit Sicherheit (ασφαλως) erkennen, dass Gott ihn zum Herrn und Christus gemacht hat, diesen Jesus, den ihr gekreuzigt habt!" (Apg 2,36). Andererseits ist ganz Israel eingeladen, durch Busse und Taufe auf Jesus die Vergebung der Sünden und die Gabe des heiligen Geistes zu empfangen, da "Israel und seinen Kindern diese

Verheissung gegeben ist, sowie allen, die fern sind, alle, die Gott unser Herr beruft!" (Apg 2,38f). In Jes 55,7 wird zur Umkehr zu Gott aufgefordert und den Büssern das Erbarmen Gottes und reiche Vergebung verheissen, in Jes 55,5 vom unbekannten Volk gesprochen, das zu Israel und so auch zu Gott kommt. David ist ja zu einem Zeugen für die Völker gesetzt (Jes 55,4), und die Apostel als Empfänger der Gnadengabe des Geistes (Jes 55,3) verrichten diesen davidischen Zeugendienst (Apg 1,8). In Apg 15,14-19 wird die Heidenmission mit dem Schriftwort Amos 9,11 f begründet, das die Wiederaufrichtung des Hauses David verheisst (vgl. Jes 55,3f).

5.4 Das Gesetz Moses und der heilige Geist als himmlische Gaben.

In Röm 6,14f erklärt Paulus, der Christ stünde nicht mehr unter dem Gesetz, sondern unter der Gnade; wie bei Jesus Gesetz und Propheten vom Kommen des Evangeliums bzw. des Gottesreiches überholt werden (Lk 16,16; Mt 12,13), so bei Paulus die Herrschaft des Gesetzes vom Leben unter der Gnade. In Joh 1,17 wird dieser Gegensatz als Thema des Vierten Evangeliums angegeben und ähnlich formuliert: "Das Gesetz ist durch Mose gegeben, die Gnade und Wahrheit sind durch Jesus Christus geworden."[22] Das Verhältnis von Gesetz Moses und der Gnade Gottes in Christus ist aber bei Paulus nicht nur ein antagonistisches, sondern auch ein analoges, vor allem, wenn man auf die Herkunft der beiden Grössen sieht. Eine Analyse dieser Analogie dient meiner These von der alttestamentlichen Grundlegung der paulinischen Charismen.

5.4.1 Das Gesetz ist nach rabbinischer Auffassung eine Gabe vom Himmel. Der Aufstieg Moses zum Berg Sinai (Ex 19,3) war auch ein Einstieg in die himmlische Welt, in der Mose die Gebote erhielt. Einen wichtigen Impuls für die spekulative Ausgestaltung des Toraempfangs gab Ps 68,19: "Du bist zur Höhe aufgefahren, hast Gefangene weggeführt, hast Gaben unter den Menschen empfangen."

Der Targum deutet diese Stelle auf Mose, der in den Himmel stieg, dort die Tora empfing und sie zu den Menschen brachte. Auch sonst wurde Ps 68,19 durchgängig auf Mose bezogen, vor allem in Midr. Tehillim z St., wonach Mose zu den Göttlichen Wesen ('Älohim Ex 19,3) hinaufstieg und dort die Tora "umsonst" (behinnam) als Gabe (mattanah) für Israel empfing. Die "Gefangennahme der Gefangenschaft" konnte auf den überwundenen Protest der Dienstengel gedeutet werden, die darüber ungehalten waren, dass ein Mensch die Tora holen und den Irdischen bringen wollte (Ex r 28, 88b).

5.4.2 Nun wird in Eph 4,7ff die Stelle Ps 68,19 auf das heilschaffende Werk Christi und auf die geistlichen Gaben der Kirche bezogen. Eph 4,7 spricht von der Gnade ($\chi\alpha\rho\iota\varsigma$), die jedem nach dem Mass der Gabe ($\delta\omega\rho\epsilon\alpha$) Christi zuteil wurde; das erinnert an Jes 55,3. Aber Ps 68,19 wird als Begründung ($\delta\iota o$)

---

[22] Zum "Werden," d.h. zur geschichtlichen Verwirklichung durch Christus, vgl. 1. Kor 1.30: Christus ist für uns zur Weisheit und zur Gerechtigkeit, zur Heiligung und zur Erlösung "geworden" ($\epsilon\gamma\epsilon\nu\eta\theta\eta$), nämlich durch sein Kreuz und seine Auferstehung.

gegeben: "Er stieg zur Höhe hinauf und nahm die Gefangenschaft gefangen; er gab Gaben (εδωκεν δοματα) den Menschen" (Eph 4,8). Das "Du" des hebräischen Textes, der Gott anredet, ist hier in ein doxologisches "Er" geändert, das Christus gilt, jedenfalls hinsichtlich des Aufstiegs und der Überwindung der Mächte. Und statt des Empfangens wird das Geben der Gaben betont, wobei die Menschen zu Empfängern werden. In Eph 4,9-16 wird dieser Psalmvers aktualisierend kommentiert. Der Aufstieg zur Höhe setzt den Abstieg in die Niederungen des Erdenlebens voraus (VV. 9-10). Man wird an die Christologie von Phil 2,6-11 erinnert: Die Menschwerdung und das Leiden des Gottgleichen sind Voraussetzung für die Erhöhung und den siegreichen Aufstieg. Denn die Überwindung der feindlichen Mächte (vgl. Mt 12,29) wird duch die Lebenshingabe des Christus am Kreuz eingeleitet. Wieder ist David der Prophet des Messias, der nach Eph 4,11f im Himmel die Freigabe von Heilsgütern erreichte. Er gab (d.h., er setzte kraft des Geistes ein) die einen als Apostel, andere als Propheten, Evangelisten, Hirten oder Lehrer, d.h. in Dienste, wie sie ähnlich in 1. Kor 12,23 als geistliche Gaben im Leibe Christi aufgezählt sind. Nach Eph 4,12 dienen sie der Erbauung der Kirche, so wie das die Charismen nach 1. Kor 14,3.5.12.26 tun. Sie führen nach Eph 4,13 zur Einheit des Glaubens ('ämunah), weil die Gnadengaben Gottes nach Jes 55,3 fest (nä'amanim) sind; deshalb bewahren sie nach Eph 4,14 vor dem Umhergeworfen- und Verführtwerden durch windige Lehren.

5.4.2.1 Wer ist das Subjekt des Gebens im Zitat Eph 4,8? Es liegt nahe, an Christus zu denken, der zum Himmel aufstieg. M.E. ist es aber Gott selbst, der Christus zu einem Mittler der Gaben macht. Das zeigt der Kontext: In Eph 4,7 ist εδοθη ein passivum divinum: Die Gnade ist von Gott gegeben. In V. 11 muss αυτος Gott sein im Unterschied zu Christus in V. 12 Ende und V. 13. Auch nach 1. Kor 12,28 setzte Gott, und nicht etwa Christus, die Eph 4,11 erwähnten charismatischen Dienste ein.

5.4.2.2 Was in Eph 4,7ff nicht eigens betont wird, ist der in 2. Kor 3 herausgestellte Gegensatz zwischen Gesetz und Geist, der Gabe Moses und der Gabe des Christus. Dem Verfasser des Epheserbriefs kommt es hier darauf an, den Ursprung der Geistesgaben aufzuzeigen, zu beweisen, dass diese bereits im Alten Testament vorhergesagt und durch den Aufstieg des Christus den Menschen gebracht worden sind. Er hat Ps 68,19 so zitiert, dass sein zweiter Teil eine Parallelaussage zu Jes 55,3 bildet: "Er hat Geschenke den Menschen gegeben." — "Ich will euch die festen Gnadengaben Davids geben." Das "Geben" Gottes — in Eph 4,8 und Apg 13,34 jeweils eingefügt — bildet die Brücke, so dass die Verheissung Gottes in Jes 55,3 durch den Davididen Jesus eingelöst wurde, der nach seiner Erhöhung die geistlichen Gnadengaben vom Vater erbat. Die Gnadengaben (hasadim) von Jes 55,3 sind gleichzusetzen mit den Geschenken (mattanoth) von Ps 68,19 und den Charismen in den paulinischen Gemeinden (Eph 4,7-12). Während für die Rabbinen das Gesetz die grosse Gabe Gottes darstellt, ist diese für die Christen der heilige Geist, der das Gesetz recht verstehen lehrt (2. Kor 3); hat der "erste Erlöser" die Tora vom Himmel für die Menschen geholt, so der "zweite Erlöser" die Geistesgaben für die christlichen Gemeinden. Jes 55,3 — in der rabbinischen Exegese wenig beachtet — wurde für die Christen zu einer Schlüsselstelle, die auch die Deutung von Ps 68,19 entscheidend beeinflusst hat. Diese Deutung ist wohl zeitlich früher als die jüdische Spekulation über den Toraempfang Moses. Denn der Plural mattanoth = "Geschenke" lässt sich gut zu den Gnadengaben Davids in Jes 55,3 (und zu den Geistesgaben bei Paulus) in Beziehung setzen, passt aber weniger zur "Gabe" (Singular) der Tora,[23] es sei denn, man denke an die Tafeln der Gebote (vgl. Midr. Tehillim z. St. [ed. Buber 160,11]), wo die mattanah der Tora auf die mattanoth von Ps 68,19 bezogen wird).

5.4.3 Wie der Empfang von Gesetz und Geist im Himmel, so wird deren Übergabe auf Erden bei den Rabbinen und den ersten Christen hier und dort ähnlich vorgestellt. Der Pfingstbericht Apg 2 lässt sich mit der rabbinischen Haggada zur Sinaigeschichte Ex 19-20 vergleichen, wobei die Frage der Priorität offen bleiben soll. Das Pfingstfest wurde in Qumran als eine Feier des Eintritts und Übertritts in den Gottesbund begangen (1 QS 1,1-3,12), und bei den Rabbinen gedachte man an diesem Tag der Gesetzgebung am Sinai. Auch in Apg 2 gibt es Einzelheiten, die sich von diesem Hintergrund her besser verstehen lassen; das betrifft vor allem die Art des Offenbarungsempfangs. So hat das von Lukas berichtete Sprachenwunder — ein Reden in "anderen Zungen" = verschiedenen Sprachen (Apg 2,3.11) — ein Gegenüber in der rabbinischen Haggadah gefunden, die von einer Teilung (halaq Niph., b Shabbat 88b) der Gottesstimme am Sinai in die Sprachen der Welt erzählt, [24] so dass jedem Volk das Gebot Gottes in seiner eigenen Sprache angeboten wurde. Am ersten Pfingstfest der Christen teilte sich (διαμερίζεσθαι V. 3) das von Hall und Wind begleitete Feuer der Theophanie in "Zungen" (γλῶσσαι), die sich auf die Apostel setzten, so dass diese, vom heiligen Geist erfüllt, in den verschiedenen "Sprachen" der Welt reden und die grossen Taten Gottes rühmen konnten (Apg 2,2-4.11).[25] Diese Teilung von Geist bzw. Gottesstimme zeigt die universale Geltung der Botschaft an. Nur werden nach den Rabbinen die Gebote, nach dem Pfingstbericht die grossen Taten Gottes verkündigt, und die endzeitliche Gabe ist

---

[23] Als mattanah wird die Tora b Ned 38a; b Mezia 59a bezeichnet. Es könnte sein, dass diese Bezeichnung sich analog zur christlichen Gnadenlehre entwickelt hat; noch in Qumran sagt man von der Tora, sie sei (von Gott) durch Mose "befohlen" (1 QS 8,15).

[24] Die qolot = "Donnerschläge, Hallstimmen" (Ex 19,16; 20,15) werden als 7 Stimmen bzw. als die 70 Sprachen der Welt verstanden, in die sich die eine "Stimme" Gottes geteilt hat. Dabei konnte man sich u.a. auch auf Ps 68,12 berufen, wonach Gott "das Wort der Verkündigung als ein grosses Heer gab" (so der Midrasch); er liess ein jedes seiner Worte sich in die 70 Sprachen der Welt teilen (b Shabbat 88b). Man verwies auch auf Jer 23,29: Gottes Wort ist wie ein Hammer, der Felsen zerschmettert und dabei Funken sprühen lässt (ibid).

[25] Wie in der rabbinischen Haggada das atmosphärische Element der Theophanie (qolot = Donnerschläge) zu einem Träger der Verkündigung wird, so auch beim Pfingstfest: Die verteilten "Feuerzungen" (γλῶσσαι πυρος) wurden in den Jüngern zu "Sprachen" (γλῶσσαι Apg 2,3f.11).

nicht ein neues Gesetz, sondern der von Christus ausgegossene Geist. Das Reden in anderen "Zungen" = "Sprachen" ist nun nicht mehr die Sache Gottes, sondern geschieht an Pfingsten durch inspirierte Menschen, ist ein Charisma. Aber in beiden Fällen vollzieht Gott eine Teilung, die eine den Menschen dienende Verschiedenheit trotz der Einheit des Offenbarungsinhalts ermöglicht.

6. Die Teilung und Zuteilung der Gnadengaben.

6.1 Beides finden wir bei Paulus: Der Teilung der Zungen (Apg 2,3) entspricht die Verteilung der Geistesgaben an die einzelnen Glieder der Gemeinde; aber es ist ein und derselbe Geist (1. Kor 12,4). Gott "teilte" (εμεριζεν = hilleq) einem jeden nach dem Mass des Glaubens zu (Röm 12,3, vgl. Eph 4,7). Darauf folgt Röm 12,4-6 der Hinweis auf die vielen Glieder eines Leibes, die verschiedene Funktionen haben und doch zusammenwirken. So sind auch die Christen, obschon viele (οι πολλοι), "ein Leib in Christus und als Einzelne wie Glieder untereinander" (V.5): "Wir haben verschiedene Geistesgaben nach der uns gegebenen Gnade" (V. 6), aber diese wirken harmonisch zusammen. Dem einen Leib mit den vielen Gliedern entspricht die eine Gnade Gottes, die sich in verschiedene Gnadengaben, Charismen, "gliedert," und deren gleicher Ursprung den sie einigenden Zweck bedingt (1. Kor 12,4-6): Man soll einander dienen, ein jeder mit der Gnadengabe (χαρισμα), die er empfangen hat, als die guten Haushalter der mancherlei Gnade Gottes (1 Petr 4,10).

6.2 Lässt sich auch diese Vorstellung von der Teilung und Zuteilung der Charismen zu Schrift und Tradition in Beziehung setzen? Der Plural "Gnadengaben Davids" (Jes 55,3) sowie "Geschenke" (δοματα = mattanoth) in Ps 68,19 konnte den Tatbestand von mancherlei Charismen biblisch rechtfertigen. Aber die Verteilung und Verschiedenheit der Geistesgaben, sowie ihre Beziehung zu den Gliedern im Leibe Christi, lässt sich mit diesen Stellen nicht belegen.

6.2.1 Wir setzen bei unserer Suche mit Lk 11,22 (vgl. Mt 12,29) ein. Jesus spricht dort von einem Starken, der seine Festung vergeblich zu verteidigen sucht: Greift ihn ein Stärkerer an, überwältigt ihn und nimmt ihm die Rüstung ab, so wird er dessen "Beute verteilen." Diese verhüllte Vollmachtsaussage Jesu geht nicht nur auf Jes 49,24, sondern in ihrer lukanischen Form auch auf Jes 53, 12 zurück: "Mit Starken wird er Beute teilen."[26] Jes 53,12 hat für Jesus, aber auch für die ersten Christen eine ähnliche Rolle gespielt wie Jes 55,3[27] oder

---

[26] Vgl. dazu W. Grimm, Weil ich dich liebe, Frankfurt-Bern 1976, S. 85-93, dazu E. Nestle-K. Aland, Novum Testamentum Graece, 26. Aufl., wo am Rand Jes 49,24f und Jes 53,12 notiert sind.

[27] Auch bei Justin (Dial. c. Tr.) sind Jes 53 und 55 miteinander zusammengesehen. Zunächst wird in Kap. 12 Jes 55,3-5 zitiert, dann folgt in Kap. 12 und 13 der Abschnitt Jes 52,10 - 54,6 als eine langes Zitat. In 1. Petr 1,18 sind Jes 55,1f und 53,12 eng miteinander verknüpft. Die Christen sind nicht durch Silber oder Gold von ihrem vergänglichen Wandel losgekauft worden (vgl. Jes 55,1f: das Angebot der freien Gnade Gottes, die Einladung zum

auch Ps 68,19, weil es auf den Sühnetod Jesu und die durch ihn erwirkten Gnadengaben bezogen werden konnte. Und an zwei Stellen bietet Jes 53,12 das Verbum "teilen" (hilleq), das für die Charismenlehre des Paulus so wichtig ist: a) Gott wird seinem Knecht unter den Vielen (einen Anteil) zuteilen ('ahalleq lo barabbim); b) der Knecht wird mit Starken Beute teilen ('ät 'asumim jehalleq shalal). Zu a): Der für Jes 53 kennzeichnende Begriff ha-rabbim = οι πολλοι meint in der Charismenlehre die Glieder der Gemeinde, denen der Dienst des Gottesknechtes zugute kommt: "Die Vielen" sind ein Leib in Christus (Röm 12,5), bilden dessen Glieder (V.4). In einem Wortspiel konnte der Apostel sagen: Ha-rabbim = 'abarim, d.h. die Vielen sind Glieder (am Leibe Christi). Gott wird sie nach Jes 53,12 seinem Knecht zuteilen, so dass sie Glieder seines Leibes bilden. Er tut dies in der Kirche dadurch, dass er die geistlichen Ämter wie Apostel, Propheten, Lehrer usw. einsetzt (1. Kor 12,28, vgl. Eph 4,7ff). Von daher erklärt sich die enge Verbindung der Charismen mit den Gliedern des Leibes Christi und die Tatsache, dass dieser Leib nicht nur ein Bild für die Wirklichkeit und für das Leben in der Kirche Christi ist, sondern auch mit ihr identisch ist: "Ihr seid der Leib Christi, und jeder ist ein Glied daran nach seinem Teil" (1. Kor 12,27). Der Leib Christi ist eine charismatische Setzung Gottes (1 Kor. 12,28), der seinem erhöhten Knecht die Vielen als Glieder zuteilt. Zu b): Nach Jes 53,12 wird der Gottesknecht mit den Mächtigen Beute teilen. Auch in der frühjüdischen Tradition dieser Zeit wird dem Messias die Aufgabe des Teilens anvertraut; das zeigt das wichtige Kap. 17 der Psalmen Salomos. Danach wird der endzeitliche König aus dem Hause David das befreite Land unter den Stämmen Israels verteilen. Keine Fremden werden in deren Nähe leben, aber er wird Völker und Nationen in der Weisheit seiner Gerechtigkeit regieren (17,28f). Das heilige Land spielt in der Zukunftserwartung des Paulus keine grosse Rolle. Deshalb ist an die Stelle einer Landverteilung die Zuteilung des geistlichen Erbteils der Heiligen durch den Christus gerückt, an der auch die Heiden beteiligt werden. Dafür schien auch Jes 53,12 zu sprechen: Mit den "Starken" ('asumim) wird der Gottesknecht Beute teilen. Wie das bei manchen Begriffen des sprachlich schwierigen Kapitels Jes 53 geschieht, so könnte der Apostel analog zu ha-rabbim = 'abarim auch bei dem Begriff 'asumim an eine zweite Bedeutung gedacht und 'asamim = Gebeine, Glieder gelesen haben: Christus teilt mit den Gliedern seines Leibes die "Beute" (vgl. Ps 68,19) der Geistesgaben. Es scheint mir, dass Paulus dabei Gen 2 interpretiert haben könnte. Für ihn war ja Christus der zweite, endzeitliche Adam, der die Kirche liebt wie ein Mann seine Frau, wie ein Mensch seinen Leib (Eph 5,27-29). Solche Vergleiche erinnern an das Verhältnis Adams zu Eva, die nach Gen 2,23 nicht nur Fleisch von Adams Fleisch (vgl. Eph 5,20), sondern auch "Bein, Knochen," von seinen Gebeinen war ('asam me'asamaj), d.h. ein Glied seines Leibes (Eph 5,30). Gott hatte ja nach Gen 2,22 eine Rippe, d.h. einen Knochen, Adams zu einer Frau für ihn

---

Kaufen ohne Geld), sondern durch das Blut Christi. Die soteriologische Kraft des Blutes Christi hat ihre Stütze in Jes 53,12, wonach der Knecht Gottes "seine Seele ausgoss," d.h. mit dem Vergiessen seines Blutes das Leben dahingab.

ausgestaltet, "gebaut" (banah). So wird nach Eph 4,12 der Leib Christi durch die Charismen "erbaut." Da der zweite Adam ein lebenschaffender Geist ist (1. Kor 15,45), so ist auch der Leib Christi ein geistlicher Leib.

6.2.2 Die Teilung und Verteilung der Geistesgaben soll der Einheit und Harmonie im Leben des Leibes Christi keinen Eintrag tun, denn gerade die Verschiedenheit der einzelnen Glieder ermöglicht das Leben eines Organismus (1. Kor 12,14-18). Und Gott selbst demonstriert auf "trinitarische" Weise die Einheit des Wirkens der Charismen, trotz ihrer Verschiedenheit (1. Kor 12,4-6). Aber es gibt auch unheilvolle Teilungen im Leibe Christi, die nicht vom dreieinigen Gott, sondern von Menschen ausgehen und sich dann als Spaltungen auswirken (σχισματα = mahalaqoth, 1. Kor 1,10). Wenn Paulus dieses Parteienwesen in Korinth kritisiert und dabei ironisch fragt: "Ist etwa Christus geteilt? Ist denn Paulus für euch gekreuzigt? Oder seid ihr auf den Namen des Paulus getauft?" (1. Kor 1,13), so müsste die Antwort lauten: Christus ist für unsere Sünden gestorben (1. Kor 15,3), und als der Erhöhte ist er nicht etwa geteilt, sondern teilt und verteilt an uns die geistigen Gaben, durch die er sich uns selbst mitteilt.

6.2.3 Die Zuteilung der Geistesgaben an die Glieder ('asamim) der Gemeinde ist begründet in der Selbstmitteilung ('asmo) des Messias am Kreuz. Diese hat Jesus beim letzten Mahl für seine Jünger sinnbildlich dargestellt. D.h.: Paulus schliesst auch hinsichtlich der Zuteilung der Charismen primär an den irdischen Jesus an. Denn dieser hat in einer Zeichenhandlung, durch das Zuteilen von Brot und Wein beim Abendmahl, gezeigt, dass er den Weg des Gottesknechtes von Jes 53 gehen und sich selbst für die Vielen in den Tod geben will (53,12). Für Paulus war der Gekreuzigte das für uns geschlachtete Passahlamm (1. Kor 5,7), und als ein solches stellte sich Jesus den Jüngern bei seinem letzten Mahl dar, das als Passah gefeiert wurde. Auch der Gottesknecht wird in Jes 53,7 einem Lamm verglichen, das zur Schlachtbank geführt wird. Beide "Vor-Bilder" hat Jesus beim Letzten Mahl in einer Zeichenhandlung zusammengefasst und auf sich bezogen: Er selbst ist das Lamm, das der Welt Sünde trägt. Er vergleicht sich dem Passahlamm, dessen Blut vor dem Verderben bewahrt, und übernimmt das Schicksal des Gottesknechts, der seine Seele für die Vielen zum Tod ausgiesst (Jes 53,12). a) Im Deutewort zum Kelch (Mk 14,24) hat Jesus Jes 53,12 gleichsam symbolisch dargestellt: Der Wein bezeichnet das Blut, das er für die Vielen vergiessen wird (Mk 14,24); Matthäus ergänzt sinngemäss: ... " zur Vergebung der Sünden." Der Gottesknecht giesst nach Jes 53,12 seine "Seele" (näphäsh = "Leben") zum Tode aus und "trägt" so "die Sünde" von Vielen (vgl. auch Mk 10,45). Da der Sitz der Seele = Lebenskraft im Blute ist, bedeutet das Ausgiessen der Seele (Jes 53,12) ein Vergiessen des Blutes (Mk 14,24). Mit dem Darreichen des Kelches wird das Heil, das durch Jesu Sühnetod erwirkt wird, als Gnadengabe angeboten. Die Gnadengabe und Stiftung des (neuen) Bundes, die mit dem Kelchwort angezeigt und mit dem sündentilgenden Opfer des Lebens verwirklicht werden, sind nicht in Jes 53,12, sondern in Jes 55,3 vorgegeben. Die Verheissung der Gnadengaben Davids und des ewigen Bundes (Jes 55,3) wird von Jesus dadurch erfüllt, dass er als der messianische Gottesknecht seine Seele = sein Blut stellvertretend vergiesst und dadurch für die Vielen die Vergebung der Sünden und die Gemeinschaft mit Gott gewinnt (Jes 53,12).

6.2.4 Jesus deutete beim Letzten Mahl das gebrochene Brot als seinen Leib, der in den Tod gegeben wird (Mk 14,22). Beide Deuteworte ergänzen einander. aa) Denn Brot (Speise) und Wein sind die beiden Hauptelemente einer Mahlzeit; der Segen wird über Brot und Wein (Most) gesprochen (1 QS 6,5; vgl. m. Ber 6,1). bb) Bei den Bestimmungen zum Passahmahl können die Begriffe "Leib" und "Kelch" nahe beieinander stehen. In m. Pes 10,3 wird vom "Leib des Passah" gesprochen (gupho shäl päsah); gemeint ist das in der Zeit des Zweiten Tempels geschlachtete Passahlamm. Es soll beim Mahl aufgetragen werden, bevor man dem Hausvater den zweiten Becher eingiesst (10,4); es folgt dann die heilsgeschichtliche Deutung der Elemente des Passahmahls (10,4f). cc): Aber auch von Jes 53,12 her fällt auf die Einheit von Brot- und Weinwort im letzten Mahl Jesu ein helles Licht. Bezeichnet Jesus, indem er den Wein darbietet, das "Ausgiessen seiner Seele" (Jes 53,12), so bildet — rein sprachlich betrachtet — die Dahingabe[28] des Leibes, die mit dem Brechen und Austeilen des Brotes dargestellt wird, einen synthetischen Parallelismus. Denn Seele und Leib machen den ganzen Menschen aus.[29] Ausserdem lässt sich auch das Brechen des Brotes als Dahingabe des Leibes auf Jes 53,12 beziehen, nämlich auf das "Tragen der Sünde der Vielen." Nach 1. Petr 2,24 hat Jesus unsere Sünden "an seinem Leib" (εν τω σωματι αυτου = begupho) zum Holz hinaufgetragen." Das Bild vom "Tragen" bezeichnet ein "leibliches" Tun; in Wirklichkeit "trug" der Gottesknecht die Sünden der Vielen dadurch, dass er seinen Leib in den Tod gab, seine Seele = sein Blut für sie vergoss. Auch beim Brotwort deutet Jesus das Verteilen und Zuteilen der Gnadengabe seines Todes sinnbildlich an. Was bei der Speisung der Fünftausend eigens erzählt wird, nämlich das Verteilen der Speise durch Jesus (Mk 6,41), gilt sinngemäss auch vom Abendmahl: Durch das Brechen des Brotes (Mk 14,22) wird das Teilen und Zuteilen angezeigt, beim Kelchwort durch die Aufforderung: "Trinkt alle daraus!" (Mt 26,27). Ebenso wird die Gemeinschaft und Einheit betont: Alle sollen essen (Mk 14,23), aber weil sie von einem Brote essen, sind die Vielen ein Leib (1. Kor 10,17).

7. Die Gnade Gottes und das Apostelamt (Röm 1,5; 12,3 und Ex 34,6-9).

7.1 Die Exegeten sehen gewöhnlich in der Rechtfertigungslehre die Mitte der paulinischen Theologie und in der "Gerechtigkeit Gottes" den

---

[28]Septuaginta und Targum haben hä'ärah = "ausgiessen" durch παραδιδοναι und masar = "übergeben, dahingeben" übersetzt.

[29]Nicht "Fleisch und Blut" (basar wadam), wie J. Jeremias meint (The Eucharistic Words of Jesus, New York 1966, S. 200f). Dieses Begriffspaar ist generisch verwendet; ein "König von Fleisch und Blut" ist der menschliche König gegenüber dem himmlischen "König der Könige."

Schlüsselbegriff, dessen existentielle Bedeutung auch die Biographie des Apostels beherrsche, da sie als Konsequenz des Damaskuserlebnisses aufgeleuchtet haben müsse.[30] Aber Paulus selbst beschreibt seine Berufung theologisch nicht als iustificatio, zumal er schon als Pharisäer "hinsichtlich der Gerechtigkeit im Gesetz untadelig geworden war" (Phil 3.6). Die im Glauben angenommene Gerechtigkeit Gottes, das Gerecht-Gewordensein und der Friede mit Gott (Röm 5,1) können zudem nicht erklären, was das Besondere der Christusvision vor Damaskus ausmacht, nämlich die Berufung des Paulus zum Apostel (vgl. 1. Kor 9,1). Für die Berufung zum Apostelamt gebraucht Paulus den Begriff χαρις; er hat durch Christus "Gnade und Apostelamt empfangen" (Röm 1.5), dessen Zweck die Verkündigung des Glaubensgehorsams unter den Heiden ist (ibid.). Die geistliche Wende und der apostolische Weg des Paulus müssen primär vom Begriff und Wesen der Gnade her verstanden und gezeichnet werden; sie sind selbst Gnadenerweis, ja "die Gnade, die mir (von Gott) gegeben wurde" (Röm 12,3; 15,15; 1. Kor 3,16; Gal 2,9).

7.2 Fragt man nach einem alttestamentlichen Vorbild für die von Gott gegebene Gnade des Apostolats, so bietet sich dafür die Perikope Ex 34 an. Sie enthält nämlich den Begriff "Gnade" (häsäd) in Verbindung mit dem Empfang der Gesetzestafeln durch Mose (V. 4); dieser Akt kann ja nicht nur analog zum Erbitten des Geistes durch Christus gesehen werden (Eph 4,7-12), sondern auch zum apostolischen Dienst des Paulus (2. Kor 3). Nach Ex 34,6 ging Gott vor dem Angesicht Moses vorüber und offenbarte sich dabei als barmherzig und gnädig, langmütig und voll von Gnade und Wahrheit (rab häsäd wä'ämät; Targum Onqelos: masge lema'bad tabewan uqeshot = "reich, Guttaten und Wahrheit zu tun"). Nach Ex 34,7 bewahrt Gott seine Gnade (häsäd) für tausend Geschlechter und trägt Vergehen, Frevel und Sünden; nach dem Targum Onqelos vergibt er denen die Schulden, die zum Gesetz umkehren. Ebenso erfuhr Paulus in der Christusvision vor Damaskus die Offenbarung der Gnade Gottes. Er sprach danach deutlich von der Gnade, die ihm mit seiner Berufung gegeben wurde, zumal er auch an eine Verheissung wie Jes 55,3 dachte: Die Gnadengaben Gottes sind zuverlässig; sie werden für tausend Geschlechter bewahrt und auch dem gegeben, der sich im Dienst für die Tora geirrt und gegen die Gemeinde Gottes gekämpft hat.

7.2.1 Warum gebraucht Paulus den Begriff χαρις, wenn er das Apostelamt als Gnadengeschenk Gottes bezeichnen will, und nicht etwa χαρισμα, das den Charakter der Gabe so deutlich zum Ausdruck bringt? Die "Gnade" ist im Röm 12,3; 15,15 u.a. — genau so wie die Gerechtigkeit Gottes als iustitia passiva — Ausdruck der Zuwendung Gottes (η χαρις η εις εμε 1. Kor 15,10), ein Geschenk für den Menschen, das jedoch in der Verfügung Gottes bleibt. Die Gnade ist die Brücke der Kommunikation, die Gott zum Menschen hin baut, den

---

[30] Vgl. dazu die wichtige Darstellung von S. Kim, The Origin of Paul's Gospel, WUNT II,4, Tübingen 1984, S. 268-335.

Der biblische Hintergrund der paulinischen Gnadengaben 97

er erwählt hat und mit einem wichtigen Dienst betrauen will; dieser ist für Paulus die Heidenmission (Röm 1,5; 15,15f; Gal 2,8f). Diese Gnade wirkte für Paulus (Gal 2,8f), sie ging in ihn ein (εις εμε) und war mit ihm (συν εμοι 1. Kor 15,10).

7.2.2 Solch ein Für-, In- und Mit-Sein der Gnade Gottes erinnert an das Verhältnis, das nach Joh 14,16f der Paraklet und "Geist der Wahrheit" zu den Jüngern Jesu haben soll: Er wird von Gott dazu gegeben, dass er "mit ihnen" sei (14,16), er soll "bei ihnen" bleiben und "in ihnen" sein (14,17). Der "Geist der Wahrheit" ist gegenüber dem ausgegossenen und die Menschen inspirierenden heiligen Geist auch als Person, als ein zweiter Zeuge neben den Jüngern (15,26f), als ein Ankläger der Welt, verstanden (16,8-11). Ähnlich scheint auch die "Gnade" des Apostelamts für die Heiden nicht einfach eine der Gnadengaben im Leib Christi zu sein, auch nicht ein Amt wie das anderer Apostel, sondern eine besondere Gnade Gottes, nicht ein χαρισμα, sondern die dem Verfolger geltende Gnadenwahl (χαρις), zu der auch das nicht von Menschen gelehrte, sondern durch eine Offenbarung Jesu Christi empfangene Evangelium gehört (Gal 1,12).

7.3 Als ungewöhnlich erscheint die allen Christen zugesprochene neue Seinsbestimmung, "unter der Gnade zu sein" (υπο την χαριν ειναι Röm 6,14f). Schon in ihrer sprachlichen Gestalt ist diese Wendung neu gegenüber dem Sein im Geist oder einem Zusammenwirken mit dem "Geist der Wahrheit," da es ein "Darunter-Stehen" und Untergeordnet-Sein unter solche geistigen Grössen nicht gibt. Vielmehr ist die Formel υπο την χαριν ειναι als Gegensatz zum "Sein unter der Tora" (υπο τον νομον ειναι Röm 6,14f) entstanden (vgl. auch Gal 3,23; 4,21). Die letztere Wendung fehlt noch im Alten Testament und auch in Qumran. Nach dem Targum zu Jes 53,11.12 "unterwirft" der Gottesknecht "viele" bzw. "rebellische Menschen" "dem Gesetz" (sha' bed le'orajetha'), da sie nur auf solche Weise Sündenvergebung und Rechtfertigung erlangen können. Dass Paulus solch "Verknechten" für die Wendung "Sein unter dem Gesetz" voraussetzt, geht aus Röm 6,16 hervor, da dort das υπο τον νομον ειναι (6,14f) mit einer allgemein geltenden Erfahrungstatsache erklärt wird: Wer sich als Knecht (δουλος) gehorsam jemandem zur Verfügung stellt (παριστανει = sha'bed napsheh), ist auch in seinem ganzen Sein ein Knecht der Macht, der er gehorcht, sei es die Sünde oder die Gerechtigkeit. Auch in Röm 7,25 wird ein "Dienen für das Gesetz Gottes" erwähnt; als Gegenteil erscheint in Phil 2,22 das δουλευειν εις το ευαγγελιον (labesorah).

7.3.1 Das "Sein unter der Gnade" begründet das Freisein von der Herrschaft der Sünde (Röm 6,14a), die ja für den fleischlichen Menschen durch das geistliche Gesetz nicht etwa aufgehoben, sondern eher aufgerichtet wird (Röm 7,7). Der Knechtung unter das Gesetz, die der Prophetentargum auch in Jes 53 entdeckt, hält Paulus die Wirkung des Leidens Christi entgegen, die er dem gleichen Text Jes 53 entnimmt: Durch seinen in den Tod gegebenen Leib hat er die Glaubenden dem Gesetz absterben lassen und sie so von dessen Forderung und

Fluch befreit.[31] Aber das Freisein von der Forderung des Gesetzes und von der Herrschaft der Sünde darf nicht als Freizügigkeit und als Freiheit zum Sündigen verstanden werden, weil dies in die alte Knechtschaft zurückführen würde (Röm 6,15f). Das "Sein unter der Gnade" bedeutet ein Freisein vom Buchstaben des Gesetzes, aber auch den Gehorsam gegenüber der Gerechtigkeit (Röm 6,16.18) und den Dienst in der Neuheit des Geistes (Röm 7,6). Die Tora als solche ist für den Christen keineswegs abgetan. Aber die Herrschaft des Buchstabens (2. Kor 3,6) und die Bedrohung durch den Fluch des Gesetzes (Gal 3,10) sind seit Christi Sühnetod für den Glaubenden unwirksam. Dank der befreienden Kraft des Geistes wird das Gesetz zum Wort Gottes, das Verheissung hat, zur Tora des Neuen Bundes, die in das Herz geschrieben ist (2. Kor 3,3). Das "Sein unter der Gnade" ist somit ein Leben in der Kraft und Freiheit des heiligen Geistes. Wer vom Geist geleitet wird, steht nicht mehr "unter dem Gesetz" (vgl. Gal 5,18). Die heilsgeschichtlich wichtige Zeit des Existierens unter dem Gesetz, das Paulus einem Zuchtmeister vergleicht, wird von der Zeit des Glaubens (Gal 3, 23-28) und der Gotteskindschaft der freien Bürger des Oberen Jerusalem abgelöst (Gal 4,21-31).

---

[31] S. Hafemann, Suffering and the Spirit, WUNT II,19, Tübingen 1986, S. 199-218.

Chapter Seven

The Magi at the Birth of Cyrus, and the Magi at Jesus' Birth in Matt 2:1-12

Roger David Aus
Christoph-Ruden-Str. 7, 1000 Berlin 47, Germany

The first scholarly book on the NT I laid hands on as a college freshman was *Understanding the New Testament,* by Howard Clark Kee and Franklin W. Young.[1] In gratitude for "heading me off in the right direction" so many years ago, I present the following study to Professor Kee with the hope that it will help elucidate one of the most popular, yet puzzling narratives in the NT, the visit to Jerusalem and Bethlehem of Magi (the "wise men" of the RSV) from the East in Matt 2:1-12.

As most commentators agree, the major background to all of Matt 2:1-23 is found in Jewish haggadic traditions on the endangered birth of Moses, Israel's first redeemer, in Exod 1:15-2:10. There Pharaoh, like Herod the Great, causes the death of innocent children so that he can retain the throne. Yet the baby Moses, like the baby Jesus, who is later to "save" Israel, miraculously escapes.[2] Another, though minor, part of the background may lie in the story of Balaam in Numbers 22-24, especially the "star of Jacob" in 24:17.[3]

---

[1] My copy was that of Englewood Cliffs, N.J.: Prentice-Hall, 1959.
[2] These traditions also provide the motif of the "census" at the time of Jesus' birth in Luke 2:1-7. See the chapter "Lukas 2, 1-20 im Licht jüdischer Traditionen vom Mose-Kind und Hirten-Messias" in my forthcoming *Weihnachtsgeschichte, Barmherziger Samariter, Verlorener Sohn.* The Matthean and Lucan birth stories are more closely related than generally thought.
[3] Cf. especially Leqah Tob on Num 24:17, where the King, the Messiah, is this star, and Isa 60:6 is cited, a verse which also informs Matt 2:11 (see the margin of the Nestle Greek NT). It is translated by A. Wünsche as "Messias-Haggada" in *Aus Israels Lehrhallen* (Leipzig: 1907; reprint Hildeshiem: Olms, 1967) 3.103-106, and in *Str-B* 2.298-99 and 1.96-97. In *The Birth of the Messiah* (Garden City, N.Y.: Doubleday, 1977) 190-96, R. Brown places special emphasis on the Balaam narrative. Yet U. Luz correctly points out that there is no clear reminiscence of the story in Matt 2:1-12. See his *Das Evangelium nach Matthäus (Mt 1-7)* (EKK 1/1; Zurich, etc., Benziger; Neukirchen-Vluyn, Neukirchener, 1985) 115. For recent and older secondary literature on Matt 2:1-12, see Luz 111 and 86.

However, "the motif of the Magi is the most difficult one," as E. Lohmeyer has stated."[4] Elsewhere in the NT a *Magos* is a negative figure, connected with magic.[5] Yet here in Matthew 2 the Magi are "wholly admirable," as R. Brown has aptly noted.[6]

How did they get into the Matthean birth narrative? I suggest that this was due primarily to their intimate connection with the birth of Cyrus of Persia, called by (Second) Isaiah the Lord's "Anointed One" or מְשִׁיחוֹ in 45:1. Indeed, the section Isa 44:24 to 45:25 was in many ways in the mind of "Matthew" when he composed 2:1-12 sometime at the end of the first century C.E.[7] Along with many other scholars, I consider Matthew to have been bilingual, or to have had at least a reading, working knowledge of Hebrew, as shown in his quotations of the "Old" Testament and in his Semitisms.[8] His familiarity with the Hebrew Bible also decisively influenced his knowledge of the Anointed One and Shepherd Cyrus, and thus also the content of Matt 2:1-12.

I shall begin this study by analyzing the Isaiah passage on Cyrus. After a brief portrait of the Persian king in Josephus, the rabbis and the pseudepigrapha, I shall point out the motif of Magi present at his birth. Finally, I shall note an event at the end of the sixties which most probably provided the decisive impetus for Matthew's use of Magi in his birth narrative.

I. Cyrus as Messiah and Shepherd

In 587 B.C.E. Jerusalem was captured and many Jews exiled to the Babylonia of Nebuchadnezzar. Yet at the latter ruler's death in 562, the empire's decline was rapid. During the reign of Nabonidus (556-39), Cyrus the Persian

---

[4]*Das Evangelium des Matthäus* (Meyer; Göttingen: Vandenhoeck & Ruprecht, 1962³) 20.
[5]Cf. Acts 13:6 and 8, as well as 8:9 and 11. See also the art. "Magos," etc. by G. Delling in *TDNT* 4.356-59. The work by G. Messina cited by him on 356 was a 1930 Berlin dissertation: *Der Ursprung der Magier und die zarathustrische Religion.* In addition, see S.V. McCasland, art. "Magi" in *IDB* 3.221-23.
[6]*The Birth* 168, after his statement that "There is not the slightest hint of conversion or of false practice in Matthew's description of the magi."
[7]For the dating, see W. Kümmel, *Einleitung in das Neue Testament* (Heidelberg: Quelle & Meyer, 1983²¹) 90, who maintains 80-100 C.E. See also F.W. Beare, *The Gospel According to Matthew* (Oxford: Blackwell, 1981) 7-8, and Luz, *Das Evangelium nach Matthäus (Mt 1-7)* 76 (not long after eighty). As Luz points out on p. 114, one can no longer get back to an earlier form of the content of Matt 2:1-12. I see no major obstacle to the gospel writer's having composed it himself on the basis of Jewish and non-Jewish traditions available to him.
[8]See, for example, Beare, *The Gospel* 10, who also posits a Greek- and Aramaic-speaking community, perhaps in Syria or Phoenicia, as the recipient of the gospel. In *Das Evangelium nach Matthäus* (NTD 2; Göttingen: Vandenhoeck & Ruprecht, 1956⁸) 17, J. Schniewind even maintained that Matt 2:1-12 was part of a section originally written in a Semitic language. There is, however, no proof of this. On possible Semitisms in 2:1-12, see the lack of the article in *en hêmerais* in v 1; *poreuthentes* in v 8; *akousantes tou basileôs* in v 9 (the Magi do not simply "hear" Herod, they "obey" his order, as in the Hebrew שָׁמַע; thus "they obeyed the king and went their way"); and "they rejoiced with exceedingly great joy" in v 10. For Matthew's knowledge of the Hebrew text of Mic 5:1,3 and 2 Sam 5:2 in v 6, see below.

conquered the Medes (550), as well as Lydia in western Asia Minor (547/6). He thereby captured the tremendous amount of gold owned by Lydia's king, Croesus, in the capital of Sardis.[9]

It was in this setting that the unknown author of Isaiah 40-55 issued his words of consolation and new hope to the exiles of Babylonia. At the time of his writing 44:24-45:25, the defeat of Babylon by Cyrus was imminent. In fact, it occurred very shortly thereafter, in 539.[10] It was the prophet's firm belief that a new age, the eschatological period, was now dawning, Cyrus would play a pivotal role in it, and the nations would convert to belief in the one God, bringing their wealth to Jerusalem.

The form of the "Cyrus Oracle" in 44:24-45:13 is that of the Near Eastern royal oracle, which borrows its imagery from the ritual of a king's enthronement. Psalms 2 and 110, also applied by early Jewish Christians in the NT to their own Anointed One, Jesus, reflect the same pattern.[11]

In Isa 45:1, the author employs an image which was shocking for the Babylonian exiles. He labels Cyrus, a Gentile, the Lord's "Anointed One," the same term later used by Jews for the "Messiah." The LXX even states that he is "My [the Lord's] Anointed One."[12] This is the only occurrence in the Hebrew Bible of a Gentile being so designated. The Lord has grasped Cyrus' right hand, subduing nations before him, and conquering other kings. This decision of God, although greatly unusual, should not be questioned by the skeptical Babylonian Jews (45:9-13). Cyrus is indeed God's chosen instrument, as expressed in different terms elsewhere.[13]

In 45:3 the Lord promises to give Cyrus the "treasures of darkness and the hoards in secret places," perhaps a reference to future booty like the captured gold and other wealth of King Croesus of Sardis.[14]

---

[9]For these dates, cf. J. Bright, *A History of Israel* (Philadelphia: Westminster, 1959) 324 and 334-35. On Croesus' gold and other great wealth, see Herodotus 1.30,51-52,92-93,153-54; 6.125; and 8.35.
[10]Bright, *A History* 342.
[11]C. Westermann, *Das Buch Jesaja. Kapitel 40-66* (ATD 19; Göttingen: Vandenhoeck & Ruprecht, 1981^4) 125, 128. He limits the royal oracle itself to 45:1-4. J. Muilenberg in "The Book of Isaiah, Chapters 40-66," in *The Interpreter's Bible* 5 (New York: Abingdon, 1956) has 44:24-45:13 as the extent of the entire Cyrus oracle, yet notes (p. 528) that "Many scholars consider vv 14-25 a continuation of 44:28-45:13." He states (p. 529) that Jerome, Ibn Ezra, Grotius, Skinner, Mowinckel and others see Cyrus addressed in 45:14, the importance of which will be shown shortly. Of course, Matthew was unburdened by present-day scholarship's division of Isaiah; he read it as a whole. Isa 45:23 is alluded to in the pre-Pauline hymn in Phil 2:10-11; see also Rom 14:11.
[12]*Isaias*, Göttingen Septuaginta 14, ed. J. Ziegler (Göttingen: Vandenhoeck & Ruprecht, 1967^2) 290.
[13]Cf. "one from the east whom victory meets at every step" in 41:2; "a bird of prey from the east, the man of my counsel from a far country" in 46:11; and "The Lord loves him" in 48:14.
[14]In Est. Rab. 2/1 on Est 1:4 (Soncino English 9.33-34), God reveals all the money in the world, which Nebuchadnezzar had amassed and hidden in the Euphrates, to Cyrus on the day he decrees the Temple should be rebuilt. Isa 45:3's "treasures of darkness" and "hidden riches"

God will employ Cyrus to rebuild the ravaged Temple (44:28) and the city of Jerusalem (45:13). The Persian will also set free the Lord's exiles in Babylon (also v 13). Yet through Cyrus' activity *all men*, "from the rising of the sun and from the west," are to know that there is no other God than the Lord (45:6; cf. vv 22-23). Second Isaiah's vision is truly universalistic, including both Jews and Gentiles. Indeed, he even has God speak of the Gentiles as "my children," "the work of my hands" (v 11).

In 45:14 the prophet employs the fem. sing. for the addressed subject, the city of Jerusalem. Egypt's wealth, Ethiopia's merchandise, and the Sabeans, from southwest Arabia,[15] on their way from Africa and Arabia along the coastal plain of Palestine, shall come over to Jerusalem and be hers.[16] They shall come over to her, "bow down to her," and "make supplication to her," acknowledging Israel's God as the only God.

This Isaianic verse influenced Matt 2:1-12 in a major way. First, I suggest Matthew read the Hebrew אנשי מדה not as "men of measure," meaning "of stature," "tall," from מִדָּה. Rather, he employed the common form of exegesis: "Read not מדה, but" אנשי מדי, "men of Media," "Medes," from מָדַי.[17] That is, not only the Arabian Sabeans are to bring Cyrus, the Anointed One, presents. The Medes, who come from the home of the Magi, as to be seen below, also are to come with their gifts to Jerusalem. While this may seem far-fetched to the modern reader, it was not then. It was a standard method of Jewish exegesis, and Matthew does the same type of thing in his use of Mic 5:1 in Matt 2:6. I shall point out the latter below.

Secondly, C. Westermann notes the "exact correspondence" of Isa 45:14 to Isaiah 60, where the nations bring their treasures to Zion and bow down at her feet (v 14).[18] Following not only the general similarities of these two chapters from the end of Isaiah, but also the catchword Seba/Sheba, Matthew appropriated from 60:6 the gold and frankincense to be brought by all those of Sheba to Jerusalem. The LXX may have encouraged him to do so, for it then reads:

---

are so interpreted. This is said by R. Tanhuma, a fifth generation Palestinian Amora. See H. Strack and G. Stemberger, *Einleitung in Talmud und Midrasch* (Munich: Beck, 1982[7]) 100.

[15]Cf. G. Van Beek, art. "Sabeans," in *IDB* 4.144-46, who notes the intimate relationship with Sheba/Seba. See also D. Harvey, art. "Sheba, Queen of," in *IDB* 4.311-12. Interestingly, in his "Dialogue with Trypho" 77-78, Justin Martyr says five times that the Magi come from Arabia. Could he have had Isa 45:14 in mind?

[16]In Isa 43:3, these three nations had been given to Cyrus by God as a ransom for the Babylonian exiles. For this interpretation of 45:14, I follow G. Fohrer, *Das Buch Jesaja. 3. Band, Kapitel 40-66* (Zurich: Zwingli, 1964) 92.

[17]For a different wordplay on *middah*, see m. Ber. 9:5 in H. Danby, *The Mishnah* (London: Oxford University, 1964) 10. "The Medes" and "the men of the East" are also variants of the same saying by Rabban Simeon b. Gamaliel II, a third generation Tanna (Strack and Stemberger, *Einleitung* 84). See, for example, Gen. Rab. Vayetze 74/2 on Gen 31:4 (Soncino English 2.677), and Eccl. Rab. 7:23 §1 (Soncino 8.203). Matt 2:1 speaks of magi "from the East," a motif repeated in vv 2 and 9. For a Jewish-Christian with knowledge of Hebrew, they thus could be thought of as Medes.

[18]*Das Buch Jesaja* 138.

"they shall proclaim as good news *(euangeliountai)* the salvation of the Lord." In addition, the Greek form of "your" *(sou)* is not feminine, as in the Hebrew, but applied to all genders, allowing the addressee to change from Jerusalem to Jesus.[19] Matthew's Magi from the east bring gold and frankincense as two of their three gifts to the king of the Jews (Matt 2:11).[20] They also expect him in Jerusalem. Indeed, they must be told to seek him elsewhere (Matt 2:1,5).

Isa 60:6 is also connected with the coming of the Messiah in the late Midrashim Bereshit Rabbati on Gen 25:19,[21] and Leqah Tob on Num 24:17.[22]

Thirdly, Isa 45:14 also speaks of the nations "bowing down" and "making supplication" to Jerusalem. The Hebrew of "bowing down" is the Hithpa. of שָׁחָה, translated by the LXX as *proskyneô*. The same Greek verb is found in Matt 2:2 and 11 of the Magis' "doing obeisance" to the newborn king, Jesus, and in v 8 of King Herod's deceitful desire to do the same. This threefold mention of the motif of obeisance shows how important it was for Matthew.

The RSV translates *proskyneô* here in Matthew 2 with "to worship," yet the baby Jesus is not worshiped by the Magi as a god. He is for them a king (v 2), and in the Near East one "does obeisance" primarily to kings. For example, 2 Sam (2 Kgdms) 9:6 says Mephibosheth came to King David "and fell on his face and did obeisance." He did not "worship" David; only God is worshiped.[23] The Magi also "fell down" and "did obeisance" to Jesus in Matt 2:11, who is the king of the Jews (v 2), as well as the son of David (1:2; v 6–the king).

Something else which was probably also influential here is the fact that in rabbinic Hebrew, the Messiah is usually designated "the King, the Messiah" (המלך המשיח). Considered by his followers to be the Messiah, Jesus was thus almost automatically also thought to be a "king."

This scene of obeisance in Matthew 2 stands in intentional contrast to the crucifixion in chapter 27, the only other place in the gospel where Jesus is described as King of the Jews (vv 11,29,37) and King of Israel (v 42).[24] There, like the Magi, Gentiles also "fall on their knees" before him (v 29). Yet Pilate's

---

[19] This applies, of course, also to Isa 45:14.
[20] The third gift, myrrh, is used to scent the robes of God's anointed one, his king, in Ps 45:8. It is thus also a gift fit for a king. For myrrh and frankincense together, see Cant 3:6; 1 Enoch 29:2; and Tanhuma B Vayera on Gen 18:1. I have an extensive discussion of rabbinic and other Jewish sources on the gifts to be made to the Messiah, at the time the nations flock to Jerusalem, in "Paul's Travel Plans to Spain and the 'Full Number of the Gentiles' of Rom. XI 25" in *NT* 21 (1979) 232-62.
[21] Ch. Albeck, ed., *Midrash Bereshit Rabbati* (Jerusalem: Mekize Nirdamin, 1940) 102-03. Here the Sabeans are descendants of Abraham via Jokshan in Gen 25:3.
[22] See n. 3 above.
[23] Against H. Greeven, who in his art. *proskyneô* etc. in *TDNT* 6.763 states: "When the NT uses *proskynein*, the object is always something – truly or supposedly – divine."
[24] Matt 21:5 also applies the term king to Jesus, yet it is a quotation of Zech 9:9.

soldiers merely mock the "King of the Jews" before their whole batallion (vv 27-31).[25]

Finally, Cyrus is not only designated the Lord's "Anointed One" by Second Isaiah in 45:1. The prophet also has God say: "He is my shepherd" (רֹעִי; 44:28). The targum translates: "that saith of Cyrus that he will give to him the kingdom" (מלכו).[26] This emphasizes the shepherd's rule, as elsewhere.[27] The LXX also avoids the term "shepherd," translating: "He who says to Cyrus, 'Be wise.'" To my knowledge there is not one single rabbinic citation of this verse, which is very probably due to Christian emphasis on Jesus as the "good shepherd."[28]

It is also worthwhile noting that the only other example of a shepherd king G. Fohrer gives in his commentary on Isa 44:28 is 2 Sam 5:2. There the Israelite tribes tell David at Hebron: "The Lord said to you, 'You shall be shepherd (תִרְעֶה) of my people Israel, and you shall be prince (נָגִיד) over Israel.'"

It is precisely this biblical verse which Matthew quotes in slightly modified form in 2:6. First he took the LXX's *hêgoumenos* (leader, guide, ruler) from 2 Kgdms 5:2b and added to it Mic 5:1's "Out of you shall come." He could have employed the term *archôn* (ruler) from Micah, but purposely chose the 2 Kgdms 5:2b expression. He then rewrote the LXX's "You shall shepherd" to "who shall shepherd," and continued on with "my people Israel."

I suggest that bilingual Matthew selected imagery from 2 Kgdms 5:2 precisely because he had the Cyrus oracle in mind for all of 2:1-12. In Second Isaiah the Persian is not only the Lord's "Anointed One," he is also God's "Shepherd." Matthew knew his Hebrew (and Greek) Bible just as well as modern-day commentators do with the aid of their concordances, and he, like them, naturally thought of 2 Sam 5:2 in regard to the "shepherd" king, David.

Matthew's modifications of Mic 5:1 (Eng. 2) in 2:6 have often been adequately described elsewhere. It suffices to note here that they also betray his knowledge of how the Hebrew text can be read in various ways through different vocalization.[29] There is thus no compelling reason to posit a collection of "messianic testimonies" here, as proposed by some commentators.[30] Via the catchword "shepherd," Matthew associated Isa 44:28 and 2 Sam 5:2. Since the

---

[25]Mark 15:19 has *proskyneô*. Here the RSV translates better: "they knelt down in homage to him."

[26]J. Stenning, *The Targum of Isaiah* (Oxford: Clarendon, 1949) 152-53.

[27]See, for example, Jer 23:1-5. The "shepherds of Israel" in Ezekiel 34 are also its kings.

[28]See J. Jeremias, art. *poimên* etc. in *TDNT* 6.489.

[29]See, for example, Klostermann, *Das Matthäusevangelium* 15, and Lohmeyer, *Das Evangelium des Matthäus* 23. One instance is אַלְפֵי, "thousands," "families," read as אַלֻּפֵי "chiefs," "princes." See *BDB* 49 on both.

[30]A. McNeile, *The Gospel According to St. Matthew* (New York: St. Martin's, 1965; original 1915) 16; Lohmeyer, *Das Evangelium des Matthäus* 23; and W. Grundmann, *Das Evangelium nach Matthäus* (THKNT 1; Berlin: Evangelische Verlagsanstalt, 1975[4]) 78.

ruler of Israel, to come forth from Bethlehem, also shall "shepherd" (וְרָעָה) his flock in Mic 5:3 (Eng. 4), Matthew could also easily employ imagery from the neighboring v 1 (Eng. 2). He knew that Jesus grew up in Galilean Nazareth (Matt 2:23).[31] Yet the messiah, the son of David, according to strong Jewish traditions was to be born in Bethlehem of Judea.[32] Mic 5:1 helped the evangelist get Jesus there.

* * *

If the above suggestions are basically correct, this means that Isa 44:24-45:25 provided Matthew with his motifs of the messianic king and shepherd, to whom gifts would be made, also by Medes, and to whom Gentiles would do obeisance in Jerusalem.

Before analyzing the other major motif in Matt 2:1-12, the Magi, it is helpful first to see how Cyrus is viewed in other Jewish writings.

II. Cyrus in Josephus, the Rabbis and the Pseudepigrapha

A. Josephus

In *Bell.* 5.389 (9.4) Josephus urges the Jerusalemites to surrender in their war with the Romans in 70 C.E. One episode he recalls to them from Israel's history is that of Cyrus: "You know, moreover, of the bondage in Babylon, where our people passed seventy years in exile and never reared their heads for liberty *(eleutheria)*, until Cyrus granted it in gratitude to God...." Through Cyrus the Jews were allowed to reestablish their Temple worship in Jerusalem.[33]

In *Ant.* 20.233 (10.2) most of this statement is repeated; here Cyrus "freed" *(apolyô)* the Jews from Babylon.

Cyrus' "gratitude to God" in Josephus is based on Ezra 1:1-2 (= 2 Chr 36:22-23), where the Lord stirs up the Persian king to make a proclamation throughout all his kingdom: "The Lord, the God of heaven, has given me all the kingdoms of the earth, and he has charged me to build him a house at Jerusalem...." In v 3 the Jews of Babylonia are encouraged to go up to Jerusalem and rebuild the Temple.

---

[31] See 13:53-58, where *patris* can also mean "home town" (BAGD 636-37). Nazareth is clearly meant, as in Luke 4:16.
[32] See John 7:42 and the rabbinic and targumic passages cited by T. Zahn, *Das Evangelium des Matthäus* (Leipzig: Deichert, 1910³) 96.
[33] I employ the *LCL* edition of Josephus, here translated by H. St. J. Thackeray.

Thus according to both scriptural and Jewish tradition it was God himself who commissioned Cyrus, his Anointed One and Shepherd, to free the Jews from their Babylonian captivity and to rebuild the Temple.

Josephus paraphrases this Ezra passage in *Ant.* 11.4 (1.1):

> Since the Most High God has appointed me king *(basileus)* of the habitable world, I am persuaded that He is the god whom the Israelite nation worships, for He foretold my name through the prophets and that I should build His temple in Jerusalem in the land of Judea.[34]

Josephus then comments on this statement of Cyrus:

> These things Cyrus knew from reading the book of prophecy which Isaiah had left behind two hundred and ten years earlier. For this prophet had said that God told him in secret, "It is my will that Cyrus, whom I shall have appointed king *(basileus)* of many great nations, shall send my people to their own land and build my temple" (11.5; 1.2).

Here Josephus, or the source he employs, interprets the Shepherd and Anointed One of Isa 44:28-45:1 to mean that Cyrus is the king commissioned by God to carry out his purpose. This is buttressed by the continuation of Josephus' remarks: "And so, when Cyrus read them [Isaiah's prophecies], he wondered at the divine power and was seized by a strong desire and ambition to do what had been written" (11.6; 1.2). He then summoned the leading Babylonian Jews and allowed them to return to Judea and rebuild the Temple.

Writing at the end of the first century C.E., and thus as a contemporary of Matthew, Josephus in his description of Cyrus thus positively associates the Persian with "liberating" the Jews from their Babylonian captivity. He also connects this liberation event with the Cyrus oracle of Isa 44:24-45:13.

B. The Rabbis

With the exception of b. Meg.12a, where Isa 45:1 is interpreted of God's raising a complaint with the Messiah against Cyrus,[35] rabbinic sources generally give a very positive portrait of the Persian king.[36] In Eliyyahu Rabbah 20 it is stated, for example: "The Holy One brought the kingdom of Media into the world and put up with it only as a reward for Cyrus, who wept and sighed when the heathen destroyed the Temple."[37] In b. Ros. Has. 3b a

---

[34] English translation by R. Marcus.

[35] Soncino English 67. This is said in the name of R. Nahman b. R. Hisda, a third generation Babylonian Amora (Strack and Stemberger, *Einleitung* 96).

[36] This agrees with Herodotus 3.89, where in contrast to the huckster Darius and the imperious Cambyses, Cyrus is labeled by the Persians "the father," "for he was kind and always brought about good things for them."

[37] Hebrew in M. Friedmann, *Seder Eliahu and Seder Eliahu Zuta (Tanna d'be Eliahu), Pseudo-Seder Eliahu Zuta* (Jerusalem: Wahrmann, 1969³; original Vienna, 1904) 114. The same Hebrew consonants appear in "as a reward for" and "Cyrus." English in W. Braude and I.

tannaitic tradition says that "Cyrus" was so called because he was a "worthy" king, a wordplay on "Koresh" and "kasher," which have the same consonants.[38] In Cant. Rab. 2:13 §3, R. Johanan, a second generation Palestinian Amora,[39] comments on v 12: "The turtle-dove (תוֹר) is heard in our land." He says this is Cyrus, the good "explorer" (תַּיָּיר).[40] Shortly after this, in §4 on "the voice of the turtle-dove," it is stated that this is the voice of the King Messiah, who calls out and says: "How beautiful upon the mountains are the feet of the messenger of good tidings" (Isa 52:7).[41]

In the latter passage we see how Cyrus, who according to Josephus was to "liberate" the Jews from Babylonia, could be described with the same imagery as the Messiah. Other rabbinic passages corroborate this. In Pirqe R. El. 11, ten kings are mentioned who have ruled or will rule from one end of the world to the other. On the basis of Ezra 1:2 (= 2 Chr 36:23), Cyrus is listed as the seventh king. The ninth, before God's final rule, will be the King Messiah, as Ps 72:8 and Dan 2:35 are interpreted.[42]

In Mek. Pisha 7 on Exod 12:11 ("And ye shall eat it in haste"), R. Eliezer (b. Hyrcanus), a second generation Tanna,[43] says this haste at the Exodus event is that of the Shekinah, the divine presence. To buttress this, he quotes Cant 2:8-9. Then he asks: One could think that in the time to come it [the deliverance] will be in haste. He then cites Isa 52:12 to disprove this.[44]

This Mekilta text shows that Cant 2:8-9 was associated with the future redemption at a very early date. Cant. Rab. 2:8 §3 states that "my beloved," who "comes," is the Messiah.[45] Other comment on 2:9 compares the Exodus

---

Kapstein, *Tanna debe Eliyyahu* (Philadelphia: Jewish Publication Society of America, 1981) 289.
[38] Soncino English 9. See also the similar statement before this by R. Abbahu, a third generation Palestinian Amora (Strack and Stemberger, *Einleitung* 94); Soncino English 8.
[39] Strack and Stemberger, *Einleitung* 91.
[40] Soncino English 9.125. The Hebrew is found in S. Donski, *Midrash Rabbah, Shir ha-Shirim* (Heb.) (Jerusalem: Dvir, 1980) 70. A parallel is found in Pesiq. Rav Kah. 5/9. English in W. Braude and I. Kapstein, *Pesikta de-Rav Kahana* (Philadelphia: Jewish Publication Society of America, 1975) 108. The Hebrew is found in B. Mandelbaum, *Pesikta de Rav Kahana* (New York: Jewish Theological Seminary of America, 1962) 1.96. The same tradition is also found in Pesiq. R. 15/13. English in W. Braude, *Pesikta Rabbati* (New Haven: Yale University, 1968) 1.325. The Hebrew is found in M. Friedmann, *Pesikta Rabbati* (Vienna, 1880; reprint Tel Aviv, 1962/63) 74b.
[41] Donski, 71; Soncino English 9.125-26. Parallels are found in Pesiq. Rav Kah. 5/9 (Braude and Kapstein 109; Mandelbaum 97, also in the name of R. Johanan), and Pesiq. R. 15/14.15 (Braude 1.326; Friedmann 75a).
[42] English in G. Friedlander, *Pirke de Rabbi Eliezer* (London: 1916; reprint New York: Hermon, 1970) 82-83. See also the relevant notes. The translation is based on a MS which belonged to A. Epstein of Vienna (xiv).
[43] Strack and Stemberger, *Einleitung* 77.
[44] See the Hebrew and an English translation in J. Lauterbach, *Mekilta de-Rabbi Ishmael* (Philadelphia: Jewish Publication Society of America, 1976) 1.52-53.
[45] Soncino English 9.117. Parallels are found in Pesiq. R. 15/7 (Braude 1.316), and Pesiq. Rav Kah. 5/7 (Braude and Kapstein 101).

redemptive event and the future redemption, as well as the first deliverer of Israel (Moses) and the future or final deliverer (the Messiah).[46]

In Cant. Zuta 2:9 it is stated that the Messiah is he who "looks through the windows." For him the gates of the east will open as soon as he comes, as it is written, "Who stirred up one from the east, on his step righteousness will follow" (Isa 41:2).[47] The Messiah is of the descendants of David, for which Ps 89:37 (Eng. 36) is quoted. When the final time (קץ) will have arrived, God will stir him up from the north and east (Isa 41:25). Finally, Isa 45:1 is interpreted to mean that the gates of the east and the south (in Jerusalem) will be opened to him.[48]

This midrashic comment cannot be dated. However, it follows the same line of interpretation of Cant 2:(8-)9 as found in the tannaitic Mekilta, applying the verse(s) to the future redemption and the Messiah. Most importantly, it applies imagery employed of Cyrus in Isa 45:1 and elsewhere to the Messiah. This shows that Matthew, a Jewish Christian, could have done the very same thing.[49]

C. The Pseudepigrapha

Chapter fifteen of "The Lives of the Prophets," a work according to D. Hare most probably Palestinian and from the beginning of the first century C.E.,[50] deals with Zechariah. In v 4 it is stated regarding the prophet while he is still in Chaldea: "And concerning Cyrus he gave a portent of his victory, and prophesied regarding the service which he was to perform for Jerusalem, and he blessed him greatly." Then in v 5 Zechariah's "twofold judgment" is mentioned. As Hare notes in the margin, this can only refer to Zech 9:12.

Yet nowhere in our texts of Zechariah does the prophet refer to Cyrus. I suggest that the author(s) of "The Lives of the Prophets" knew of a Jewish tradition which applied 9:9-10 to him, verses adjacent to v 12, which is definitely alluded to. Here Jerusalem is told: "Lo, your king comes to you; triumphant (צַדִּיק) and victorious is he.... He shall command peace to the

---

[46] Cf. Cant. Rab. 2:9 §§ 1, 3-4 (Soncino 9.118-21). See also Num. Rab. Naso 11/2 on Num 6:23 (Soncino 5.412-13).

[47] In the original setting, צֶדֶק meant victory; here it more probably stresses the Messiah's righteousness.

[48] See S. Buber, *Midrasch Suta*. Haggadische Abhandlungen über Schir ha-Schirim, Ruth, Echah und Koheleth (Berlin: 1893/94; reprint Tel Aviv) 24.

[49] See also Yalqut Shem'oni § 1085 on 2 Chr 36:23, which states on the basis of a "midrash": "In this world you were saved by flesh and blood [Cyrus] and return and do service, but in the world to come you will be saved by God with an eternal redemption." In Midr. Ps. 7/17 on Ps 7:1, the redemption under Cyrus (2 Chr 36:22-23) is compared with the future redemption (Isa 63:4). English in W. Braude, *The Midrash on Psalms* (New Haven: Yale University, 1959) 1.115-16. The Hebrew is found in S. Buber, *Erläuterungen der Psalmen Haggada* (Wilna: Romm, 1891; reprint Jerusalem, 1965-66) 71.

[50] J. Charlesworth, ed., *The Old Testament Pseudepigrapha* (Garden City, N.Y.: Doubleday, 1985) 2.380-81. Chapter fifteen is on p. 394.

nations; his dominion shall be from sea to sea, and from the [Euphrates] River to the ends of the earth."

This well-known passage was applied by the rabbis to the Messiah, and by the gospel writers to the Messiah Jesus at his entry into Jerusalem.[51] It is indeed a "great blessing," which could have been interpreted as a portent of Cyrus' victory, including worldwide dominion.

If this is true, it again shows how a biblical text usually applied to the Messiah could also be applied to the Lord's "Anointed One," Cyrus.

Sib. Or. 3.285-86 also states:

> And then the heavenly God will send a king and will judge each man in blood and the gleam of fire. There is a certain royal tribe whose race will never stumble. This, too, as time pursues its cyclic course, will reign, and it will begin to raise up a new temple of God. All the kings of the Persians will bring to their aid gold and bronze and much-wrought iron. For God himself will give a holy dream by night and then indeed the temple will again be as it was before.[52]

J. Collins dates book three of the Sibylline Oracles as written ca. 160-50 B.C.E.; it was definitely composed by Egyptian Jews.[53] He believes that Cyrus is most probably meant here, and the "royal tribe" is the Jews. He also calls attention to Isa 44:27-45:1 in the margin.[54]

"A holy dream by night" most probably refers to Daniel 7, the vision which this official of Cyrus (6:28; 10:1; Bel 1-2) had "by night": vv 1, 2, 7 and 13. In Cant. Rab. 3:4 §2,[55] regarding the Babylonian kingdom's being given over to the Medes and Persians (Dan 5:28), it is related that the Israelites ask Daniel when the seventy years of Jer 29:10 are to be accomplished. At that time they are to return to Jerusalem (and rebuild the Temple with Cyrus' permission). Daniel asks for a copy of Isaiah and reads until 21:1, including the word "sea." Since Isa 21:1-10 is an oracle regarding the fall of Babylon, it is connected here by the rabbis to the night vision of the rise and fall of the four world kingdoms, including the Babylonian, by the catchword "sea" in Dan 7:2-3. Dan 7:3 and 15 are then quoted in this midrash.[56]

A variant of this tradition is found in Midrash Panim Aherim 2 on Est 1:12.[57] There Darius, in phraseology dependent on Isa 21:5, tells Cyrus: "Arise and take the kingdom. You are worthy of it because Daniel says

---

[51] See *Str-B* 1.842-44 on Matt 21:5, as well as John 12:15.
[52] J. Charlesworth, *The Old Testament Pseudepigrapha* (1983) 1.368.
[53] Charlesworth 1.355-56.
[54] Charlesworth 1.368. See also his reference to Sib. Or. 5.108 (p. 395) on Cyrus as "a certain king sent from God." In 1.355, n. 11, reference is made to an article by J. Nolland, who considers Sib. Or. 3.282-94 to refer to a Davidic messiah.
[55] Soncino English 9.145
[56] Ibid., and 147.
[57] S. Buber, *Aggadic Books on the Scroll of Esther* (Hebrew; Vilna: Romm, 1886) 60.

regarding you that you should take it." Daniel had told Cyrus, who was on the official staff[58] of Belshazzar, that in the future God would give him the kingdom. In addition, Isaiah had already prophesied regarding Cyrus that he would reign and give permission to rebuild the Temple, as Isa 45:1 is interpreted.[59]

The above midrashim, connecting the rebuilding of the Temple under Cyrus, Isa 45:1, and the night vision of Daniel 7, provide a probable explanation of the above passage from the Sibylline Oracles, where after a "night dream" the Temple will be rebuilt. If so, Josephus' statement in *Ant.* 11.4 that God foretold Cyrus' name through the prophets (pl.) would include not only Isaiah and Zechariah, but also Daniel. Although the book of Daniel in the Hebrew Bible is found in the hagiographa and not with the prophets, he was definitely considered a prophet by Josephus[60] and the Palestinian rabbis.[61]

III. The Magi at the Birth of Cyrus

The Greek historian Herodotus of Halicarnassus, born at the beginning of the fifth century B.C.E.,[62] writes in his first book of the very unusual birth of Cyrus. At the very end of his life, for example, the king was eager to lead his army against an enemy for many weighty reasons, the first among them being "his birth, whereby he seemed to be something more than mortal man" (1.204).

Herodotus relates Cyrus' birth as follows. His grandfather, the Median king Astyages, had a dream about his daughter Mandane. Enough water flowed from her to fill his city and overflow all Asia. Having asked those Magi who interpret dreams to ascertain its meaning, he was terrified *(phobeomai)*. When his daughter grew old enough to marry, he still "feared" *(deidô)* the vision. Instead of marrying her to a Mede, he therefore chose a Persian named Cambyses as his son-in-law.

In the first year of his daughter's marriage, Astyages saw a second vision:

> He dreamt that there grew from his daughter a vine, which covered the whole of Asia. Having seen this vision, and imparted it to the interpreters of dreams, he sent to the Persians for his daughter, then near her time, and when she came, kept her guarded, desiring to kill whatever child she might bear: for the interpreters declared that the meaning of his dream was that his daughter's offspring should rule in his place.

---

[58] See S. Krauss, *Griechische und lateinische Lehnwörter in Talmud, Midrasch und Targum* (Berlin: Calvary, 1898-99) 2.1 on אאפיקון as *officium*, "der Beamtenstab."

[59] For part of this discussion, see also Est. Rab. 3/4 §2 in Soncino 9.148.

[60] Cf., for example, *Ant.* 10.246, 249, 266-67 (his books, probably the "additions" to Daniel).

[61] See the sources cited in L. Ginzberg, *The Legends of the Jews* (Philadelphia: Jewish Publication Society of America, 1968) 6.413, n. 76. In the LXX the Daniel writings follow the prophet Ezekiel.

[62] Cf. the *LCL* edition of his nine books, translated by A. Godley. For the dating, see I, vii.

In order to prevent the grandson's usurpation of his kingship, Astyages then summoned his most faithful servant and steward Harpagus to take the newborn son, kill it, and bury it. However, Harpagus instead gave the infant to a cowherd in the mountains. His wife had just given birth to a stillborn child, which they then substituted for Cyrus, placing the infant in an *angos,* a cradle/coffin, and exposing it in the most desolate part of the mountains.

Having discovered that he was tricked by Harpagus, Astyages in revenge had the latter's own son slaughtered and cunningly made him eat of the flesh. Then he again called the Magi and asked them to repeat their interpretation of his vision. "They answered as before, and said that the boy must have been made king *(basileusai)* had he lived and not died first." Astyages then informed the Magi that Cyrus was indeed alive, and his boyfriends had made him king in a game, which role he played very well. Concerned that Astyages' rule *(archê)* should continue, the Magi declared their prophecy fulfilled in this game. Thereupon the king released his grandson. Cyrus, however, later became head of the Persian army and defeated that of the Medes. Because the Magi who interpret dreams had persuaded Astyages to let Cyrus go free, he at this point impaled them.

Referring to the above events in his speech to the Persians in order to get them to join his army and fight the Medes, Cyrus argued: "For I think that I myself was born by a marvelous providence to take this work in hand."[63]

The above narrative resembles that of King Herod and the Magi in Matt 2:1-12 (and 13-23) in many respects. Magi inform the ruling king that a child to be born soon will become king (Matt 2:2). In order to prevent this, the terrified king (2:3) orders the child to be killed (2:13). Yet it miraculously escapes (2:14), whereupon the king takes terrible revenge (2:16).

Herodotus admits in 1.95 (cf. 214) that already in his time there were three other accounts of Cyrus which he could have given, presumably also including the future king's miraculous birth. Other early writers seem to have known additional, or different, sources.[64]

Elsewhere (7.37) Herodotus notes that the Magi not only interpreted dreams. They also concerned themselves, for example, with celestial phenomena for King Xerxes. The Greek historian states that while the sun is the prophet of the

---

[63]Herodotus 1.107-28. For the Magis' predicting at the birth of Alexander the Great that he would become (king of all of) Asia, see Cicero, *De Div.* I.23 (47). He calls them "wise and learned men among the Persians" (46). See the *LCL* translation of W.A. Falconer.

[64]See G. Binder, *Die Aussetzung des Königskindes. Kyros und Romulus* (Beiträge zur klassischen Philologie, 10; Meisenheim am Glan: Hain, 1964) 17-28, with a list of sources on p. 175: Ktesias, Deinon, Ephoros, Aelian, Xenophon, Plutarch and Strabo. Binder has nothing on Matt 2:1-12. Many of these sources are analyzed in G. Messina, *Der Ursprung der Magier,* and in the art. "Kyros II" by F.H. Weissbach in PWSup 4 (1924) 1129-77. In his *Das Evangelium nach Matthäus,* Luz has a special chart between pp. 84-85 summarizing the motif of the persecuted and rescued child of the king. To it could be added Herodotus 5.92 on the birth of a future ruler of Corinth.

Greeks, for the Magi it is the moon. That is, they deal primarily with the nocturnal heavens. When the Magi from the east in Matt 2:2 state that they have seen (at night) the star of him born king of the Jews and then follow it (at night) to Bethlehem in vv 8-9, it thus belonged to a normal realm of their concern.

I suggest that Matthew was aware of the account of the Magi present at (the Anointed One) Cyrus' birth. Josephus, for example, quotes Herodotus a number of times, even by book.[65] Matthew's Greek is quite good, and as an educated person of the time he may have read the famous historian's works himself.

Yet another possibility also exists, that Matthew became aware of the Magi at Cyrus' birth from another source. Herod the Great appointed Nicolaus of Damascus as his official court historian. This historian-philosopher was also his counselor in family difficulties and his ambassador to, and advocate with, Augustus in Rome.[66] Because of his non-Davidic, Idumean lineage, Herod even had Nicolaus make him a distinguished Jewish genealogy.[67] In addition, the historian wrote a special history of the world for Herod, certainly also containing an account of Cyrus.[68] Nicolaus, however, from whom Josephus borrows a number of times, also wrote a work in which he recounted Cyrus' birth, primarily drawing on the "Persika" of Ktesias.[69] This too may have been available and known to Matthew, whom many scholars would place in nearby Syria.[70]

IV. The Obeisance Done by Magi from the East to Emperor/King Nero

The decisive impetus for Matthew's employing Magi from the east, who do obeisance to the newborn king of the Jews, Jesus, probably derived from a spectacular event of the year 66 C.E.[71] Dio Cassius relates in his "Roman

---

[65] See, for example, *Ant.* 10.18, as well as *Ap.* 1.168.
[66] A. Schalit, *König Herodes. Der Mann und sein Werk* (Studia Judaica 4; Berlin: de Gruyter, 1969) 412, with the relevant references to Josephus.
[67] Schalit 476, citing *Ant.* 14.9. According to 2 Kgs 24:14, only the poorest people remained in Judea; the rest were taken to Babylon. Perhaps Nicolaus wanted to imply that Herod was a descendant of the "princes" of Jerusalem *(ibid.)*, i.e., that he was of Davidic descent. See also Schalit's article "Die frühchristliche Überlieferung über die Herkunft der Familie des Herodes" in *ASTI* 1 (1962) 109-60, which deals primarily with Jewish sources such as b. B. Bat. 3b-4a (Soncino 10 and 12). Interestingly, Schalit also considers the birth of Cyrus in Herodotus 1.107-08 as closest to Matthew 2 of all non-Jewish sources. Yet he mentions this only in a footnote (148, n. 29), and does not develop it.
[68] Schalit, *König Herodes* 412, with the sources given in notes 929-30.
[69] See Nicolaus' Frg Hist 90F66, cited by Binder, *Die Aussetzung* 19, 25 and 175; Weissbach, "Kyros II" 1131 and 1134; as well as Messina, *Der Ursprung* 82.
[70] See Kümmel, *Einleitung* 90, as well as Luz, *Das Evangelium nach Matthäus* 73-75.
[71] This has been known since A. Dieterich, "Die Weisen aus dem Morgenlande" in *ZNW* 3 (1902) 1-14, who notes the relevant sources.

History," composed ca. 200-220 C.E.,[72] that the Armenian King Tiridates traveled by horseback from the Euphrates to Naples in what was like a triumphal procession. Together with his relatives, servants, 3000 horsemen and numerous Romans, he was received in festively decorated cities all along the route of his journey, which took nine months in one direction. The emperor, Nero, paid for his daily expenditures of 800,000 sesterces. Arriving in Naples, Tiridates knelt upon the ground, called Nero "master" *(despotês)* and "did obeisance" to him *(proskyneô)*. Nero then took him to Rome, which had been festively decorated especially for this occasion. There Tiridates and his entire entourage passed by the emperor, members of the senate and the Praetorians, "doing obeisance" to Nero again. Calling the emperor "Master," Tiridates says he is his slave. "And I have come to thee, my god, to worship *(proskyneô)* thee as I do Mithras." Nero then declared him king of Armenia, placing a diadem on his head. Afterwards there was a celebration in the theatre, which was completely covered with gold for the occasion, having the effect that people "gave to the day itself the epithet of 'golden.'" After other festivities, Tiridates and his immense following returned home by a different route from the one taken in coming.[73]

Suetonius, probably born in 69 C.E., notes in his "Lives of the Caesars" that Nero had lured Tiridates to Rome through great promises. He also mentions the Armenian's "falling at his feet" and "doing obeisance" to Nero, who was then hailed as "imperator."[74]

In his "Natural History" XXX.6, Pliny, who died at the eruption of Mt. Vesuvius in 79 C.E., also describes the above event, calling Tiridates a *Magus*. He notes that the Armenian king also brought Magi with him and initiated Nero into their banquets.[75]

Matthew, living within the Roman Empire and probably close to the route taken westward by Tiridates and the Magi, certainly knew of this event, which occurred only some years before the writing of his gospel. Magi from the east, who fall on their knees and do obeisance to the king/emperor of the entire empire on a "day of gold," returning home by a different route, most probably gave him the idea to relate his birth narrative of the King of the Jews, Jesus, in a similar way. In contrast to the despotic and immoral Nero, whom Tiridates and the Magi actually despised and rejected,[76] Jesus, and not Caesar, is the true king. In order to fill out his narrative, Matthew also borrowed imagery and motifs from

---

[72] Cf. the *LCL* English translation by J.C. Cary on LXIII 1.1-7.1. For the dating, see vol. I, xi.
[73] This motif of returning home by a different route was probably decisive for Matt 2:12, and not 1 Kgs 13:9-10, as some commentators note.
[74] Cf. the *LCL* English translation by J.C. Rolfs, "Nero" XIII.1 and XXX.2. For the dating, see vol. I, ix.
[75] I employ the *LCL* translation of W.H.S. Jones. For the dating, see vol. I, vii.
[76] See Dio Cassius, LXIII 6.4 and 6, and Pliny XXX.6, respectively.

the Lord's Anointed One and Shepherd, Cyrus, in Second Isaiah, at whose marvelous birth the Magi were also present.

Chapter Eight

Thomas and Aesop

John Priest
The Florida State University

Several writers have called attention to alleged parallels between at least four Sayings in the gospel of Thomas and sayings/fables in the Aesopic tradition.[1] This paper examines each of the alleged parallels and cognate Synoptic material where appropriate. Further, one of the most significant contributions of Thomas research, according to many scholars, is the substantive confirmation of the existence of Sayings Collections in late antiquity. Therefore, the second part of the paper will focus on the nature and function of such collections, particularly those associated with Aesop, and propose some exegetical consequences for interpreting both Thomas and the Synoptics.

The following procedure underlies the first section. Although the materials are available in scattered sources, I shall, for sake of convenience, cite in full the Saying in Thomas, the proposed Synoptic parallel[s], and the Aesopic saying/fable. Then a brief interpretation, or representative interpretations, of each will be given.[2] The paper has sharply defined perimeters. Since I do not presume to be a specialist in Nag Hammadi studies, the intricacies of Thomas interpretation and the question of the relationship between Thomas and the Synoptics will be mentioned only insofar as those matters pertain directly to sayings collections in general and the Aesopic tradition in particular. The point of departure is that of classical study rather than New Testament scholarship, though I believe that emphasis on the former does not preclude some contribution to the latter.

---

[1] Aesopic tradition refers both to fables attributed to Aesop and to fables couched in an Aesopic format. Also in this paper I am making no distinction among fable, proverb, parable, saying, etc. For discussion of these two matters, see Ben Perry, *Aesopica I* (Urbana: University of Illinois Press, 1952), *passim* and *Studium Generale* 12 (1959), pp. 17-37. For discussion of refinement of the genres, see J.D. Crossan, *In Fragments* (San Francisco: Harper and Row, 1983), esp. pp. 3-25, and J.G. Williams, *Those Who Ponder Proverbs* (Sheffield: The Almond Press, 1981), esp. pp. 78-80.
[2] Since the focus of this paper it not on Thomas interpretation as such, I shall include only representative interpretations from works which contain extensive additional bibliography.

I

Thomas Saying 8

And he said, "The man is like a wise fisherman who cast his net into the sea and drew it from the sea full of small fish. Among them the fisherman found a large fine fish. He threw all the small fish back into the sea and chose the large fish without difficulty. He who has ears to hear, let him hear."[3]

Although many scholars consider this saying to be totally independent of the Synoptic tradition, others relate it to a Matthean parable which we shall include without prejudging the question of dependency.[4]

Matthew 13:47-50

Again, the kingdom of heaven is like a net which was thrown into the sea and gathered fish of every kind; when it was full, men drew it ashore and sat down and sorted the good into vessels but threw away the bad. So will it be at the end of the age. The angels will come and separate the evil from the righteous, and throw them into the furnaces of fire; there men will weep and gnash their teeth.[5]

The alleged Aesopic parallel is found in the collection of Babrius who flourished in the late first or early second century C.E. It is fable 4 in the Loeb edition.[6]

A fisherman drew in the net he had cast a short time before and, as luck would have it, it was full of all kinds of delectable fish. But the little ones fled to the bottom of the net and slipped through its many meshes, whereas the big ones were caught and lay stretched out in the boat. It's one way to be insured and out of trouble, to be small; but you will seldom see a man who enjoys a great reputation and has the luck to evade all risks.

The only element common to all three is the act of fishing itself. Thomas and Matthew share the motif of retaining some fish and throwing back others, though in the former only one fish is retained while in the latter unspecified numbers are retained and returned. Further, there is a distinction between good and bad in Matthew, large and small in Thomas. Aesop differs considerably from both. The fisherman neither retains or returns, the small fish escape through the meshes of the net while the large fish are secured safely in the boat. Aesop does share with Thomas the motif of large and small, but with Matthew

---

[3]All Thomas sayings are from the translation by Thomas Lambdin in *The Nag Hammadi Library*, ed. James M. Robinson (San Francisco: Harper and Row, 1981).

[4]The question of dependency will also be bracketed in the treatment of the other three sayings examined. Some tentative suggestions on the matter appear in the concluding section of the paper.

[5]All Biblical quotations are from the *Revised Standard Version*.

[6]*Babrius and Phaedrus*, tr. Ben Perry (Cambridge: Harvard University Press, 1965), pp. 8-11.

the emphasis on the multiplicity of fish retained rather the one large fish of Thomas.

Commentators on Thomas differ widely in their interpretation of Saying 8, the crucial point being the extent to which they consider Thomas to be essentially Gnostic in nature. Then the "Man" is the true Gnostic and the one "large fine fish" is Gnostic wisdom.[7] This reading is certainly possible, but one might also interpret the saying in connection with Saying 76 (the Pearl) and perhaps also 109 (the Treasure), stressing the overwhelming value of the kingdom. If the present text is correct,[8] reference to the man rather than to the kingdom would seem to call the latter interpretation into question, but no consensus has yet been reached.

The Matthean parable, in its present form at least, clearly refers to the eschatological judgment when the righteous will be separated from the wicked. It is difficult, if not impossible, to discern any eschatological dimension in the Thomas saying.[9] The moral in Babrius, stated explicitly, counsels that public prominence entails risks while relative anonymity insures a high degree of safety. Since there seems to be no common ground of interpretation among the three, may we nevertheless infer divergent uses of a common source? Or are the common elements fishing, big/small fish so universal as to be simply a part of the popular domain of popular wisdom? An attempt to address these questions will be deferred until the other three examples have been examined.

---

[7] The literature on this Saying, regarding its Synoptic dependence/independence, its "authenticity" and its interpretation has reached enormous proportions. The primary issue for interpretation hinges on the question of whether the Saying is "gnostic." Most scholars agree that, to some extent it is "gnostic" but there is no consensus as to degree nor to the "correct" Gnostic interpretation. Representative interpretations may be found in G. Quispel, "Gnosis and the New Sayings of Jesus" *Eranos Jahrbuch* 38 (1969), pp. 26-296, esp. pp. 272-275 (Quispel also deals with the issue in a number of articles in *VC* and *NTS*); Jacque E. Menard, *L'Evangile Selon Thomas* (Leiden: E.J. Brill, 1975) esp. pp. 88-91; R. McL. Wilson in a number of articles and in *Studies in the Gospel of Thomas* (London: Mowbray, 1960), esp. pp. 40f., 94f., Hugh Montefiore, *Thomas and the Evangelists* (London: SCM Press, 1962), esp. p. 55; J. Jeremias, *The Parables of Jesus*, tr. S.H. Hooke (New York: Charles Scribner's Sons, 1963), esp. pp. 201f., and *Unknown Sayings of Jesus*, tr. R.H. Fuller (London: SPCK, 1964), pp. 88-90; and J. Leipoldt, *Das Evangelium Nach, Thomas* (Berlin: Akademie-Verlag, 1967), esp. p. 57. The list could be extended almost infinitely. Gnostic interpretations have not gone unchallenged. Early in Thomas research, Kendrick Grobel, "How Gnostic is the Gospel of Thomas?" NTS 8 (1963), pp. 367-373, expressed his doubts, and recently Stevan L. Davies has totally rejected a Gnostic provenance, *The Gospel of Thomas and Christian Wisdom* (New York: Seabury Press, 1983). See also Helmut Koester's apparent modification of earlier observations, "Three Thomas Parables" in *The New Testament and Gnosis*, ed. A.H.B. Logan and A.J.M. Wedderburn (Edinburgh: T&T Clark, 1983), pp. 195-203, esp. p. 201. The issue, though of great importance for Thomas studies, does not affect directly the thesis of this article.

[8] J. Jeremias, *Unknown Sayings of Jesus*, tr. R.H. Fuller (London: SPCK, 1964) pp. 88-90, maintains that "man" is a scribal error for "kingdom."

[9] If one agrees with the interpretation proposed, for example, by C.H. Dodd and T.W. Manson that the eschatological theme is secondary, then the original parable in Matthew may be much closer to the tradition underlying Thomas than the present Matthean redactions.

Thomas Saying 82

Jesus said, "he who is near me is near the fire, and he who is far from me is far from the kingdom."

The Synoptics

It is difficult to adduce definite Synoptic parallels and most scholars, either explicitly or implicitly, indicate that the Thomas saying is independent of the Synoptic tradition. The parallels which have been suggested[10] – Mark 9:49, "For everyone shall be salted with fire;" Mark 12:34, "And when Jesus saw that he answered wisely, he said to him, 'You are not far from the kingdom of God;'", Luke 12:49-50, "I am come to case fire upon the earth; and would that it were already kindled! I have a baptism to be baptized with; and how I am constrained until it is accomplished;", and Matthew 3:11, "I baptize you with water for repentance, but he who is coming after me is mightier than I, whose sandals I am not worthy to carry; be will baptize you with the Holy Spirit and with fire;" – seem strained indeed. Mention of "fire" in Matt. 3:11, Mark 9:49, and Luke 12:49, and "kingdom" in Mark 12:34 hardly bears enough weight to sustain a clear claim for interdependence.[11]

Aesop

He who is near Zeus is near the lightning.

Although this saying is not found in any Aesopic *collection* earlier than the 14th century C.E.,[12] a close parallel, "Far from Zeus and his lightning" was certainly current in the 4th century C.E. and probably may be attested as early as the 2nd century C.E..[13] The meaning of the Greek sayings is patent, a warning not to venture too near Zeus, that is any source of power or authority, lest one come into peril. The meaning in Thomas, however, is far from clear and depends, as was the case with Saying 8, to a large extent to which one considers Thomas to be a "Gnostic" writing. For instance, one line of interpretation minimizes the Gnostic element and affirms simply that the meaning is to be near Jesus is to be near danger (the risk of discipleship), but that such nearness also brings one near the kingdom. This interpretation is supported by a number of sayings in the patristic literature which are almost identical with Thomas 82.

---

[10]See the list in the original English translation, *The Gospel According to Thomas*, ed. Guillamont, Peuch, Quispel and al Masih (New York: Harper and Bros. 1959), p. 59.

[11]One should not overlook, however, ancient exegetical techniques which seem "strange" to our methodology.

[12]Codex Florentinus Laurentius LVII, 24. See *Aesopica I*. pp. 262 f., 290; and Ben Perry, *Studies in the Text History of the Life and Fables of Aesop* (Lancaster: Lancaster Press, 1936), pp. 230f.

[13]See, for example, the references cited in Menard, *L'Evangile Selon Thomas*, pp. 182f.; Jeremias, *Unknown Sayings*, pp. 70-71; and Robert M. Gant and David Noel Freedman, *The Secret Sayings of Jesus* (London: Collins, 1960), p. 170.

Origen, in Latin translation, and Didymus the Blind in Greek, reproduce the Thomas Saying almost exactly, and Ignatius of Antioch wrote to the Smyrneans (4,2), "Why have I given myself up to death, to fire, to sword, to wild beasts. But near sword is near God, with wild beasts is with God."[14]

A second, "Gnostic" interpretation, proposes that the Thomas saying refers to the illumination of the believer, perhaps even to a rite which was considered to seal the light of knowledge which nearness to Jesus imparts. (If this interpretation be adopted, then the allusion to "baptism with fire" in Matt. 3:11 might not be so farfetched.)[15] A third suggestion is that the Thomas saying alludes to insight into the divinity of the self achieved by nearness to Jesus.[16] Be that as it may, some observations about the possible connections among the saying, in Thomas, the Greek sayings, and the patristic citations are in order.

First, it seems certain that Origen and Didymus drew upon Thomas or, at least, a tradition parallel with Thomas. Whether Didymus is directly indebted or only indirectly through Origen is not, for our purposes significant. If the more oblique reference in Ignatius does stem from the tradition underlying Thomas, the relative antiquity of some form of the saying is confirmed. This supposed antiquity is used by Jeremias, for example, to argue for the "authenticity" of the saying,[17] but how do the Greek sayings fit into the tradition complex? One position states that since some form of the saying was attributed to Jesus, it would have been impossible for a pagan proverb to have been transferred to him. Thus, either there is no relationship between the "Aesopic" saying and the tradition behind Ignatius (and Thomas?), or the Aesopic version is secondary and "obviously produced under the influence of our saying."[18] On the other hand, the "authenticity" of the saying has been urged on the grounds that since the Greek sayings were anterior to Jesus we should assume that he could have used them and that he did use them.[19] Rather than arguing about "authenticity" it seems more fruitful to recognize that the saying in Thomas reflects use and expansion of a proverbial statement identical with or closely akin to "He who is near Zeus is near the lightning." This conclusion will be a datum in the concluding section of this paper.

---

[14]This view is championed by J. Jeremias. See *Unknown Sayings*, pp. 66-73; *The Parables of Jesus*, tr. S.H. Hooke (New York: Charles Scribner's Sons, 1963), p. 164, 196.

[15]Jacques E. Menard, "Les Problems de L'Evangile Thomas" in *Essays on the Nag Hammadi Texts in Honour of Alexander Boehling*, ed. M. Krause (Leiden: E.J. Brill, 1972), p. 61; and Menard, *L'Evangile Selon Thomas*, p. 184. This interpretation is strengthened if one assumes, with Menard, a thematic connection between Thomas 82 and the following sayings, 83-85.

[16]By implication at least, H. Koester, *Introduction to the New Testament*, Vol. 2 (Philadelphia: Fortress Press, 1982), p. 153.

[17]*Unknown Sayings*, p. 70.

[18]*Unknown Sayings*, p. 71.

[19]See Menard, "Les Problems ..." p. 61, and *L-Evangile* ..., p. 183 and the references cited there. The article by J.B. Bauer, "Echte Jesusworte" in W.C. van Unnick, *Evangelien aus dem Misland* (Frankfurt am Main: 1960), pp. 108-150, broke fresh methodological ground although his conclusions are now questioned by most commentators.

Thomas Saying 102

Jesus said, "Woe to the Pharisees, for they are like a dog sleeping in the manger of oxen; for neither does he eat nor does he let the oxen eat."

Strictly speaking only Saying 102 contains an Aesopic referent, but the obvious connection between it and Saying 39 requires that the latter be included in our analysis.

Thomas Saying 39

Jesus said, "The Pharisees and the scribes have taken the keys of knowledge and hidden them. They themselves have not entered, nor have they allowed to enter those who wish to. You however, be wise as serpents and innocent as doves.

Matthew 23:13

But woe to you scribes and Pharisees; hypocrites! because you shut out the kingdom against men; for you neither enter yourselves, nor allow those who would enter to go in.

Luke 11:52

Woe to you lawyers! for you have taken away the key of knowledge; you did not enter yourselves, and you hindered those who were entering.

Aesop

A dog lying in the manger does not eat, nor does he permit the ass (to eat). Its interpretation: The wickedness of a shameful (greedy) man is to close (shut out) another from the food he does not make use of.[20]

Unlike the Thomas Sayings 8 and 82 which *may* have a hidden, esoteric, (Gnostic?) implication, this saying seems to admit of a straightforward interpretation. The Pharisees, who may not be the historical Pharisees but rather religious leaders opposed to the community which produced/preserved the Gospel of Thomas, have neither utilized the knowledge they have received nor permitted others to have access to it. Thus, they may be compared with the dog lying in the manger. Since the interpretative problem in Thomas seems negligible, we may concentrate on the issues raised by the Aesopic allusion.

The story of the Dog in the Manger is so much a part of the Aesopic tradition that it is somewhat surprising to discover that it does not appear in any extant Aesopic *collection* prior to the 14th century C.E. Its occurrence in three 2nd century C.E. writings, however, is of considerable consequence for the present study. The Dog in the Manger allusion is found twice in the works of Lucian and once in Strato, though neither Lucian nor Strato specifically

---

[20] My translation of the text in *Aesopica I*, p. 276.

attributes the saying to Aesop. As we shall see later this is a not common attribute of sayings collections. Both Lucian and Strato flourished in the 2nd century C.E., had connections with Egypt, particularly Alexandria, and were born and reared in the eastern Mediterranean basin. The chronological time frame and the generally similar geographical provenance of Lucian/Strato and the Gospel of Thomas may be purely coincidental, and some commentators have so concluded. Perhaps more than coincidence is involved.[21]

Sayings 39, 102 and the Synoptic parallels (Matt. 23:13=Luke 11:52) have been perceptively analyzed by Crossan in terms of their development. He proposes four stages: (1) woe/proverb in Saying 102; (2) woe/nonproverb in an unknown source which was incorporated (3) in Q, woe/nonproverb; and (4) nonwoe/nonproverb in Saying 39.[22] I suggest the possibility of another stage, perhaps anterior to the others, proverb/nonwoe. Such a stage would coincide precisely with the Aesopic version. To this possibility we shall return in the second section of this paper.

Thomas Saying 109

> Jesus said, "The Kingdom is like a man who had a treasure in his field without knowing it. And after he died he left it to his son. The son did not know (about the treasure). He inherited the field and sold (it). And the one who bought it and went plowing and found the treasure. He began to lend money at interest to whomever he wished.

Jewish Parallels

> R. Simeon b. Yohai taught [The Egyptians were] like a man who inherited a piece of ground used as a dung hill. Being an indolent man, he went and sold it for a trifling sum. The purchaser began working and digging it up, and he found a treasure there, he began going about in public followed by a retinue of servants – all out of the treasure he found in it. When the seller saw it he was ready to choke, and he exclaimed, "Alas, what have I thrown away." So when Israel were in Egypt ... (*Cant. Rab.* 4. 12. 1) R. Rimon, the son of Yohai, giving a parable, says: To what can this be compared? To a man to whom there had fallen as an inheritance a residence in a far off country which he sold for a trifle. The buyer, however, went and discovered in it hidden treasures and stones of silver and gold, of precious stones and pearls. The seller, seeing this, began to choke with grief. So also did the Egyptians ... (*Mek.* Exodus 14.5)[23]

---

[21] For a fuller discussion of tradition history of the Dog in the Manger, see my article "The Dog in the Manger: In Quest of a Fable," *The Classical Journal* 8 (1985), pp. 49-58; and Martin Rist, "The Fable of the Dog in the Manger in the Gospel of Thomas," *Ilier Review*, 25 (1968), pp. 13-25.

[22] *In Fragments*, p. 35.

[23] The translations are those found in J.D. Crossan, *Finding is the First Act*, (Philadelphia: Fortress Press, 1979), pp. 65f.

Matthew 13:44

> The kingdom of heaven is like a treasure hidden in a field, which a man found and covered up; then in his joy he goes and sells all that he has and buys that field.

Aesop

> A farmer who was about to die and wanted to familiarize his sons with the farm, called to them and said, "Boys, a treasure is buried in one of my vineyards." After he died they took plows and mattocks and dug up their whole farm. They didn't find the treasure but the vineyard repaid them with a much increased crop. (Moral) The story shows that work is a treasure for men.[24]

Analysis of this complex of sayings, within the context of this paper, is complicated by two factors. First, stories of hidden treasure are so much a part of many cultures, as Crossan has amply illustrated,[25] that one might simply dismiss the question of interdependence. The second complication is the introduction of alleged parallels from yet another st of sayings collections. The latter, however, may prove to be a blessing in disguise in that it provides an addition to the data base for setting the relationships among Thomas, the Synoptics, and the Aesopic tradition within the broader issue of sayings collections as such. Before pursuing that line of investigation a brief summary of the probable interpretations of the sayings in Matthew, Thomas, and Aesop is in order.

While contemporary parable research is in a state of considerable flux, it seems that Matt. 13:44 is either a call to give up all that one has to obtain the inestimable value of the kingdom or that it conveys the sense of the immense joy which overwhelms one when confronted with the treasure of the kingdom.[26] Both nuances, indeed, may be present. There is as yet no consensus interpretation of Thomas 109, but three representatives views may be noted: (a) the father, son, and buyer represent the three types of mankind, i.e., material, psychic, and spiritual; (b) they represent Jews, Christians, and Gnostics; and (c) the stress is on the treasure as the divine self which only the Gnostic recognized. (The last may easily be incorporated into either of the first two.[27] The meaning of the saying in Aesop is unambiguous and the appended moral, "The story

---

[24] The translation is that of L.W. Daly, *Aesop Without Morals* (New York: Thomas Yoseloff, 1961), p. 111. It is numbered 42 in *Aesopica I*.

[25] *Finding is the First Act*.

[26] With these views we may associate, for example, C.H. Dodd, *Parables of the Kingdom*, reprint edition (London: Collins, 1961) pp. 84f. (first edition in 1936) and J. Jeremias, *The Parables*, pp. 200f. Recent parable research has not, in my judgment caused a serious revision of the conclusions of Dodd and Jeremias with respect to his parable.

[27] Some representative discussions of this ambiguous saying may be found in Menard, *L-Evangile*, pp. 46f., 207f.; R. McL. Wilson, *Gnosis and the New Testament* (Philadelphia: Westminster Press, 1968), pp. 78f.; B. Gaertner, *Theology of the Gospel of Thomas* (New York: Harper and Row, 1962), pp. 237f.

shows that work is a treasure of men," is a fully adequate summary.

Because of the radical differences between the versions of the parable in Matthew and Thomas, most commentators have concluded that Saying 109 is not related to the tradition underlying Matthew but to the Jewish parallel(s). There are the common elements that the original owner did not know of the treasure and that the buyer uncovered the treasure by laboring. At this point any similarity ceases. While the interpretation of Thomas remains in doubt, it clearly has nothing in common with the Midrashic stories which illustrate relations between the Egyptians and the Israelites. Thus, though superficially Thomas seems closer to the Jewish parallel(s) than to either Matthew or Aesop, no direct dependence should be inferred. What may be inferred, however, is the probability of a current folk tale about a buyer who found a treasure which had been unknown to the original owner or owners. It is this inference which leads directly to the second part of this paper.

II

It is a commonplace of New Testament scholarship that the canonical gospels utilized sayings collections, both oral and written, and there is no need to rehearse the history of that research. But the discovery of the Gospel of Thomas has provided a new dimension in that we now have extant a sayings collection almost certainly contemporary with those which have previously been hypothetically reconstructed from analysis of a common tradition underlying Matthew and Luke.[28] Later collections, such as those of Sextus and Silvanus, both found now in the Nag Hammadi library,[29] provide additional confirmation of the conclusion that early on sayings collections played a significant role in communities which were later deemed "orthodox" and those which subsequently were considered "heretical." Thomas is clearly our best exemplar of this stage of Christian literature.

Quite early in the study of the Gospel of Thomas Turner remarked that it "seems probable that the Gospel of Thomas was intended to serve as a kind of gnostic Testimony Book ..."[30] One might demur from the adjective "gnostic," but the designation "Testimony Book" is clearly on target. The import of that recognition is put succinctly by Hunzinger:

> In the process [of studying the parables in Thomas] the modern critical

---

[28] It is not necessary to enumerate the lengthy list of scholars who espouse this view. James M. Robinson's "*Logoi Sophon*" in *Trajectories Through the New Testament*, with Helmut Koester (Philadelphia: Fortress Press, 1971) pp. 71-113 is a model. Cf. also now his resume of the conclusions of Vielhauer, "[the Gospel of Thomas] transmits words that Jesus had spoken or was supposed to have spoken during his earthly life, and to this extent is a companion of Q." "The Nag Hammadi Library and the Study of the New Testament" in *The New Testament and Gnosis*, p. 6.

[29] Sextus, *Nag Hammadi Library*, pp. 454-459; Silvanus, pp. 346-351.

[30] *Thomas and the Evangelists*, p. 86.

research on the Synoptics is confirmed in a remarkable way: The existence of the *genre* of sayings collections postulated by literary criticism is now demonstrated; the small isolated units transmitted without framework or situation that form criticism postulated stand here before us in just that form; the secondary elements of a predominantly allegorical or moralizing nature detected especially in the analysis of the parables as secondary (especially also the generalizing conclusions of the parables) are almost completely absent from the Gospel of Thomas.[31]

James M. Robinson in his by now classic article "Logoi Sophon: on the Gattung of Q" proposed "to confirm, clarify, and carry further Bultmann's association of *logia* and *meshalim* under the concept of 'wisdom teacher,' by working out a name for the gattung of Q. 'logoi sophon,' 'sayings of the sages,' or 'words to the wise' ..." "He noted that a more thorough investigation of Greek literature with regard to this gattung is a still further need."[32] The remainder of this paper will focus on the nature and function of such sayings collections as might have been available to the traditions underlying Thomas and the canonical gospels with specific reference to Aesopic material.

The history of the Aesopic tradition[33] is not as clear as one might wish and Aesopic specialists are not in complete agreement as to the literary form or forms in which it first appeared, but I believe that the following resume is a fair reflection of the main points in the development of the Aesopic tradition. Although a few fables are found scattered in Greek literature before Aesop (traditionally dated in the late 7th/early 6th centuries B.C.E.), it is with his name that the fable became preeminently associated. Fables attributed to him are used by Greek authors from the 5th century B.C.E. onward, and there may have been a collection of his sayings as early as the end of that century. We are told in the *Phaedo* (59E-61B),[34] that while he was in prison Socrates began to compose poetry, including a hymn to Apollo and "metrical versions of Aesop's fables [*logous*]." He said that "a poet, if he is to be a poet, must compose myths [*muthous*] and not speeches [*logous*], since I was not a maker of myths, I took the myths of Aesop, which I had at hand and knew, and turned into verse the first came upon." If the somewhat ambiguous words "had at hand and knew ..." refer to a collection available to Socrates, than a date before the end of the 5th century B.C.E. is established. This seems likely, but Socrates may have been referring to his knowledge of the fables through oral sources.

---

[31]C.-H. Hunzinger, *ThLZ* 85 (1960), cols. 844-846. The translation is that of James M. Robinson, in *Gnosis*, ed. B. Aland (Goettingen: 1978), p. 143.
[32]"Logoi sophon" esp. pp. 73f.
[33]I have relied heavily on the work of Ben Perry in the writings already mentioned and in the works cited in the following notes. The critical edictions of the French specialist Chambry; *Aesopi Fabulae* (Paris: Bude, 1925) and *Fables, Texte Etablie et Traduit* (Paris: Societe d'Edition Les Belles Lettres, 1960) and the German specialist, August Haustrath, *Aesopus: Corpus Fabularum Aesopicarium*, 4th ed. (Leipzig: Teubner, 1970), should also be consulted.
[34]Loeb, *Plato I*, tr. H.N. Fowler (Cambridge: Harvard University Press, 1914), pp. 208-213.

There is unambiguous reference to an Aesopic collection compiled by Demetrius of Phalerum at the end of the 4th or beginning of the 3rd century B.C.E.[35] Demetrius' political career was ended by a shift of power in Athens in 307 B.C.E. and he was forced to flee Greece. He became librarian in Alexandria in 297 B.C.E. and died in Egypt c. 280 B.C.E. Diogenes Laertius,[36] in his list of the literary works of Demetrius mentions one book of Aesopica and characterizes it as "a collection of the words [*logon*] of Aesop." The work is no longer extant, though it seems that it was still in circulation as the 10th century C.E. Perry has maintained, on the basis of a series of careful text analyses, including the texts of first century C.E. fable fragments now in the John Rylands library, that a number of fables from the collection of Demetrius can be detected in later versions and that the Rylands Papyri almost surely reflect the literary form used by Demetrius.[37] Thus, there is clear evidence that sayings collections associated with Aesop were current in the Mediterranean world centuries before the beginning of the common era and it is probable that the literary form and purpose of those collections had already undergone considerable transformation by that time.

There seem to have been three phases of the fable in Greco-Roman antiquity, "each of which is conditioned by a different outlook and purpose on the part of the authors concerned."[38] The first is the insertion of a fable or part of a fable, for illustrative purposes into a historical narrative, oration, philosophical discourse, or some other form of literature. The second is a collection of disconnected sayings without setting or context. In the final state the fables are presented by an author as self-conscious literary works in their own right. This phase is found already in Phaedrus in the middle of the 1st century C.E. and Babrius in the first part of the next. It is the proposed in-between form that primarily concerns us. Here we find collections of sayings without setting or context and with no specific moral attached. What was the purpose of such collections?

No doubt one purpose was simply to preserve sayings attributed to famous persons in the past as a part of the cultural heritage of the age. (It is to be noted that many sayings collections in addition to Aesopic ones were in wide circulation.) The collections had another more pragmatic purpose. They were designed "to provide a repertoire of materials compiled for the benefit of writers and speakers"[39] for illustrative purposes in their own writings and orations.

---

[35] For the most thorough treatment of Demetrius with the Aesopic tradition, see Perry, "Demetrius of Phalerum and the Aesopic Fables," *TAPA* 93 (1962), pp. 287-346.

[36] Loeb, *Diogenes Laertius I*, tr. R.D. Hicks (Cambridge: Harvard University Press, 1925), pp. 530-535.

[37] In addition to the evidence given in Note 35, see also Perry, *Studium Generale* 12 (1959), esp. pp. 29-31. The Rylands Papyri are catalogues by C.H. Roberts, *Catalogue of the Greek and Latin Payri in the John Rylands Library* (Manchester: 1938), III 19ff., no. 493.

[38] Perry, *Studium Generale*, p. 28.

[39] Perry, *TAPA* 93 (1962), p. 340.

This is interestingly confirmed in two plays of Plautus (late 3rd/early 2nd centuries B.C.E.). The full plot of the plays is not, for our purposes, important, but in the first, the *Persian* (Act III, Scene 1) a father is comforting his daughter who fears that lack of a dowry will preclude a good marriage. He assures her that she does have a dowry in his collection of books, saying, "I'll give you a good six hundred witticisms out of 'em for a dowry, and all Attic ones, without a single Sicilian quip amongst 'em." An even clearer example is in *Stichus* (Act III, Scene 2) where the lead character fears that he is losing favor with his patron. His spirits revive, however, after he does some homework: "I've consulted my books; I'm absolutely sure I can hold my patron, I'll be so comical." (This may be our earliest reference to joke books!)[40]

Confirmation comes also directly from the Aesopic tradition. A manuscript family of the Augustana recension has a preface stating the purpose of the collection. One section of that preface specifically notes that the collection is "For the benefit of public speakers in their contests and revelries with each other"[41] and goes on to say that many other such collections have been made from the poets and dramatists. I would infer that the collection was designed for writers as well as speakers.

I now draw attention to three specific points about the Aesop tradition which, in my judgment, have direct bearing upon the study of Thomas within the context of sayings collections. The first relates to the literary form of the collections. It is to be admitted that evidence on this item is largely inferential and thus problematical, but I believe that the following schema is defensible. The first collections were simply that, a random selection without context, order, or moral. The hypothetical Demetrius collection *may* have had this form or it may already have shown the development confirmed in the Rylands Papyri, where each fable is introduced by a promythium which gives an index to the fable's contents.[42] This was, surely, designed to facilitate ready reference for speakers and writers seeking an apt illustration. Phaedrus, in the earlier part of his collection where he is following Aesop more closely, also uses the promythium. But in the later parts of his work, and in Babrius, the promythium is dropped and replaced by an epimythium which is designed to explain explicitly the meaning of the fable, its "moral." The shift from promythium to epimythium and the later confusion of the functions of each, while important for students of the development of the Aesopic tradition, need not deter as at this point.[43] I would suggest, however, that if such a development may be considered a general literary phenomenon, and I believe that it can, then the

---

[40]The references in Plautus may be found in Loeb Plautus III, tr. P. Nixon (Cambridge: Harvard University Press, 1924), pp. 466-467 for the *Persian* and Loeb Plautus V, tr. P. Nixon (Cambridge: Harvard University Press, 1938), pp. 54-55 for the *Stichus*.
[41]Perry, *Studium Generale* 12, p. 34.
[42]Ibid., p. 35.
[43]On the development of the epimythium, see Perry *TAPA* 71 (1940) pp. 399ff.

absence of explanations, epimythia, in Thomas may very well reflect a stage in the sayings collections earlier than many sayings in the Synoptics. This is, I emphasize, a cautious suggestion which needs to be examined with respect to each single Thomas saying and its alleged Synoptic parallel.

Our second specific observation pertains to the words used to denote Aesop's sayings, *muthous* and *logos*. The words were at times used interchangeably and the later rhetoricians preferred *muthous*, but in the earliest collections *logos* is certainly predominant.[44] A title early ascribed to Aesop is "Aesop the Wise" and in his biography which dates from the late 1st or early 2nd century C.E. we are told that it was the goddess Isis who removed his speech impediment and "persuaded the Muses as well to confer on him each something from her own endowment. They conferred on him the power to devise stories and the ability to conceive and elaborate tales in Greek." ("Stories and tales" are in the Greek text *logon kai mython*.)[45] Thus, though the formulation does not actually appear in any manuscript, the early Aesopic collections could be called "The Sayings of Aesop the Wise, inspired by a goddess and the Muses." We might well include the Aesopic collections among the *Logoi Sophon*.

The third specific observation about the Aesopic collections leads us directly to the concluding section of this paper. Aesopic collections circulated not only in Greek but were, probably quite early, translated into Syriac and perhaps other Semitic languages.[46] This translation process was a two-way street since Democritus (mid-5th century B.C.E.) made, or commissioned to be made, a translation of Ahikar, and Theophrastis, the teacher of Demetrius of Phalerum by the way, wrote both a book on Ahikar and one on Democritus (Diog., Laert. 5, 2, 49-50).[47] The interpenetration of sayings collections – Greek, Jewish, and non-Jewish Semitic – was pervasive in the eastern Mediterranean basin, and thus well known in Syria, Palestine, and Egypt, all of which have been proposed as the geographical provenance of the Gospel of Thomas.[48]

The relationship between Thomas, the Synoptic traditions and Aesop can be formulated in the following way. (1) Could Thomas and the Synoptics have used Aesopic materials? (2) Would they have used them? (3) Did they use them? The answer to the first question can be brief and clearly affirmative.

---

[44]Perry, *TAPA* 1962, pp. 336-338.
[45]For Aesop the Wise, cf. Babrius, Loeb, p. 139 and somewhat less direct allusion on p. 3. Aristophanes often refers to Aesop in this manner. The passage referring to Isis and the Muses is in *Life of Aesop*, ch. 7, *Aesopica I*, pp. 37f, and in Daly's translation, p. 34.
[46]On Syriac translations of Aesopic materials see Perry, *TAPA*, 1962, esp. pp. 310, 322f.; *Aesopica I*, pp. 52-523; *Life and Fables*, pp. 185-190.
[47]See my observations in connection with respect to Thomas 102, "Dog in the Manger," pp. 57f.
[48]R. Bultmann, *History of the Synoptic Tradition*, tr. John Marsh (New York: Harper and Row, 1963), p. 105. The entire section of Jesus as Teacher of Wisdom, pp. 69-108 is seminal.

Aesopic collections, certainly in Greek and probably in Semitic translation, were current centuries before the beginning of the common era. The second, unless one adopts an extraordinary theological bias, should also be answered affirmatively. Referring only to 20th century scholarship we may note that Bultmann pointed out that the "tradition has taken many logia from popular wisdom and piety into itself, and it has done so now and then because Jesus has made use of or coined such a saying." He isolated twenty-six secular *meshalim* set forth as dominical sayings in the canonical tradition and many others which reflected contemporary Jewish popular piety and are paralleled in *"Jewish and oriental literature generally"* (emphasis his).[49] Other scholars have demonstrated convincingly that some canonical sayings have not only Jewish and oriental parallels but also Greek ones.[50] There is no reason to assume that Aesopic sayings might not have been among those used. Thus, Thomas and the Synoptics *could* have used Aesop and the evidence indicates that they *would* have. There remains the question, "Did they?"

We shall limit response to this question to the sayings in Thomas for which Aesopic parallels have been alleged although it is obvious that a much broader spectrum needs to be investigated. Since each of the four sayings which may have affinity with the Aesopic tradition has been discussed in the first section of this paper we may proceed directly to summary conclusions of that evidence. Saying 8 is independent of though not unrelated to the Matthean parable. Each has drawn upon a common fable tradition and adapted it to his own theological purpose. With some diffidence I suggest that the Aesopic version, in some form, was prior to and known by both Matthew and Thomas. Saying 82 is independent of the Synoptic tradition but shows a clear awareness of some form of the Aesopic proverbs discussed earlier. It is equally clear that Thomas has radically modified their meaning for his theological purpose. If the proposed Synoptic parallels to reflect knowledge of one of the Greek proverbs, they have used it in a most fragmentary manner, adapting its elements in widely divergent theological context. Sayings 39 and 102 provide provocative evidence. As I indicated above, Crossan's paradigm of movement from woe/proverb (Thomas 102) to woe/nonproverb (Matthew and Luke), to nonwoe/nonproverb (Thomas

---

[49] Ibid., p. 102. W.D. Davies, *The Setting of the Sermon on the Mount*, (Cambridge: Cambridge University Press, 1963), pp. 457-460 examined the secular sayings isolated by Bultmann and agreed that Jesus could have used such sayings, but Davies concluded that they are used in their present setting to "illumine the crisis caused by his coming" (460). (See also W. Beardslee, "Use of the Proverb in the Synoptic Gospels" *Interpretation*, 24 (1970), pp. 61-73.

[50] See Saul Lieberman, *Greek in Jewish Palestine* 2nd ed. (New York: Philip Feldheim, Inc. 1965), esp. pp. 144-160; *idem.*, "How Much Greek in Jewish Palestine?" *Texts and Studies*, (New York: KTAV, 1974), pp. 216-234); Arnold Ehrhardt, "Greek Proverbs in the Gospel" The Framework of the New Testament stories (Cambridge: Harvard University Press, 1964), pp. 44-63; *idem* "Lass die Toten ihre Toten begraben" *ST* 6 (1952), pp. 128-163; W.A. Beardslee, "Proverb in the Gospel of Thomas" in "Proverbs in the Gospel of *Thomas,* ed. D.E. Aune (Leiden: E.J. Brill, 1972), pp. 92-103. This list could be considerably expanded, but the preceding works indicate sufficiently the lines of research currently progressing.

39) is patently susceptible of an additional, and initial, stage; proverb/nonwoe, and this is precisely what we find in the Aesopic tradition. Thus, I suggest that Thomas, surely, and the Synoptics, probably,[51] knew the Aesopic saying and modified it within their specific theological context.

Saying 109 requires a more extensive summary since the Jewish parallels add a new dimension for our comparative study and provide an important clue for understanding the hermeneutical process involved the use of sayings collections. The differences among the versions of the Hidden Treasure in Thomas, Matthew, and the rabbinic materials, are so great that it would, in my judgment, demand a remarkable *tour de force* to propose any direct literary dependence. They each adapted a widespread motif, hidden treasure, to make a specific theological or homiletical point. One might simply let the matter rest there, but can anything more be said? The Aesopic version differs significantly from the others in two respects. First, in Aesopic there is only an alleged treasure, and second, the interpretation (moral) is a straightforward secular one, "The story shows that work is a treasure of men." Even if there is no direct dependence of Thomas Matthew, or the rabbinic stories on Aesop, which might itself reflect a secondary adaptation of an older hidden treasure story, the movement from secular to theological or homiletical is worthy of note.

Koester[52] has called attention to this development in comparing Thomas 39 with Matt. 7:6. The saying in Thomas "is a perfect form of a proverb without any religious or Christian application, whereas Matt. 7:6 shows signs of an application of this proverb to the situation of the church." An even more specifically Christian application is made in Did 9:5b. Consequently, when we find, or can plausibly reconstruct, a popular saying without religious connotations which has been given a different theological adaptation by two or more subsequent authors (or traditions), then the *tendenz* of the latter may be set forth in sharper detail. There is, certainly, the danger that our own theological *tendenz* may obscure the evidence, but is, I believe, a risk worth taking.

I have in this paper, with the exception of a brief comment on Saying 82, avoided the thorny question of "authenticity" and, indeed, the issue is peripheral to the present investigation. But a question posed by Quispel cannot be totally ignored: "Can we imagine a Jesus familiar with Greek wisdom, using the

---

[51]C.E. Carlson, whose important article, "Proverbs, Maxims, and the Historical Jesus" *SBL* 99 (1980), pp. 87-105, raises sharply the historical and theological issues of the presence of tradition sayings attributed to Jesus, maintains that the Aesopic proverb was known to the Synoptic Tradition (p. 100), and it is so cited in J.D. Crossan, *Sayings Parallels* (Philadelphia: Fortress, 1986), p. 181, and R.W. Funk, *New Gospel Parallels* (Philadelphia: Fortress, 1985), p. 129. Because of the absence of reference to "the dog in the manger" in the Synoptics, many others do not call attention to the parallel, e.g., the latest edition of *Gospel Parallels*, ed. B.H. Throckmorton (Nashville: Thomas Nelson, 1979), p. 149, cites a parallel between the Synoptics and Thomas 39 but omits 102.

[52]"One Jesus and Four Primitive Gospels" in *Trajectories*, p. 182.

material of popular folktale and wisdom?"[53] I believe that the evidence presented in this paper provides modest confirmation of previous writers who have maintained that the question should receive an affirmative answer. Though Jesus was not only, perhaps not even primarily, a sage, there should be no doubt that some of his words ought to be included in the *logoi sophon*.[54] That not only Thomas and the Synoptic traditions could have used Aesop, but that such use by Jesus himself is readily credible.

Careful scrutiny of Aesopic materials and other contemporary sayings collections which are extant or which can be reconstructed, can make, to be sure, only a small contribution to our understanding of the canonical and noncanonical literature which is the primary concern of Biblical scholarship, but even small contributions are to be welcomed in that complex task. Such scrutiny will also expand our understanding of the Hellenistic cultural setting of Judaism and early Christianity which has long occupied Professor Kee and to which he has made most substantial contributions.

Addendum

Robert L. Wilken, in dealing with a different issue, has remarked that "... like many historical questions the matter of origins may not be the most interesting or significant. The more important question is what the redactor though he was doing with the material he received" ("Wisdom and Philosophy in Early Christianity" p. 149, in *Aspects of Wisdom in Judaism and Early Chrimsriah Literature* [Notre Dame Press, 1975].

That, above all, is what I have tried to point out in this article. What can we learn from alterations which diverse authors have made of a common tradition? I offer the following fantasy as an illustration.

The Fisherman and the Small Fish

This Aesopic fable is found in three ancient collections. The shortest, and probably the most original, is in the Augustana recension (number 18 in Perry's enumeration). "A fisherman threw his net and brought out a minnow. When the minnow begged him to throw it back for the present, since it was small, and catch it again when it was grown up, the fisherman said, 'I would certainly be a great simpleton if I let go the gain I have in hand and sent chasing after some vague hope.'" The moral is, "The story shows that present advantage is preferable, even though slight, to any anticipation, no matter how great" (Daly, *Aesop Without Morals,* 101, 269). Both Babrius and Avaianus expand the

---

[53]Gnosis and the New Sayings of Jesus," p. 275.
[54]Although the authenticity of the passage is much disputed, the reference to Jesus as a wise man (*sophos*) in Josephus, *Antiquities* XVIII, 63 is interesting. For a recent discussion of the historical value of Josephus with respect to early Christianity, see G.H. Twelftree, "Jesus in Jewish Traditions", in I 5 ed., David Wenham (Sheffield: JSOT Press, 1984), pp. 289-310.

Thomas and Aesop 131

narrative considerably, but the basic point remains the same. (The Babrius fable is number 6 in the Loeb edition and the Avaianus version is number 20 in the Loeb edition of *Minor Latin Poets*.)

A series of recent manuscript discoveries may be of enormous value and consequence for studies of the Synoptic gospels and the Gospel of Thomas. In each of them is found a saying attributed to Jesus which is manifestly dependent upon, or at least related to, the Aesopic fable. I am not at liberty to disclose details about these finds, lest the finder, the dealer, and the present owner be placed in jeopardy. I can assure you, however, that each bears the mark of authenticity and each appears to dae from the late 1st or early 2nd century C.E.. I shall reproduce each *in extenso*. Since no formal designations have yet been assigned to the manuscripts I shall refer to them simply as Fragments A, B, C, and D.

Fragment A. Almost surely a lost section of the Gospel of Thomas.

> The man is like a Wise Fisherman who threw in his net and brought out one small fish. The Wise Fisherman said, "I may not eat of you, but you shall eat of me." Whoever has ears to hear, let him hear.

Fragment B. Probably a Matthean saying, though a Q provenance cannot be ruled out. See comment on Fragment C.

> Again, the Kingdom of Heaven is like a net which was thrown into the sea, and when men drew it ashore, it contained but one small fish. Since it was small it was eaten at once. So will it be at the close of the age. He whose faith is slight and has done small things will perish, but he whose faith is great and has done large things will abide. He who has ears, let him hear.

Fragment C. Undoubtedly this was once included in Luke or Proto-Luke. While it bears some incidental parallels with the new Matthean fragment, the differences are so great that one is inclined to assume independent traditions. Further, since an additional parallel is found in the Markan fragment, see below, the likelihood that Luke and Matthew are here using Q is slender.

> So he told them this parable. A man cast his net into the sea and drew in but one small fish. Though it was small, he rejoiced; for better one sinner who repents than the rest who need to repentance. He who has ears to hear, let him hear.

Fragment D. That this was once a part of Mark (Secret Mark?) is beyond dispute.

> And he taught them many things in parables, and in his teaching he said to them, "Listen! A fisherman cast his line into the sea and drew in one small fish. He hid that small fish till it became great." Then he said,

"So shall it be in the day of the Son of Man." He who has ears to hear, let him hear.

There is a considerable gap in the manuscript at this point, but preliminary examination suggests that the immediately following lines may have contained an interpretation of the parable for the disciples.

While it is far too early to draw definitive conclusions about the intertextuality of the new passages, my present tentative observations are:

1. The priority of the Aesopic saying, in the Augustana Recension, seems clear.
2. Thomas is not dependent upon the Synoptic versions and may very well reflect the setting in life of Jesus better than the synoptics.
3. Mark has clearly adapted the saying into his theology of the parables as mystery (riddle).
4. The versions in Matthew and Luke are entirely in keeping with the redactional tendencies of those authors as are known from other studies.

These tentative observations, of course, may be modified when other scholars have had an opportunity to study the facsimiles which are in course of preparation. For the present additional comment is not warranted.

Chapter Nine

Outside/Inside:
Celsus on Jewish and Christian *Nomoi*

Harold Remus

Jewish-Christian dialogue is often illuminated when viewed as a three-way conversation, with paganism as the third – the silent or shadowy – partner.[1] Similarly, in pagan-Christian dialogue or polemic the continuing presence in antiquity of Jewish communities observant of Jewish *nomoi* is an important, albeit often neglected, factor in study of such exchanges.[2] In Celsus' attack on Christianity, the *Alethēs Logos,* preserved in part in Origen's *Contra Celsum,* the same three partners (or opponents) appear. Celsus' polemic both denigrates Judaism and invokes it against Christianity, in defense of paganism.

Celsus' wide-ranging polemic, which on first reading might appear as diffuse and desultory[3] and lacking in consistency, turns out on closer examination to be focused on a defense of ancient tradition, epitomized in the terms *logos* and *nomos*.[4] "There is an ancient, primal doctrine *[logos]* that has always been a concern of the wisest peoples and of cities and of wise men" (*C. Cels.* 1.14c).[5]

---

[1] For an illustration see Harold Remus, "Justin Martyr's Argument with Judaism," in S.G. Wilson (ed.), *Anti-Judaism in Early Christianity*, vol 2, *Separation and Polemic*, Studies in Christianity and Judaism/Etudes sur le christianisme et le judaisme 2/2 (Waterloo, Ontario: Wilfrid Laurier University Press for the Canadian Corporation for Studies in Religion, 1986), 59-80.
[2] See Robert L. Wilken, *Judaism and the Early Christian Mind: A Study of Cyril of Alexandria's Exegesis and Theology*, Yale Publications in Religion, 15 (New Haven and London: Yale University Press, 1971), ch. 1; "The Jews and Christian Apologetics after Theodosius I *Cunctos Populos,*" *Harvard Theological Review* 73 (1980), 451-71; "The Christians as the Romans and the Greeks Saw Them," in E.P. Sanders (ed.), *Jewish and Christian Self-Definition,* vol. 1, *The Shaping of Christianity in the Second and Third Centuries* (Philadelphia: Fortress Press, 1980), 100-25, esp. 120-23.
[3] Thus A. Miura-Stange, *Celsus und Origenes: Das Gemeinsame ihrer Weltanschauung nach den acht Büchern des Origenes gegen Celsus. Eine Studie zur Religions- und Geistesgeschichte des 2. und 3. Jahrhunderts*, Beihefte zur Zeitschrift für die neutestamentliche Wissenschaft, 4 (Giessen: Töpelmann, 1926), 18 (a "polemische Planlosigkeit").
[4] Carl Andresen, *Logos und Nomos: Die Polemik des Kelsos wider das Christentum*, Arbeiten zur Kirchengeschichte, 30 (Berlin: de Gruyter, 1955).
[5] I cite the Greek text of Celsus from R. Bader (ed.), *Der Alethes Logos des Kelsos,* Tübinger Beiträge zur Altertumswissenschaft, 33 (Stuttgart and Berlin: Kohlhammer, 1940); the

And every people, asserts Celsus, has a *nomos* and should live according to it. These two motifs are then pursued in the various parts of Celsus' treatise.[6] In the third part (5.2-7.61), Celsus presents Jews, for whom he has no particular fondness, as like other peoples of the Greco-Roman world in that they at least possess and maintain their own *nomos* (5.25). Christians, by contrast, have no *nomoi*, or derivative ones at best. In this they stand apart from other peoples and groups in the Empire. That in Celsus' polemic we see not simply arguments over words and concepts – disputing over an ass's shadow, as he puts it in denigrating Jews and Christians (3.1) – but confrontation between rival communities I have sought to demonstrate elsewhere,[7] and I will recur to it again in what follows. This essay will ask in what way Celsus' vantage point as an outsider both to Judaism and Christianity offers insights into these two religions and relations between them, then and now, as well as into paganism of that day. It will also consider, on the other hand, the significance of Christianity's position as both outside and inside the system to which Celsus is an insider.

1. Celsus as an Outsider

A long and respectable tradition contends that the insider, perhaps indeed only the insider, truly understands a religion. Those Jews, writes Philo, who actually keep and observe the laws, in addition to interpreting them allegorically, come to a closer understanding of what the laws symbolize (*De migr. Abr.* 89-93). That observation he might well have applied to what his contemporary, the apostle Paul, says about circumcision as a matter of heart and spirit rather than letter (Rom. 2:28-29),[8] rejecting it as a requirement for non-Jews. The *Midrash Rabbah Exodus* 30.12 portrays the Emperor Hadrian as telling Aquila, then a potential convert, to study the Jewish law, if he wishes, but not to be circumcised, to which Aquila replies, "Unless one is circumcised even the wisest in your kingdom, and even an old man of a hundred years, cannot study their Torah."[9] Anselm's *Credo ut intelligam* is echoed in Leszek Kolakowski's recent

---

translations are my own.

[6]T. Keim, *Celsus' Wahres Wort: Ältester Streitschrift antiker Weltanschauung gegen das Christentum vom Jahre 178 nach Christus. Wiederhergestellt, aus dem Griechischen übersetzt, untersucht und erläutert, mit Lucian und Minucius Felix verglichen* (Zurich: 1873; reprinted, Aalen, Germany: Scientia Verlag, 1969), discerned a preface and four parts in Celsus' treatise, a judgment concurred in by P. Koetschau, the editor of *Contra Celsum* in *Origenes Werke*, Die griechischen christlichen Schriftsteller, 2, 3 (Leipzig: Hinrich, 1899) (see vol. 2, xlix-lv, and his article, "Die Gliederung des ἀληθής λόγος des Celsus," *Jahrbücher für protestantische Theologie* 18 [1892], 604-32), as well as by scholars generally; see Andresen, *Logos und Nomos*, 32.

[7]Harold Remus, *Pagan-Christian Conflict Over Miracle in the Second Century*, Patristic Monograph Series, 10 (Cambridge, MA: Philadelphia Patristic Foundation, 1983), chs. 8-9.

[8]For precedents and parallels to this view cf., e.g., Lev. 26:41; Deut. 10:16, 30:6; Jer. 4:4, 9:26; Ezek. 44:7, 9; 1QS 5.4-5; Plutarch, *Isis and Os.* 352c; *Ps.-Barn.* 9.4-5.

[9]Cited in Wilken, "Christians as the Romans and Greeks ...," 103. Cf. Theophilus of

study which asserts that "'belonging to' precedes all proofs" and that understanding comes through "real participation in a religious community."[10]

In the academic study of religion in the second half of the twentieth century, the idea that only insiders can understand and teach a religion, and its corollary, the "'zoo' theory, according to which religion can be dealt with only by exhibiting representative members of the various species,"[11] have been generally rejected by religious studies scholars. It is true, of course, as Arnold Band observes, that while persons who teach Judaism, for example, need not be Jews, yet "since extensive familiarity with different sources is crucial for professional competence, it is only natural that the qualified candidates for posts would be men [sic] who had studied these sources before their graduate training, and these are likely to be Jews."[12] Not commitment to a religious tradition, but knowledge and empathy – expertise – are requisite for understanding and interpreting a religious tradition. Thus, today scholars who are Jews teach courses in and write books about Christianity, scholars who are Christian do the same for Judaism, Buddhism, etc. Part of their expertise lies in treating the truth claims of a religion as just that – claims – and providing students with perspective – including data and methodology – on how to assess such claims.[13]

Another counterpoise to the insider theory is the observation that the outsider often perceives truly – Galen's comment that, though Christians are not philosophically schooled, they live the kind of life urged by philosophy is a case in point[14] – and may indeed perceive precisely what insiders do not. Thus Porphyry, against the contemporary Jewish and Christian consensus that the book of Daniel was composed by a sixth-century B.C.E. figure, anticipated modern scholarship in dating it to the reign of Antiochus Epiphanes in the second century B.C.E.;[15] in general, by applying canons of literary and

---

Antioch's assertion (*Ad Autolycum* 2) that God can be seen only by those who have had the eyes of their soul opened, and he is manifested only to those who have put away evil deeds (which might be viewed as a commentary on Matt. 5:8).

[10]Kolakowski, *Religion: If there is no God ... On God, the Devil, Sin and Other Worries of the So-called Philosophy of Religion* (New York and Oxford: Oxford University Press, 1982), 165, 176.

[11]Claude Welch, *Graduate Education in Religion: A Critical Appraisal* (Missoula: University of Montana Press, 1971), 16; on the "insider" theory, see further, pp. 16-17; in the study of Judaism, Jacob Neusner, *The Public Side of Learning: The Political Consequences of Scholarship in the Context of Judaism*, AAR Studies in Religion, 40 (Chico, CA: Scholars Press, 1985), ch. 8, "Being Jewish and Studying About Judaism" (on the "insider," pp. 91-93).

[12]Band, "Jewish Studies in American Liberal-Arts Colleges and Universities," *American Jewish Yearbook* 67 (1966), 6.

[13]Cf. John H. Whittaker, "Neutrality in the Study of Religion," *Council on the Study of Religion Bulletin* 12/5 (1981), 129-31.

[14]In R. Walzer, *Galen on Jews and Christians*, Oxford Classical and Philosophical Monographs (London: Oxford University Press, 1949), 15.

[15]Porphyry, *Adv. Christ.*, fragment 43 in A. Harnack (ed.), *Porphyrius, "Gegen die Christen," 15 Bücher: Zeugnisse, Fragmente und Referate*, Abhandlungen der königlich preussischen Akademie der Wissenschaften (1916), philosophisch-historische Klasse, 1 (Berlin: George

historical criticism, he was able to point out flaws and contradictions in the Jewish and Christian scriptures.[16] The Enlightenment, placing itself in the position of outsider to much of traditional Christianity, came to similar conclusions.[17] That parade example, perhaps – Friedrich Nietzsche – with perception heightened by hate and loathing, discerned in Christianity elements to which most Christian insiders in his day were blind.[18]

Celsus writes as a polemicist, not as a religious studies scholar striving for a fair degree of objectivity in approaching and assessing his subjects. Nevertheless, he is not uniformed, as the continued combing of his work for data on second-century Jews and Christians by modern scholars attests.[19] With respect to Jews Celsus stands in the tradition of other *literati* of the Greco-Roman world who possessed a fair amount of information about Judaism, some of it reliable, some not, some reported with hostile intent, some not.[20] Nor is Celsus undiscerning: he does not repeat some of the more blatant slanders against Jews, such as misanthropy[21] or worship of an ass,[22] or against

---

Reimer, 1916).

[16] Ibid., fragments 1-72.

[17] Perhaps the most trenchant critique, reminiscent in some respects of Porphyry's criticisms, is H.S. Reimarus, "Von dem Zwecke Jesu and seiner Jünger," published posthumously by Lessing (Braunschweig: 1778) and trans. by R.S. Fraser in Charles H. Talbert (ed.), *Reimarus: Fragments*, Lives of Jesus Series (Philadelphia: Fortress Press, 1970). On the Deistic predecessors of the Enlightenment, see now Henning Graf Reventlow, *The Authority of the Bible and the Rise of the Modern World*, trans. by J. Bowden (Philadelphia: Fortress Press, 1985), Part III.

[18] Cf. Jaroslav J. Pelikan, *Fools for Christ: Essays on the True, the Good, and the Beautiful* (Philadelphia: Muhlenburg Press, 1955), 133-44.

[19] For example, Walther Völker, "Die Kritik des Celsus am Leben Jesu und die Korrekturen der Gnostiker," *Theologische Blätter* 5 (1626), 25-39, and *Das Bild vom nichtgnostischen Christentum bei Celsus* (Halle [Salle]: Buchhandlung des Waisenhauses, 1928); Eugene V. Galagher, *Divine Man or Magician? Celsus and Origen on Jesus*, Society of Biblical Literature Dissertation Series, 64 (Chico, CA: Scholars Press, 1982); Robert L. Wilken, "Christians as the Greeks and Romans ..." (cited above, n. 2), 116-23; Gary T. Burke, "Walter Bauer and Celsus: The Shape of Late Second-Century Christianity," *The Second Century* 4/1 (1984), 1-8.

[20] See John G. Gager, *The Origins of Anti-Semitism: Attitudes toward Judaism in Pagan and Christian Antiquity* (New York and Oxford: Oxford University Press, 1983), chs. 3-5.

[21] Apollonius Molon, *De Iudaeis* (in Josephus, *Contra Apionem* 2.148, μισανθρώπους); Diodorus Siculus, *Bibliotheca Historica* 34.1.2 (τὸ μῖσος τὸ πρὸς τοὺς ἀνθρώπους), 3 (τὰ μισάνθρωπα καὶ παράνομα 'έθη ... τὴν μισανθρωπίαν), 4 (τὰ μισόξενα νόμιμα). Christians also came to be charged with misanthropy: Tacitus, *Annals* 15.44 (*odio humani generis*). The texts of these and many of the other sources cited in succeeding notes are collected in Menahem Stern (ed. and trans.), *Greek and Latin Authors on Jews and Judaism*, 3 vols. (Jerusalem: Israel Academy of Sciences and Humanities, 1974); I cite the pages in Stern for the less familiar or less accessible sources.

[22] The first extant reference (see Stern, *Greek and Latin Authors*, vol 1, 97) is Mnaseas of Patara, in Josephus, *Contra Apionem* 2.114; others repeating the story include Apion (in ibid., 2.80) and Damocritus, *De Iudaeis*, in the Suda, s.v. Δαμόκριτος (both texts in Stern, *Greek and Latin Authors*, vol. 1, nos. 170 and 247; other, related references in Stern, vol .1, p. 97). Christians, too, came to be charged with ass-worship: Tertullian, *Apol.* 16.1-3 (Tertullian traces the slander to Tacitus, *Hist.* [5.3-4], whence it came to be applied also to Christians); *Ad nationes* 1.11 (cf. 1.14); Minucius Felix, *Octavius* 9.3; on a crucified figure with an ass's head, see Martin Hengel, *Crucifixion in the Ancient World and the Folly of the*

Christians, such as cannibalism[23] or orgies.[24]

Yet as an outsider, and as a polemicist, Celsus clearly misunderstands or misrepresents Judaism and Christianity in significant ways. The Jews' departure from Egypt was one of the items of common knowledge about Jews among pagan writers, some of whom report it nonjudgmentally, other not.[25] Celsus falls in the second category: the Jews' exodus was an unwarranted rebellion (3.5-6). Circumcision as a mark of Judaism was also common knowledge in Greco-Roman paganism. That Egyptians practiced it was also known at least to some,[26] including Celsus. He uses this piece of information to show the derivative character of Judaism (1.22; 5.41). Similarly with abstention from pork,[27] which the Egyptians also practiced (5.41).[28] Unlike the comparisons that modern students of religion make between religions, Celsus' comparisons of Jewish *nomoi* with those of other peoples diminish rather than further understanding. True, Egyptians practiced circumcision, but Celsus' polemic displays no interest in the distinctive role this particular *nomos* played in Egyptian religion and Judaism respectively. As with the pan-Babylonians at the

---

Message of the Cross (Philadelphia: Fortress Press, 1977), 19 (with further literature cited).

[23]Hinted in Pliny the Younger, *Ep.* 10.96 (the Christians interrogated by Pliny say that when they assemble they eat ordinary, harmless food *[cibum promiscuum ... et innoxium]*); explicit in Justin, *1 Apol.* 26.7, *2 Apol.* 12.2, *Dial.* 10.1; Athenagoras, *Legatio pro Christianis* 3; Theophilus of Antioch, *Ad Autolycum* 3.4; Tertullian, *Apol.* 4.11, 7.1, 8.2, 7; Minucius Felix, *Octavius* 9; Eusebius, *Hist. Eccl.* 4.7.11, 5.1.52. Origen, *C. Cels.* 6.27, 40, says Celsus acts toward Christians like those who spread such rumors, but he does not say Celsus actually repeats them. Jews had also been accused of ritual murder (Josephus, *Contra Apionem* 2.95), and in the Middle Ages, Christians begin to accuse Jews of this crime; see Léon Poliakov, *The History of Anti-Semitism* (New York: Vanguard Press), vol. 1, trans. by R. Howard (1965), 56-64; vol. 2, trans. by N. Gerardi (1973), 196-97.

[24]The charge often appears with that of cannibalism; thus in the texts cited in n. 23: Justin (all three texts), Athenagoras, Theophilus, Tertullian, Minucius Felix, Eusebius (4.7.11).

[25]*Non-judgmentally:* Manetho, in Josephus, *Contra Apionem* 1.89-90; Strabo, *Historica Hypomnemata,* in Josephus, *Anti.* 14.118, and *Geographica* 61.2.35-36. *Negatively:* Hecataeus of Abdera, *Aegyptica* (in Diodorus Siculus, *Bibliotheca Historica* 40.3.1-2: because of a plague, which is ascribed to neglect of traditional Egyptian rites, the Egyptians expel aliens who are seen as responsible for such neglect); Manetho, in Josephus, *Contra Apionem* 1.228-29, 233 (the Jews are associated with lepers); Diodorus Siculus, *Bibliotheca Historica* 34.1.1-2 (the Jews as impious, hated by the gods, and leprous); Pompeius Trogus, *Historica Philippicae* 36 as summarized in Justin, *Epitome* 2.12-13 (in Stern, *Greek and Latin Authors,* vol. 1, 335; the Jews as diseased and leprous); Apion, *Aegyptiaca,* in Josephus, *Contra Apionem* 2.15 (the Jews as lepers, blind, and lame); Chaeromon, *Aegyptiaca Historia,* in Josephus, *Contra Apionem* 1.289-90 (the Jews as polluted and diseased); Tacitus, *Hist.* 5.3.1 (the Jews are expelled during a plague because they are hateful to the gods).

[26]As early as Herodotus, *Hist.* 2.104.2; also Diodorus Siculus, *Bibliotheca Historica* 1.28.3; Strabo, *Geographica* 17.2.5.

[27]The Egyptians, says Herodotus, abstain from pork except on special occasions (*Hist.* 2.47); see also Josephus, *Contra Apionem* 2.137-38, 141.

[28]Celsus (5.34) cites Herodotus as his authority for abstention from pork (Herodotus, *Hist.* 2.47) and other animals (ibid., 2.42) by various unspecified peoples (οἱ μὲν ... οἱ δέ). In 5.41 he asserts (without citing Herodotus) that Egyptians abstain from pigs as well as from goats, sheep, oxen, and fish.

beginning of the twentieth century,[29] citing of an antecedent parallel to Judaism is sufficient in Celsus' eyes to relativize and thus discredit the latter. Whereas Herodotus (*Hist.* 2.47.2) says he knows the reason why Egyptians detest pork but declines to reveal it, for the sake of propriety, and whereas Plutarch's discussion of Jewish abstinence from pork, for example, manifests an attempt to understand the practice – is it because Jews revere the pig or abhor it? (*Quaestiones convivales* 4.5) – Celsus is interested only in citing the same custom among Egyptians in order to discredit Jews.[30] His observation (5.41) that Egyptians also abstain from goats, sheep, oxen, and fish only obscures understanding further by ignoring the question – fruitfully investigated in modern study[31] – why Jews abstain from pork and not from the flesh of goats, sheep, and oxen.

It is clear that Celsus knows some of the basic *nomoi* that demarcate Jew from non-Jew, but, viewing them from the outside, and with little effort to understand them,[32] he quite misunderstands them.

Similarly with what he says about Christianity. His knowledge of Christianity is extensive and detailed. He is aware not only of what he calls "the great church" (ἀαπὸ μεγάλης ἐκκλησίας, 5.59a; ἀπὸ τοῦ πλήθους, 5.61d) but of a broad spectrum of Christian groups – Christians who observe the Jewish *nomos* (5.61); some who are Jewish in origin, but have forsaken the *nomos* of their fathers (2.1); allegorizing Christians (1.17, 27; 4.38, 48-50); Christians who have some (mistaken) knowledge of Plato (6.19a); Marcionites (5.54, 61, 62; 6.53); gnostics (5.61; 6.27) and various species of gnostics (5.62). He knows Christian writings and teachings sufficiently to dwell on them in detail.[33] If Carl Andresen is correct, the *Alethēs Logos* is occasioned by

---

[29]Herbert F. Hahn, *The Old Testament in Modern Research* (Philadelphia: Muhlenberg Press, 1954; expanded ed., Fortress Press, 1966), 89-91.

[30]Thus in 5.41; in 5.34 he says that some (unspecified) peoples abstain from pigs because they detest them.

[31]Mary Douglas, *Purity and Danger: An Analysis of Concepts of Pollution and Taboo* (Routledge & Kegan Paul: 1966; Baltimore et al.: Penguin Books, 1970), chs. 2-3, with many citations of scholarly literature.

[32]By contrast, cf., in addition to the efforts cited in the text of various pagan authors to understand and explain Jewish *nomoi*, Pompeius Trogus' explanation that Jews keep apart from other peoples so as to avoid the reputation, acquired in Egypt, of spreading infection to non-Jews, *Historiae Philippicae* 36 as summarized in Justin, *Epitome* 2.1.15 (in Stern, *Greek and Latin Authors*, vol. 1, 335-36). Also Apion (in Josephus, *Contra Apionem* 2.20-21), who explains the Jewish sabbath as deriving from the Jews' resting after a six-days' trek from Egypt to Judea in order to recover from a disease of the groin, the Egyptian word for which is similar (he says) to "sabbath."

[33]Jesus' appearing in fulfillment of prophecy (1.50, 57; 2.28); his genealogy (2.32b); his parents and birth (1.28, 32, 29); the star at his birth (1.34); the visit of the Chaldeans (Magi) and Herod's slaughter of the infants (1.58); the flight into Egypt (1.66) where Jesus subsequently learned thaumaturgy (1.28, 38); his baptism by John and the appearance of the dove (1.41) and the voice from heaven (2.72); his title of God (1.28, 38) or Son of God (1.61, 66, 67; 2.6, 47a, 72); the calling of tax collectors and sailors as followers (1.62, 63, 65; 2.46) and his meals with them (2.20, 21, 22); his role as teacher (2.9) and various

Celsus' reading of Justin.[34] One of Celsus' misunderstandings of Christianity is to take a part for the whole, i.e., one particular Christian group for the whole of Christianity.[35] This may be deliberate on his part (it is useful polemically[36]), and if it is not, it is a misunderstanding often repeated since, also by insiders to Christianity. Also useful polemically are Celsus' assertion that Jesus spent time in Egypt and thus learned magical arts (1.28, 38),[37] his bagatellizing of the cross with his jest that had Jesus pursued an occupation other than carpenter, the materials of that trade would have constituted the Christian symbol (6.34), and his frequent claims that Christians derived their teachings from (mis)reading the Greek sources.

That what Celsus writes about Judaism and Christianity is polemical – a hostile view from outside – becomes clear to anyone reading the *Aleth ēs Logos* even casually.[38] The fact that it is polemic, and its very bulk, may obscure the keen insights Celsus offers into Christianity and Judaism and the relations between them – and into the paganism he represents. Celsus may bagatellize the cross; on the other hand, he, along with much of the Greco-Roman world, sees the cross for the offense it is to pagan conceptions of deity and of order, i.e, *nomos*. A deity too weak to resist arrest (2.9, 55; 6.10c) lacks one of the essential requisites of deity: power. A deity that dies (2.68), and is in fact now

---

elements of his teaching (6.16; 7.18); his style of rhetoric ("woe to you" and "I say to you," 2.76), and his itinerant ministry (1.61); the Jews' demand for a sign (1.67); his foreknowledge (2.13b, 15, 17, 18, 19a,b, 20, 21, 44); his working of miracles (1.68; 2.48); his agony in Gethsemane (2.24); his betrayal (2.9, 19b) and denial by his followers (2.19b, 45); his capture, conviction, passion (2.34c, 37), and death by crucifixion (2.31a, 36, 58, 68) at the hands of the Jews (2.4, 5, 9, 12) while Jesus offers no resistance (2.9, 55, 59); his resurrection (2.54, 55, 59, 61, 70b). Celsus of course reports these data pejoratively, and Origen is at pains to correct him. Celsus (2.74a) refers to the Christians' own writings as sufficient refutation of their claims about Jesus.

On Christians, Celsus notes, e.g., their appeal to prophecy (2.28; 3.1) and how they differ from Jews in this respect (3.1); their possession of multiple gospels (2.27); their claim that Jesus is the Logos (2.31a) and suffered for the benefit of humans (2.38); and Christians' martyrdom (2.45). Celsus accepts the view (cf. Acts 2.44, 4.32; Hegesippus in Eusebius, *Hist. Eccl.* 3.32.7, 4.22.4) that Christians (now badly divided) were once of one mind (3.10).

[34] Andresen, *Logos und Nomos* (cited above, n. 4); general concurrence with Andresen's contention in Henry Chadwick, *Early Christian Thought and the Classical Tradition: Studies in Justin, Clement, and Origen* (Oxford: Clarendon Press, 1966), 132, n. 59, who also lists further affinities between Celsus' and Justin's argumentation noted by himself and in A.D. Nock's review of Andresen in *Journal of Theological Studies* N.S. 7 (1956), 316, n. 4.

[35] For example, Ophites (6.28) or Marcion(ites) (6.52-53).

[36] Hence, Origen frequently seeks to distinguish himself and his (mainstream) Christianity from Marcionites and various gnostic groups to which Celsus refers (see, e.g., 6.24, 26, 27, 29, 30). Origen says (6.24, 32) he has had to go to some pains to acquire information about some of the groups and teachings Celsus describes, i.e., persons who teach such strange doctrines surely could not be Christians.

[37] One of Celsus' sources for his characterization of Jesus as a thaumaturgist may have been Justin's report in *Dial.* 69.7 that Jesus' fellow Jews accused him of being a μάγος who practiced φαντασίαν μαγικήν.

[38] Cf. 1.12: Celsus says he does not inquire of Christians as one trying to come to understanding, for "I know all things" (about them).

dead (7.36, 68), lacks another: immortality.[39] And a crucified deity falls in the category of the worst offenders and lowest strata of society, for whom crucifixion was reserved.[40] Paul had described the message of the cross as foolishness (μωρία) to those outside the fold, and Justin acknowledges that pagans judge it to be "madness" (μανία) that Christians accord a crucified person a place second to the unchangeable and eternal God and maker of all things (*1 Apol.* 13.4). Miracle claims, even a resurrection, were divine *aretai* that pagans could understand,[41] a crucified deity not. Thus Celsus asserts that to introduce what he calls their innovations (καινοτομῆσαι) the Christians should have chosen someone who died nobly (γενναίως) and acquired a divine myth (θεῖον μῦθον), for example, Heracles or Asclepius; instead, they say that a man of most infamous life and most pitiable death (θανάτῳ δὲ οἰκτίστῳ) was a god (7.53).[42] Consequently, we find Christians going to some lengths to defend and explain the crucifixion. Sons of Zeus suffered and died, says Justin, and in various ways, so why should Jesus be singled out because of the particular manner of his suffering and death (*1 Apol.* 22.3-4)?[43] Even so, Christians would not be persuaded that a crucified man was the first-begotten of the unbegotten God (πρωτότοκος τῷ ἀγεννήτῳ θεῷ) had it not been thus prophesied (*1 Apol.* 53.2). The crucifixion is a solid piece of evidence in Celsus' case against the Christians as devoid of *nomos:* What other people has been so foolish as to worship a crucified deity?

Certainly not the Jews, against whom the Christians rebelled, thus cutting themselves off from the Jewish *nomos.* Justin is aware of the issue: Trypho's repeated charge against Christians in the *Dialogue* is that, though professing to

---

[39] The difference between the ephemeral nature of human life and the immortal deities is eloquently put in Homer, *Iliad* 6.138-49.

[40] Hengel, *Crucifixion* (cited above, n. 22), has collected the evidence in support of this judgment.

[41] Celsus, 2.55 and 3.26, 32, cites some stock pagan resurrection accounts.

[42] Other examples of pagan incomprehension and abhorrence of claims of a suffering and crucified deity in Walter Bauer, *Das Leben Jesu im Zeitalter der neutestamentliche Apokryphen* (Tübingen: Mohr [Siebeck], 1909), 476-77; Hengel, *Crucifixion,* ch. 1. The comment by John Reumann, *Jesus in the Church's Gospels: Modern Scholarship and the Earliest Sources* (Philadelphia: Fortress Press, 1968), 48, is apt: "early Christians felt they had to *explain the death* of Jesus whereas they simply *declared the resurrection.*"

[43] Significantly, Justin states that the demons, in (proleptically) imitating Christian teachings, did not put forth that any of the sons of Zeus who suffered and died (see *1 Apol.* 22.3-4) were crucified; the reason is that the demons failed to comprehend the prophecies of Jesus' crucifixion, which were uttered symbolically (συμβολικῶς *1 Apol. 55*); Justin thus turns a lack of pagan support for his case into an argument in favor of it and, indeed, develops a quite elaborate *apologia crucis* (see Remus, *Pagan-Christian Conflict* [cited above, n. 7], 140-41). There is in fact an account of a crucified pagan deity, in Lucian of Samosata, *Prometheus;* see the commentary in Hengel, *Crucifixion,* 11-12; Lucian was a younger contemporary of Justin and hostile to Christians (see his *Alexander of Abonoteichos* 25, 38; *Peregrinus* 11-13), and Hengel (*Crucifixion,* 12) aptly observes that it does not seem to be a coincidence that the man who refers to Christians as "poor devils" who worship "that crucified sophist" (*Peregr.* 13; cf. 11) also satirizes the death of Prometheus using the technical terms of crucifixion.

know God, they "do not keep the law." The Jewish persona whom Celsus invokes against Christians asserts the same: When we punished Jesus, you Christians of Jewish descent "gave up the law of your fathers" (τοῦ πατρίου νόμου; 2.4a). "How is it that you take your origin from our holy rites [ἱερῶν], but then – as though you are making an advance – despise them, although you are unable to name any other source of your belief than our law?" (2.4b). Why did they desert "the law of their fathers" (τὸν πάτριον νόμον) for "another name and another life" (2.1)? Christians say they accept the Jewish *nomos;* yet, when the *nomoi* of Jesus and Moses conflict, they turn to another God (6.29). An example is the antithesis between Moses' imparting of *nomoi* (νομοθέτει) which predict that Jews would become rich and powerful and Jesus' giving of contradictory *nomoi* (ἀντινομοθέτει) which say that the rich or power-loving person cannot come to the Father (7.18). "Is Moses or Jesus lying? Or when the Father sent Jesus, did he forget what he had bequeathed to Moses? Or having condemned his own laws [νόμων] and changed his mind, did he send his messenger for opposite purposes?" (7.18)

In these passages about the crucifixion and Christians' failure to observe Jewish *nomoi* Celsus is needling Christians at two of their most sensitive and vulnerable points. One of the hidden warrants in Celsus' polemic on these points is that there are people – both pagans and Jews – who embody the views that serve as foils to Christian teachings and behavior. For these people, as well as for Celsus, Christians are the outsiders.

2. Christians as Outsiders

To Western moderns looking back from the standpoint of centuries of Christianity as the majority religion of the West, Celsus is often viewed as the outsider peering into Christianity. But to Celsus and most of his contemporaries he was the insider and Christians the outsiders. The numerical strength and growth of the Christian movement may alarm Celsus, but a more sober view is that Christians were still definitely a minority, both statistically and culturally.[44]

---

[44]Scholars have disputed the meaning of Celsus' statements regarding the numerical growth and strength of the Christian movement (3.10, 12, 73; other passages sometimes cited, such as 8.39 and 69 which speak of persecution, or 8.55 which states that such a despicable group as the Christians deserves to die out, reveal little, if anything about Celsus' view of the Christians' numerical strength); see Völker, *Das Bild* (cited above, n. 19), 27-29. πλῆθος as a designation of Christian numbers (3.10, 12) is an elastic term (see the examples cited in Völker, *Das Bild,* 28) and should not be pressed too far. Moreover, the context of the contrast Celsus draws between the Christians' meager beginnings (3.10, ἀρχόμενοι ... ὀλίγοι τε ἦσαν and the present πλῆθος of Christians, enough to divide into competing factions, should be kept in mind: he is attempting to demonstrate (Bk. 3) that Christianity originated in a revolt and is a fissiparating movement (cf. Andresen, *Logos und Nomos,* 39-40). Yet that Celsus was aware of Christian success in winning converts, as is indicated by 3.73b (τοῦ

Applied to Christians the term "outsider" must be used with care. Christians are indeed distinct from, often distinctly opposed to, the dominant system and its ethos and one glimpses them as such in various pagan writers of the second century.[45] On the other hand, Christians are still very much a part of the Greco-Roman world: they are still insiders, and, even as today, the degree to which they are distinct from the surrounding world is related to social and cultural factors and the kind of Christianity they profess. The apostle Paul and other early Christian writers may contrast the "before" and "after" states of pagans who have entered Christianity.[46] But the fact that he and these other writers go to such trouble to exhort these new Christians to leave their pagan past behind or to distance themselves from their environment, and also offer guidance on how to do so, indicates how much Christians lived and breathed in an environment whose ethos was not Christian and in many respects continued thus for centuries.

At the end of the second century, for example, Tertullian asserts that a mark of a Christian is that he or she stays away from the big public entertainments that are permeated with pagan religion (*De spectaculis* 24). That he goes to such lengths to argue his case suggests strongly that in this respect many Christians were still very much insiders to the inherited, pagan system. The guidance various Christian writers give to fellow Christians on what occupations are suitable for Christians and which not,[47] or on how to carry out acceptable

---

πλήθους τῶν προσερχομένων αὐτῷ [scil. τῷ λογῳ]), is suggested at least in part by the vehemence of his attack and would seem to be substantiated by other sources (see the second-century texts cited in A. Harnack, *Mission und Ausbreitung des Christentums in den ersten drei Jahrhunderten*, vol 2, *Die Verbreitung* [Leipzig: Hinrichs, 1924], 530ff., and the commentary, 546-48). With these passages by Celsus one may compare Origen's statements in the third century: the number of Christians in the Empire is still only πάνυ ὀλίγοι (*C. Cels.* 8.69), but in comparison with their beginnings they are (as Celsus says) a πλῆθος (3.10).

[45] In addition to Celsus: Tacitus, *Annal.* 15.44; Suetonius, *Nero* 16; Pliny the Younger, *Epp.* 10.96; Lucian of Samosata, *Alexander of Abonoteichos* 25, 38, and *Peregrinus* 11-13; Galen, in Walzer, *Galen on Jews and Christians* (cited above, n. 14), 15.

[46] For example, 1 Thess. 5:4-5; 1 Cor. 6:9-11; 1 Pet. 4:3-4; Justin Martyr, *1 Apol.* 53.5; *2 Apol.* 2.1-7; *Dial.* 63.5, 119.5, 123.5; Tertullian, *De spectaculis* 4, 24; *Acts of Thomas* 12-15.

[47] Excluded by the rigorists, either by explicit prohibition for Christians of by general condemnation, and at least frowned upon by other Christians were any functions or crafts related to pagan worship, such as priesthood or fashioning of images or amulets (Tertullian, *De idololatria* 8, 11, 17; Hippolytus, *Apost. Trad.* 16.11, 16, 21); prostitution (1 Cor. 6:14-16; Athenagoras, *Supplicatio* 33-34; Hippolytus, *Apost. Trad.* 16.20) and pimping (Tertullian, *De idol.* 11; *De spectaculis* 23; Hippolytus, *Apost. Trad.* 16.10); acting (Tatian, *Oratio* 22, 24; Clement of Alexandria, *Paedagogus* 3.11.76-77; Tertullian, *De spect.* 10, 17, 22; Hippolytus, *Apost. Trad.* 16.12; Minucius Felix, *Octavius* 37); working as a charioteer (Clement of Alexandria, *Paed.* 3.11.76; Tertullian, *De spect.* 23; Hippolytus, *Apost. Trad.* 16.14; Minucius Felix, *Octav.* 37), a boxer (Tatian, *Oratio* 23.1; Tertullian, *De Spect.* 22), a gladiator (Tatian, *Oratio* 23.2; Irenaeus, *Adv. haer.* 1.6.3 [Harvey ed., 1.1.12]; Hippolytus, *Apost Trad.* 16.15; Minucius Felix, *Octav.* 37), or a trainer of gladiators or any work connected with gladiatorial shows (Tertullian, *De idol.* 11; Hippolytus, *Apost. Trad.* 16.15); an astrologer (Tertullian, *De idol.* 9; Hippolytus, *Apost. Trad.* 16.22) or a diviner (Clement of Alexandria, *Paed.* 3.4.28;

occupations,[48] indicates the pains it took to develop a Christian ethos. So also the attention to details of daily life, such as eating and drinking, bathing, dress, speech, and letter writing.[49] Even so, it is often only small details that mark these Christian guidelines off from contemporary Stoic ethical exhortations.[50] Tertullian can defend Christians against pagan slander by describing how fully they live and move in pagan society, though with certain distinguishing characteristics (*Apol.* 42; cf. *Epistle to Diognetus* 5-6).

As late as the fourth century, Antioch – where the Emperor Julian noted a strong Christian presence – was still predominantly pagan in its art, architecture, literature, and civic symbols and rhythms, and what Christian art there was drew heavily on pagan styles and motifs.[51] Christians there took part in pagan festivals, celebrated marriage according to pagan custom and pagan law, and named their children after forbears with pagan names.[52] Robert Wilken has shown how social factors enter into the degree to which Christians at Antioch are set off from pagans. The Christians ranged from uneducated celibate monks of rural peasant origin to a celibate and sometime monk like Chrysostom who, himself of the urban upper social stratum, excoriates those Christians who look down on the monks as inimical to Greek culture and its matrix, the *polis,* and, over against the monastic ideal and ethos, insist on an education for their children that will prepare them to fit into the same social and cultural stratum as themselves.[53] Education for the Antiochene Christians of the upper social strata meant worldly opportunity. For other early Christians education was profoundly disturbing because it was so permeated with pagan cult, pagan lore about the

---

Alexandria, *Paed.* 3.4.28; Tertullian, *De idol.* 9; *De spect.* 10; Hippolytus, *Apost. Trad.* 22). Celsus urges Christians to fight as soldiers for the emperor (8.73) and to accept public office (8.75); Origen, in response, defends Christians' refusal to do either (cf. Tertullian, *De idol.* 17, 19; Hippolytus, *Apost. Trad.* 16.17-19.

[48]There were the examples of Jesus (Mark 6:3) and Paul (1 Thess. 2:9; 1 Cor. 4:12; Acts 18:3, 20:34), working as craftsmen, to follow, and the exhortations to Christians to work so as not to be a burden to others (2 Thess. 3:8-12), to pay laborers their due (James 5:4), and render honest service to masters (Col. 3:22) and proper treatment to slaves (Col. 4:1).

[49]These are only a few of the many details treated in Clement of Alexandria's *Paedagogus,* which is a sort of combination of Christian etiquette book, ethical text, and guide to healthful living, with an upper-class bias (see John Ferguson, "The Achievement of Clement of Alexandria," *Religious Studies* 13 [1976], 75). There are New Testament precedents, of course (1 Tim. 2:9-10; 1 Pet. 3:3-4). A goodly number of Tertullian's writings are concerned with marking off Christian from pagan behavior and appearance: *De idololatria, De spectaculis, De corona, De pallio,* etc. Later, one sees Augustine continuing this tradition of making such distinctions: he proscribed apotropaic amulets but sanctioned earrings worn by women to please men (Peter Brown, *Augustine of Hippo: A Biography* [Berkeley and Los Angeles: University of California Press, 1969], 266).

[50]See Ferguson, "Achievement," 74-75; Hans Lietzmann, *A History of the Early Church,* trans. by B.L. Woolf (rev. ed.; Cleveland and New York: Meridian Books, 1961), vol 2, *The Founding of the Church Universal,* 153-54.

[51]Robert L. Wilken, *John Chrysostom and the Jews: Rhetoric and Reality in the Late 4th Century* (Berkeley et al.: University of California Press, 1983), 18-19, 25.

[52]Ibid., 19, 21, 25.

[53]Ibid., 26-29.

gods, and pagan values. Still, in order to be able to profit from the scriptures, Christians had to know how to read. Aside from catechetical schools, Christians established no schools in antiquity,[54] and so Christians had to attend pagan schools, but with appropriate cautions.[55] Tertullian advises Christians in pagan schools to behave like persons who know they are being given poison and must avoid drinking it (*De idololatria* 10). Later, Basil the Great devoted a whole treatise to instructing Christian young men on how to read pagan Greek authors without endangering their eternal salvation.

Though Celsus is aware – painfully so – that Christians are indeed so much a part of pagan society, he views them as outsiders, and himself as insider. Unlike adherents of pagan religions, Christians deliberately shut themselves off from other people. They shirk military service (8.73) and exercise of public office which sustains laws and piety (8.75). They constitute secret societies, contrary to the laws (1.1), and practice and teach their doctrines in secret (1.3, 7). Their aniconism is symptomatic of secret societies (8.17) and accords with their general rejection of and contempt for pagan cult evident in their intolerance of temples, altars, and images (7.62), their actual ridicule of pagan cult and cult narratives (3.43), of deities (3.19), and of images (8.38, 41), and their designation of the latter as phantoms or idols (7.36; 8.24). Their incomprehension of, and alienation from, pagan culture is shown by their euhemerizing (3.22) and demonizing (7.62) interpretations of pagan deities.

While familiar to educated pagans, such theories were not necessarily employed by them, as they were by many Christians, to nihilate pagan cult. For Celsus such attitudes on the part of Christians are pathognomic symptoms of Christian rejection of that ancient *nomos* that he sees as vital to life in the ancient world. Christians' intolerance of pagan cult places them among other, similarly intolerant peoples, the most impious and most lawless sorts (τὰ δυσαγέστατα καὶ ἀνομώτατα, 7.62). This rejection is not surprising, however, in view of the origin of Christians in a revolt from Judaism (3.5, 14; 5.33; 8.2). They are plagued with the disease of rebellion (8.49). Christians are nouveaux, unable or unwilling to reveal their origins or the originator of their hereditary laws. In point of fact, their origins lie with the Jews (5.33). Yet since they have rebelled against the Jews (5.33), what ancient *nomoi* can they possibly have? Rebellion against society brings novelty (3.5).

In a passage that is revealing of his view of a necessary relation between religion and society, Celsus argues that since Christians choose to participate in the institutions of society such as marriage and family, then they should offer homage to the deities or daimons placed over these institutions.[56] "For it is

---

[54] See Harnack, *Die Verbreitung* (cited above, n. 44), 999-1,000.
[55] See the examples cited in H.I. Marrou, *A History of Education in Antiquity*, trans. by G. Lamb (New York: New American Library, 1964), 428-29.
[56] Celsus regards the cosmos, the various peoples of the earth, social institutions, and even parts of the body as allotted to the administration of deities or daimons (5.25; 7.68; 8.28, 35,

unjust for those who share in what one knows is their [scil. the daimons'] possession not to offer something to them" (8.55). But Christians do not do so, and indeed do quite the opposite, and therefore constitute a threat to the pagan system. Similarly, with the ancient doctrine *(logos)* taught by the wise men of various peoples and vital to ancient culture. Christians are among those whose belief is uninformed by *logos* (1.9, τοὺς ἀλόγως πιστεύοντας), as is evident (a) from their rejection of questioning and of providing of warrants for their beliefs in favor of implicit belief (1.9) and (b) from their deliberate appeal to the immature, the ignorant, and those unschooled in Greek thought (1.27; 3.44, 49, 50, 55, 59, 72, 74, 75; 6.12-14). Their making a virtue of foolishness (1.9) and of ignorance (3.44) sets them apart from a person of Celsus' background and from the ideals of Greek *paideia*. "Why is it bad to have been educated and to have studied the best doctrines and to be and to seem intelligent?" (3.49).

By rejecting pagan education, specifically, Greek *paideia*, Christians exclude an essential element in the process of socialization through which the ancient *nomos* and *logos* are transmitted from one generation to the next. In one passage (3.55) Celsus gives a glimpse of how he sees this occurring, to the undermining of pagan culture and its social matrices. Christians, likened by Celsus to disreputable persons seen in the marketplace, are not found in the company of intelligent men (φρονίμων ἀνδρῶν) but rather with adolescent boys and slaves and stupid people (3.50); they prey upon vulnerable sorts – women and children – when they are alone with them in private houses. There they urge disobedience to fathers and to teachers but obedience to themselves, who alone are able to tell their victims how to live and arrive at perfection (τὸ τέλειον) and how to achieve well-being in their homes. They vilify fathers and teachers as foolish and senseless, occupied with empty talk, and capable of nothing good. But when actually confronted by a father or teacher or any intelligent person, they either scatter in all directions or whisper to the children that in the presence of such empty-headed and corrupt persons (who punish children!) they are unwilling and unable to give any instruction.

In this vignette one sees two systems in conflict, each contending for the loyalty of the next generation. It also offers an example of Celsus' view of the subversive nature of the Christian movement, in accord with its origins in a revolt. The Christians represented in 3.55 as leading women and children astray are, by occupation, woodworkers, shoemakers in leather (σκυτοτόμους), and bleachers or fullers (κναφεῖς). How preposterous that persons of such lowly occupation and education, from whom one would properly expect only silence in the presence of their elders and owners, should undertake to instruct the young. And how incongruous that when this furtive Christian instruction in private houses encounters difficulties with the persons entrusted with this responsibility it should adjourn to the shops where these menial slaves pursue their

---

35, 53, 58, 60, 63).

occupations and that there the children, and the women who accompany them, will attain perfection (τὸ τέλειον), a term associated in Greek tradition with high and holy things such as deity and the mystery religions (3.55)! With this passage may be compared others in which Celsus says that Christians, in contrast to Socrates who claimed only human wisdom (6.12), claim to impart divine wisdom – and to whom? To the most uneducated and most ignorant persons and to slaves (6.13b). By contrast persons of culture (χαριεστέρους) are not prepared to be deceived (6.14) and, if they are like Celsus, follow Plato who provides a foil to the Christians' mode of teaching in that, unlike Christians, he does not fail to supply warrants (λογισμόν) – even when speaking of the ineffable (6.10a) – and discloses the source of his teaching (6.10b), and, unlike Jesus, does not claim to have come down from heaven (6.10b).

3. Jews as Insiders

Celsus, as was indicated in section one, misunderstands Judaism at some fundamental points. In general, he is not fond of Jews. They originated in a revolt (3.5). Originally goatherds and shepherds, they were deceived by Moses into thinking, without cause (ἀλόγως), that there is only one God. With obvious sarcasm Celsus speaks of the Jews as that "illustrious and extraordinary race" (λαμπρὸν καὶ θεσπέσιον Ἰουδαιων γένος) who were commanded by their leader to dwell and pasture their flocks on worthless lands somewhere outside of Egypt (4.47). Their escape from Egypt was a flight of runaway slaves (δράπετας) who never did anything worth mentioning and have never been held in regard or esteem, as is evident from Greek silence on their history (4.31). The details in the biblical traditions are cleverly employed by Celsus, as Andresen observes, *"um das soziale Milieu der Juden möglichst abträglich zu schildern."*[57]

Celsus' portrayal of Jews as rebellious comports with other similar charges by pagans in light of the two Jewish rebellions of recent memory.[58] The unsympathetic tone in his portrayal of Jews is also common among *literati* of the Greco-Roman world.[59] Yet a number of such *literati*, for whatever reasons, view Jews with dispassion and even favorably.[60] There is one characteristic of Jews that Celsus looks on with favor: like other peoples of the Greco-Roman world they have their own *nomos* (τὸν ἴδιον νόμον, 5.41).[61] On becoming a distinct people (ἔθνος ἴδιον), the Jews made laws befitting themselves (κατὰ

---

[57] Andresen, *Logos und Nomos*, 177, n. 16.
[58] Cf. Gager, *Origins of Anti-Semitism* (cited above, n. 20), 62-64, 66.
[59] Ibid., 59, 63-65.
[60] Ibid., chs. 3-5.
[61] *C. Cels.* 5.34, a long quotation from Herodotus, is an extended statement of the view that each people has its own distinctive *nomos*. Celsus states this in a general way in 5.25 (τὰ πάτρια and τὰ ἐξ ἀρχῆς κατὰ τόπους νενομισμένα) and 8.75 (νόμων); with respect to Romans in 8.69 (τῶν νενομισμένων) and Jews in 2.1 (τὸν πάτριον νόμον), 2.4a (idem). 5.25 (νόμους), 5.41 (τὸν ἴδιον νόμον).

τὸ ἐπιχώριον νόμους θέμενοι), which they preserve along with their worship, as other peoples do (5.25). Whatever else Jewish worship may be, it is traditional (ὁποίαν δή, πάτριον δ'οὖν, 5.25). Like other pagans who are repelled by pagans who become Jewish proselytes, Celsus looks with disfavor on pagans "who have abandoned their own traditions and professed those of the Jews" (5.41). Jews err in presumptuously thinking their *nomos* is superior to the *nomoi* of other peoples, but they cannot be faulted for adhering to their own *nomoi*, because, for Celsus, that fits them into the system he is defending. They are insiders who serve their native country (τῆς πατρίδος) "for the sake of the preservation of *nomoi* and religion" (ἕνεκεν σωτηρίας νόμων καὶ εὐσεβείας, 8.75).[62] In so doing, they serve the common *nomos* (τὸν κοινὸν νόμον, 1.1).

For Celsus, as for many other pagans, Judaism – unlike Christianity – was, despite its repellent features, a known quantity. By contrast with Christians, Jews had a history that located them in their own land where they had erected a renowned (though strange[63]) sanctuary, had fought wars, and then, many of them dislocated from that land, had settled in other parts of the *oikoumene* where they enjoyed certain rights and privileges and were protected by the laws of the cities and the Empire.[64] Unlike Jesus, Moses, the Jews' founder and lawgiver, was no newcomer: he was widely known and for some pagans ranked along with other cultural heroes of the past.[65] Nor was knowledge of Jews something derived simply from hearsay or from reading of Pliny the Elder or Strabo and

---

[62]Origen aptly summarizes Celsus' thinking: "all persons ought to live according to their ancestral ways [τὰ πάτρια] and should not be reproached for this; but Christians, who have forsaken ancestral ways and are not one discrete people like the Jews, incur blame for assenting to the teaching of Jesus" (*C. Cels.* 5.35).

[63]In addition to the reports that the Jews worshipped an ass's head in their temple (see n. 22 above), pagan authors point out that the temple had no images, in accord with the Jews' aniconism (Hecataeus of Abdera, in Josephus, *Contra Apionem* 1.199; Strabo, *Geographica* 16.2.35; Tacitus, *Hist.* 9.1).

[64]Because of the distinctive characteristics of Judaism such as Sabbath observance and monotheism, the rights and privileges accorded Jews, often cited by Jewish apologists (Philo, *De legatione ad Gaium* 138, 155-61; *In Flaccum* 50, 74; Josephus, *Antiquities* 12.145-46, 148-53; 19.280-91, 303-11), set them apart from other peoples of the Hellenistic and Roman empires. However, as the same apologists also point out at times (Philo, *De legatione* 153; Josephus, *Contra Apionem* 2.73), these rights did not differ in principle from the right granted to other peoples of these pluralistic empires to live (within certain limits) according to their ancestral laws; see the detailed discussion and citation of sources in Victor Tcherikover, *Hellenistic Civilization and the Jews,* trans. by S. Applebaum (Philadelphia: Jewish Publication Society of America and Jerusalem: Magnes Press, 1959), 82-89, 297-308 (on the distinction between "rights" and "privileges," 509, n. 36). On the continuation of Jewish rights and privileges by various Roman emperors see J. Parkes, *The Conflict of the Church and the Synagogue: A Study in the Origins of Anti-Semitism* (London: Soncino Press, 1934), 177, 188-89, 201-03, 207-09, 275-76, and Robert L. Wilken, "The Jews and Christian Apologetics" (cited above, n. 2), 464-66.

[65]John G. Gager, *Moses in Greco-Roman Paganism,* Society of Biblical Literature Monograph Series, 16 (Nashville and New York: Abingdon Press, 1972); *Origins of Anti-Semitism,* 69, 74-76, 108-11.

other ethnographers:

> To the Greeks and the Romans the ways of the Jews were familiar from *first hand experience* extending over several centuries. Because Jews had been living in the cities of the Mediterranean world long before Christianity arose, in some cases before the time of Alexander the Great, the inhabitants of those cities had a sense of what the Jews were like and what distinguished them from others. In comparison the Christians were not only unknown, but were themselves searching for a clearly defined identity.[66]

Because Judaism was a living, thriving presence in the Empire,[67] a vigorous embodiment of the Mosaic *nomos* which Celsus saw as essential to inclusion in the Greco-Roman system but which mainstream Christians reinterpreted to accommodate their own nonobservance of that *nomos,* Celsus is able, in effect, simply to point to the contrast between Jews whom one could observe around one as a people of *nomos* – and therefore of tradition and order – and Christianity as (in the words of Justin's Trypho) a lawless sect (αἵρεσις ... ἄνομος, *Dial*. 108.2) that has put itself outside the system. That way lies chaos, as the Christians' rebellion from Judaism and their fissiparating proclivities make clear.

4. Continuity and Change

Viewed with the spectacles of twentieth-century sociology, Celsus could be labeled a functionalist: the inherited system is a given, and its continued functioning without significant or sudden change is the *desideratum*.[68] As a Platonist Celsus would not say his was the best of all possible world, but if change for the better were to come it would not be by embracing novelty but by adherence to the ancient *nomos* and *logos* and especially to Plato, from whom the title and theme of the *Alethēs Logos* probably derive.[69] As an insider to the

---

[66]Wilken, "Christians as the Romans and Greeks ..." (cited above, n. 2), 104; emphasis added. Cf. Minucius Felix, *Octavius* 10.2-5, which contrasts the clandestine nature of Christian worship, devoid of altars, victims, and temples, with that of the Jews, which has all of these and is conducted openly.

[67]See Remus, "Justin Martyr's Argument" (cited above, n. 1), 72-74.

[68]"For Celsus it is axiomatic that nothing can be both new and true" (Chadwick, *Early Christian Thought* [cited above, n. 34], 23). On system, function, and dysfunction, as seen by functionalists, see Talcott Parsons, *The Social System* (London: Collier-Macmillan and New York: Free Press, 1951), 19, 24, 26-36, and Robert K. Merton, *Social Theory and Social Structure* (enlarged ed.; London: Collier-Macmillan and New York: Free Press, 1968), 104-08; for a critique, see Irving M. Zeitlin, *Rethinking Sociology: A Critique of Contemporary Theory* (Englewood Cliffs, NJ: Prentice-Hall, 1973), 6-7, 9-10, 64-65 105, and Ian Robertson, "Functionalism," in *The Encyclopedia of Sociology* (Guilford, CT: DPG Reference Publishing, 1981), 117-18.

[69]See *C. Cels*. 6.9, where Celsus cites Plato, *Ep*. 7.342A: ἔστι γὰρ τις λόγος ἀληθής; cf. also *Meno* 81A (τίνα λόγον ...; ἀληθῆ) and other Plato references cited in A. Wifstrand, "Die wahre Lehre des Kelsos," *Bulletin de la Société Royale des Lettres de Lund* (1941-42), 398-400.

prevailing system, Celsus sees clearly the threat posed by Christianity.

But in the late second century the system was showing various signs of dysfunction, with Christianity as only one of a variety of causes of, and responses to, the dysfunction.[70] Had Celsus known of Alexander of Abonoteichos, the founder and impressario of a cult of the "new Asclepius," which attracted Platonists as well as members of other philosophical schools,[71] he might well have identified with the Celsus to whom Lucian of Samosata addresses his piece on Alexander and whose skepticism Lucian lauds.[72] The pagan Platonists of the third and fourth centuries – Plotinus, and then especially Porphyry and Iamblichus – are no less devoted to Plato than Celsus but sometimes in ways he would hardly have countenanced.[73]

The system was changing, despite Celsus – but also in part because of Celsus or because of pagan-Christian-Jewish dialogue. To pagan critiques of a crucified deity some Christians responded with a docetic Christ who does not suffer and die,[74] while others took up the Platonic theme of a crucified just man (*Republic* 361E-362A) and applied it to Jesus.[75] Rather than being nonplussed by Celsus' claim that Greek philosophers anticipated Christian ethical thinking, Origen sees it as a point in its favor (*C. Cels.* 1.4).[76] To pagan critiques of Judaism, Christianity responded by representing itself as the true Israel, devoid of those elements pagans found offensive in Judaism. Moving into the Roman sphere, Christianity, it has been argued, is in time transformed into Roman religion.[77] Distancing itself from the Judaism that gave it birth, and, thanks to

---

[70] E.R. Dodds, *Pagan and Christian in an Age of Anxiety: Some Aspects of Religious Experience from Marcus Aurelius to Constantine* (New York: Norton, 1970).
[71] Lucian of Samosata, *Alexander* 25.
[72] Ibid., 21, 61.
[73] Detailed demonstration of this claim extends beyond the bounds of this paper. One may, e.g., contrast Celsus' pejorative references to ritual manipulations (γόης, *C. Cels.* 1.68, 71; γοητεία, 1.6b; μαθήματα, 1.6b) with Plotinus' philosophical treatment of γοητεία, μαγεία, φάρμακα, and ἐπῳδαί (*Enneads* 4.4.40-44) and of magicians' arts (ταῖς μάγων τέχναις, 4.26.3), relating all of these to prayer; see further A.H. Armstrong, in Armstrong (ed.), *The Cambridge History of Later Greek and Earlier Medieval Philosophy* (Cambridge: Cambridge University Press, 1967), 207-08, 260; also with Porphyry's flirtation with theurgy, and the later Neoplatonists' embrace of theurgy; see M.P. Nilsson, *Geschichte der griechischen Religion*, vol. 2 (2d ed.; Munich: Beck, 1961), 431-66; E.R. Dodds, *The Greeks and the Irrational* (Berkeley and Los Angeles: University of California Press, 1951), App. 2, "Theurgy." A.C. Lloyd's observation in Armstrong (ed.), *Cambridge History*, 277, is apt: "it was no longer the myth which was regarded as philosophically relevant but the ritual."
[74] See the sources cited in Hengel, *Crucifixion* (cited above, n. 22), ch. 3.
[75] See Ernst Benz, *Der gekreuzigte Gerechte bei Plato, im Neuen Testament und in der Alten Kirche*, Akademie der Wissenschaften und der Literatur in Mainz, Abhandlungen der geistes- und sozialwissenschaftlichen Klasse (1950), 12 (Wiesbaden: Franz Steiner Verlag, 1950), 31-46.
[76] Cf. Chadwick, *Early Christian Thought* (cited above, n. 34), 104-05.
[77] Thus John Helgeland, "The Transformation of Christianity into Roman Religion," in Peter Slater et al. (eds.), *Traditions in Contact and Change: Selected Proceedings of the XIVth Congress of the International Association for the History of Religions* (Waterloo, Ont.:

those roots, also from paganism, and yet an insider both to Judaism and paganism, it emerges as a new or third race or people[78] increasingly forgetful of its Jewish roots and those ties that might have bound it to Judaism and yet stressing to pagans those elements that pagans found attractive in Judaism: antiquity, monotheism, morality. Jews, for their part, defined themselves over against such a Christianity and so distanced themselves from it. Perhaps conflict is essential to demarcating groups from one another – especially groups close to one another. If they are now to understand one another, and achieve some rapprochement, then study which attempts to understand religions both from inside and outside can perhaps arrive at a more holistic picture than Celsus and his Jewish and Christian counterparts achieved.

Wilfrid Laurier University Press for the Canadian Corporation for Studies in Religion, 1983), 337-45.

[78] καινὸν γένος, *Ep. Diognetus* 1.8; see the sources and detailed discussion of "Die Botschaft von dem neuen Volk und dem dritten Geschlecht" in Harnack, *Verbreitung* (cited above, n. 44), 259-89.

Chapter Ten

Who Is "Israel"?
The Jewish-Christian Confrontation in Fourth Century Iran

Jacob Neusner
Brown University

In the fourth century, beginning with the conversion of Constantine in 312 and ending with the recognition of Christianity as the religion of the Roman Empire in the Theodosian Code of 387, Christianity reached that position of political and cultural dominance that it would enjoy until the twentieth. In that same fourth century, in response to the triumph of Christianity in the Roman Empire, Judaism as shaped by sages in the Land of Israel defined its doctrines of history, Messiah, and who is Israel. Those doctrines successfully countered the challenge of Christianity from then to the point at which Christianity lost its status as self-evident truth in the West. So the age of Constantine was marked by the interplay of issues as defined in the same way by Judaism and Christianity. What we shall see in the present instance is that, on the Iranian side of the frontier, in the empire of Shapur II (307-379), the confrontation between Judaism and Christianity in the aftermath of the legalization of Christianity in Rome went forward along precisely the lines that guided discourse within Rome itself. When we recall that Constantine had written to Shapur II and had declared himself the protector of Christians within the Sasanian empire, we understand why the Christian party fo the debate, represented by Aphrahat, should have taken his place comfortably within the position outlined on the Roman side of the frontier.

Constantine told Shapur II that it is with "joy" that he heard "tidings so in accordance with my desire, that the fairest districts of Persia are filled with those men on whose behalf alone I am at present speaking, I mean the Christians. I pray therefore that both you and they may enjoy prosperity, and that your blessings and theirs may be in equal measure...I commend these persons to your protection....Cherish them with your wonted humanity...."[1] No wonder, then, that from the viewpoint of Christians in Iran, events in Rome were seen to mark that caesura in time, that validation of the faith, that Christians in Rome itself perceived. In Homily 23, Aphrahat, for his part, despairs of seeing an Iranian Constantine. Seeing Rome as Esau, Aphrahat identified that kingdom with Jesus: "The kingdom of the children of Esau is being kept safe for its giver, doubt not about it, that that kingdom will not be conquered. For a mighty champion whose name is Jesus shall come with power, and bearing as his armor all the power of the kingdom...." When in 337 Shapur II decreed that the Christians pay double the normal head tax, it marked the beginning of a systematic persecution of Christians, which lasted for nearly a half century.

In our setting, we ask whether living in Iran, rather than in Rome, persuaded Aphrahat that the issues separating Judaism from Christianity were to be read in some way other than that of Christian theologians represented, in the time of Constantine, by Eusebius, who found in the conversion of the emperor, then the Roman state, proof for the validity of Christianity. The answer, as we shall now see, negative. While in Iran, Aphrahat saw things precisely as did his counterparts in Rome, and that is shown, as I shall now demonstrate, by his framing of the issues in the received terms of Christianity in Rome, without the slightest revision of matters to accommodate the condition of Christianity in Iran. Since, when Aphrahat took up other questions than those in the Judaic-Christian confrontation, he found reason to revise the received viewpoint to accommodate the facts of his own time and place, the persistence of the received formulation of the debate becomes suggestive. Specifically, it tells us that once matters had reached theological definition, political circumstances would not greatly affect the framing of issues. Where Aphrahat stood in a line beginning, as we shall see, with Paul, there he repeated, in Iran, viewpoints far more pertinent to the Christian situation in now-Christian Rome than in anti-Christian Zoroastrian Iran.

I. The Issues of the Confrontation in the Age of Constantine and Shapur II

We find in the Judaism of the sages who redacted the principal documents of Judaism that reached closure in the century beyond the conversion of Constantine both a doctrine and an apologetic remarkably relevant to the issues presented to Christianity and Judaism by the crisis of Christianity's worldly triumph. A shared program brought the two religions into protracted confrontation on an intersecting set of questions. A struggle that has continued until our own time originated in the fact that, to begin with, both religions agreed on almost

---

[1] Trans. Ernest Cushing Richardson in *Select Library of Nicene and Post-nicene Fathers. Second Series* (Grand Rapids, repr. 1961), 1:543-544; see also Georg Bert, *Aphrahat's des persischen Weisen Homilien* (Leipzig, 1888), pp. 69-88, and my *History of the Jews in Babylonia* (Leiden, 1969) 4:21-2).

everything that mattered. They differed on little, so made much of that little. Scripture taught them both that vast changes in the affairs of empires came about because of God's will. History proved principles of theology. In that same Torah prophets promised the coming of the Messiah, who would bring salvation. Who was, and is, that Messiah, and how shall we know? And that same Torah addressed a particular people, Israel, promising that people the expression of God's favor and love. But who is Israel, and who is not Israel? In this way Scripture defined the categories shared in common, enabling Judaism and Christianity to engage, if not in dialogue, then in two monologues on the same topics. The terms of this confrontation continued for centuries because the conditions that precipitated it, – the rise to political dominance of Christianity and the subordination of Judaism, – remained constant for fifteen hundred years.

We know the fourth century as the decisive age in the beginning of the West as Christian. But to people of the time, the outcome uncertain. The vigorous repression of paganism after Julian's apostasy expressed the quite natural fear of Christians that such a thing might happen again. Bickerman states matters in a powerful way:

> Julian was yesterday, the persecutors the day before yesterday. Ambrose knew some magistrates who could boast of having spared Christians. At Antioch the Catholics had just endured the persecution of Valens...and unbelievers of every sort dominated the capital of Syria. The army, composed of peasants and barbarians, could acclaim tomorrow another Julian, another Valens, even another Diocletian. One could not yet, as Chrysostom says somewhere, force [people] to accept the Christian truth; one had to convince them of it.[2]

Although matters remained in doubt, the main fact remains: In the beginning of the fourth century Rome was pagan, in the end, Christian. In the beginning Jews in the Land of Israel administered their own affairs. In the end their institution of self-administration lost the recognition it had formerly enjoyed. In the beginning Judaism enjoyed entirely licit status, and the Jews, the protection of the state. In the end Judaism suffered abridgement of its former liberties, and the Jews of theirs.

From the viewpoint of the Jews, the shift signified by the conversion of Constantine marked, as I said, a *caesura* in history. The meaning of history commencing at Creation pointed for Christians toward Christ's triumph in the person of the Emperor and the institution of the Christian state. To Israel, the Jewish people, what can these same events have meant? The received Scriptures of ancient and recent Israel – both Judaic and Christian – now awaited that same sort of sifting and selection that had followed earlier turnings of a notable order, in 586 B.C., and after 70, for example: which writing had now been proved right, which irrelevant? So Christians asked themselves, as they framed the

---

[2] Cited by Wilken, pp. 32-33

canon of the Bible, both Old and New Testaments. Then to Israel, the Jewish people, what role and what place for the received Torah of Sinai, in its diversity of scrolls? The dogged faith that Jesus really was Christ, Messiah and King of the world, now found vindication in the events of the hour. What hope endured for the salvation of Israel in the future. In the hour of vindication the new Israel confronted the old, the one after the spirit calling into question the legitimacy of the one after the flesh: what now do you say of Christ? For Israel, the Jewish people, what was there to say in reply, not to Christ but to Christians? These three issues frame our principal concerns: the meaning of history, the realization of salvation, definition one's own group in the encounter with the other. In the case of Aphrahat, it was the matter of the definition of "Israel" that comes to the fore. Elsewhere I present all of the three issues in a systematic way.[3]

II. The Issue: Who Is Israel

The legacy of ancient Israel consisted not only of Scriptures but also of a paramount social category, Israel, God's people and first love. The Church from its origins in the first century confronted the task of situating itself in relationship to "Israel," and Paul's profound reflections in Romans constitute only one among many exercises in responding to that question. For the society of the Church, like the society of the Jews, required a metaphor by which to account for itself. And revering the Scriptures, each group found in "Israel" the metaphor to account for its existence as a distinct social entity. It follows that within the issue Who is Israel? we discern how two competing groups framed theories, each both of itself and also of the other. We therefore confront issues of the identity of a given corporate society as these were spelled out in debates about salvation. The salvific framing of the issue of social definition – who is Israel today (for Judaism)? what sort of social group is the Church (for Christianity)? – served both parties. We deal with a debate on a single issue. It finds its cogency in the common premise of the debate on who is Israel. The shared supposition concerned God's favor and choice of a given entity, one that was *sui generis*, among the social groups of humanity. Specifically, both parties concurred that God did favor and therefore make use of one group and not another. So they could undertake a meaningful debate on the identity of that group.

The debate gained intensity because of a further peculiarity of the discourse between these two groups but no others of the day. Both concurred that the group chosen by God will bear the name, Israel. God's choice among human societies would settle the question, which nation does God love and favor. Jews, who saw themselves as the Israel today joined in the flesh to the Israel of the scriptural record. Christians explained themselves as the Israel formed just now,

---

[3] See my *Judaism and Christianity in the Age of Constantine. Issues in the Initial Confrontation* (Chicago, 1987: University of Chicago Press).

in recent memory, even in the personal experience of the living, among those saved by faith in God's salvation afforded by the resurrection of Jesus Christ. We therefore must not miss the powerful social and political message conveyed by what appear to be statements of a narrowly theological character about salvation and society. In these statements on who is Israel, the parties to the debate chose to affirm each its own unique legitimacy and to deny the other's right to endure at all as a social and national entity.

But both parties shared common premises as to definitions of issues and facts to settle the question. They could mount a sustained argument between themselves because they talked about the same thing, invoked principles of logic in common, shared the definition of the pertinent facts. They differed only as to the outcome. Let us turn to the articulation of the question at hand. The issue of who is Israel articulated in theological, not political, terms covers several topics: are the Jews today "Israel" of ancient times? Was, and is, Jesus Christ? If so, who are the Christians, both on their own and also in relationship to ancient Israel? These questions scarcely can be kept distinct from one another.

First, was, and is, Jesus Christ? If so, then the Jews who rejected him enjoyed no share in the salvation at hand. If not, then they do. The Christian challenge comes first. If Jesus was and is Christ, then Israel "after the flesh" no longer enjoys the status of the people who bear salvation. Salvation has come, and Israel "after the flesh" has denied it. If he is Christ, then what is the status of those – whether Jews or gentiles – who did accept him? They have received the promises of salvation and their fulfillment. The promises to Israel have been kept for them.

Then there is a new Israel, one that is formed of the saved, as the prophets had said in ancient times that Israel would be saved. A further issue that flowed from the first – the rejection of Jesus as Christ – concerns the status of Israel, the Jewish people, now and in time to come. Israel after the flesh, represented from the Gospels forward as the people that rejected Jesus as Christ and participated in his crucifixion, claims to be the family of Abraham, Isaac, Jacob.

Then further questions arise. First, does Israel today continue the Israel of ancient times? Israel maintains that Israel now continues in a physical and spiritual way the life of Israel then. Second, will the promises of the prophets to Israel afford salvation for Israel in time to come? Israel "after the flesh" awaits the fulfillment of the prophetic promise of salvation. Clearly, a broad range of questions demanded sorting out.

But the questions flow together into a single issue, faced in common. The Christian position on all these questions came to expression in a single negative: no, Israel today does not continue the Israel of old, no, the ancient promises will not again bear salvation, because they have already been kept, so, no, the Israel that declines to accept Jesus' claim to be the Christ is a no-people.

The response of Israel's sages to these same questions proves equally unequivocal. Yes, the Messiah will come in time to come, and yes, he will come to Israel of today, which indeed continues the Israel of old. So the issue is squarely and fairly joined. Who is Israel raises a question that stands second in line to the Messianic one. And, it must follow, the further question of who are the Christians requires close attention to that same messianic question. So, as is clear, the initial confrontation generated a genuine argument on the status and standing, before God, of Israel "after the flesh," the Jewish people. And that argument took on urgency because of the worldly, political triumph of Christianity in Rome, joined, as the fourth century wore on, by the worldly, political decline in the rights and standing of Israel, the Jewish people.

Before Christianity had addressed the issue of who the Christians were, Paul had already asked what the Jews were not. Christians formed the true people of God.[4] So the old and lasting Israel, the Jewish people, did not. Paul had called into question "Israel's status as God's chosen people," because (in Ruether's words) "Israel had failed in its pursuit of righteousness based on the Torah...had been disobedient...[so that] the privileged relation to God provided by the Mosaic covenant has been permanently revoked". So from its origins, Christianity had called into question Israel's former status, and, as Gager says, held that "Israel's disobedience is not only not accidental to God's plan of salvation, it has become an essential part of its fulfillment." The Christian position on one side of ,the matter of who is Israel, namely, who is not Israel, had reached a conclusion before the other aspect of the matter – the Christians' status as a New Israel – came to full expression.[5]

That matter of status closely follows the issue of salvation. As soon as Christians coalesced into groups, they asked themselves what *sort* of groups they formed. They in fact maintained several positions. First, they held that they were a people, enjoying the status of the Jewish people, and that, as Harnack says, "furnished adherents of the new faith with a political and historical self-consciousness." So they were part of Israel and continued the Israel of ancient times, not a new group but a very old one. But the further defined themselves as not only a new people, but a new *type* of group, recognizing no taxonomic counterpart in the existing spectrum of human societies, peoples or nations. The claims of the Christians varied according to circumstance, so Harnack summarizes matters in a passage of stunning acuity:

> Was the cry raised, "You are renegade Jews" – the answer came, "We are the community of the Messiah, and therefore the true Israelites." If people said, "You are simply Jews," the reply was, "We are a new creation and a new people." If again they were taxed with their recent origin and told that they were but of yesterday, they retorted, "We only seem to be the younger People; from the beginning we have been latent;

---

[4] Ruether, pp. 64ff.
[5] Ruether, pp. 64ff., Gager, pp. 256-8.

we have always existed, previous to any other people; we are the original people of God." If they were told, "You do not deserve to live' the answer ran, "We would die to live, for we are citizens of the world to come, and sure that we shall rise again."[6]

These reflections on the classification of the new group – superior to the old, *sui generis*, and whatever the occasion of polemic requires the group to be – fill the early Christian writings. In general there were three: Greeks or gentiles, Jews, and the Christians as the new People.

When Christians asked themselves what sort of group they formed, they answered that they constituted a new group, and a group of a new type altogether. They identified with the succession to Israel after the flesh, with Israel after the spirit, with a group lacking all parallel or precedent, with God-fearers and law-keepers before Judaism was given at Sinai. The dilemma comes to expression in Eusebius:

> In the oracles directed to Abraham, Moses himself writes prophetically how in the times to come the descendants of Abraham, not only his Jewish seed but all the tribes and all the nations of the earth, will be deemed worthy of divine praise because of a common manner of worship like that of Abraham.... How could all the nations and tribes of the earth be blessed in Abraham if no relationship of either a spiritual or a physical nature existed between them?...How therefore could men reared amid an animal existence...be able to share in the blessings of the godly, unless they abandoned their savage ways and sought to participate in a life of piety like that of Abraham?...Now Moses lived after Abraham, and he gave the Jewish race a certain corporate status which was based upon the laws provided by him. If the laws he established were the same as those by which godly men were guided before his time, if they were capable of being adopted by all peoples so that all the tribes and nations of the earth could worship God in accordance with the Mosaic enactments, one could say that the oracles had foretold that because of Mosaic laws men of every nation would worship God and live according to Judaism....However since the Mosaic enactments did not apply to other peoples but to the Jews alone..., a different way, a way distinct from the law of Moses, needed to be established, one by which the nations of all the earth might live as Abraham had so that they could receive an equal share of blessing with him.[7]

Since, with the advent of Constantine, a political dimension served to take the measure of the Christian polity, we have to ask about the political consciousness of the Church in its original formulation. In this matter Harnack points out that the political consciousness of the Church rests on three premises, first, the political element in the Jewish apocalyptic, second, the movement of the gospel to the Greeks, and third, the ruin of Jerusalem and the end of the Jewish state. He says, "The first of these elements stood in antithesis to the two

---

[6] Harnack, pp. 241, 244.
[7] *The Proof of the Gospel* I 2:, cited by Luibheid, p. 41.

others, so that in this way the political consciousness of the church came to be defined in opposite directions and had to work itself out of initial contradictions."[8] From early times, Harnack says, the Christians saw Christianity as "the central point of humanity as the field of political history as well as its determining factor." That had been the Jews' view of themselves. With Constantine the corresponding Christian conception matched reality.

Now the Christians formed a new People, a third race. When the change came, with the Christianization of the Empire at the highest levels of government, the new people, the third race, had to frame a position and policy about the old people, enduring Israel "after the flesh." And, for its part, the Jewish people, faced with the Christian *défi*, found the necessity to reaffirm its enduring view of itself, now, however, in response to a pressure without precedent in its long past. The claim of the no-people that the now and enduring Israel is the no-people knew no prior equivalent. The age of Constantine marked the turning of the world: all things were upside down. How to deal with a world that (from the perspective of Israel, the Jewish people) had gone mad? Israel's answer, which we shall reach in due course, proves stunningly a propos: right to the issue, in precisely the terms of the issue. But first let us see how a substantial Christian theologian phrases the matter in the polemic at hand.

III. Aphrahat

To show us how a fourth century Christian theologian addressed the question at hand, namely, who is Israel in the light of the salvation of Jesus Christ, we turn to Aphrahat, a Christian monk in Mesopotamia, ca. 300-350, who wrote, in Syriac, a sustained treatise on the relationship of Christianity and Judaism. His demonstrations, written in 337-344, take up issues facing the Syriac speaking Church in the Iranian Empire. The church then – ca. 337-345 – was suffering severe persecution on the part of the Government, for the monks and nuns, maintaining they had no property, could not pay taxes. Since at that time Jews enjoyed stable and peaceful relationships with the Iranian government while Christians did not, the contrast between weak Christianity and secure Judaism required attention as well. Aphrahat presents his case on the basis of historical facts shared in common by both parties to the debate, Judaism and Christianity, that is, facts of Scripture. He rarely cites the New Testament in his demonstrations on Judaism. Moreover, when he cites the Hebrew Scriptures, he ordinarily refrains from fanciful or allegoristic reading of them, but, like the rabbis with whom Jerome dealt, stressed that his interpretation rested solely on the plain and obvious, factual meaning at hand. His arguments thus invoked rational arguments and historical facts: this is what happened, this is what it means. Scriptures therefore present facts, on which all parties concur. Then the argument goes forward on a common ground of shared reason and mutually-

---

[8] Harnack, p. 256-7.

agreed-upon facts. Still more important, the program of argument – is Israel, the Jewish people, going to be saved in the future, along with the issue of the standing and status of the Christian people – likewise follows points important to both parties.

Here, as I claimed at the outset, we find Judaic and Christian thinkers disagreeing on a common set of propositions: who is Israel? Will Israel be saved in the future, or have the prophetic promises already been kept. We take up Aphrahat's explanation of "the people which is of the peoples,"the people "which is no people," and then proceed to his address to Israel after the flesh. The two issues complement one another. Once the new people formed out of the peoples enters the status of Israel, then the old Israel loses that status. And how to express that judgment? By denying the premise of the life of Israel after the flesh, that salvation for the people of God would come in future time. If enduring Israel would never enjoy salvation, then Israel had no reason to exist: that is the premise of the argument framed in behalf of the people that had found its reason to exist (from its perspective) solely in its salvation by Jesus Christ. So what explained to the Christian community how that community had come into being also accounted, for that same community, for the (anticipated) disappearance of the nation that had rejected that very same nation-creating event.

Let me point to Aphrahat's *Demonstration Sixteen, "On the Peoples which are in the Place of the People."* Aphrahat's message is this: "The people Israel was rejected, and the peoples took their place. Israel repeatedly was warned by the prophets, but to no avail, so God abandoned them and replaced them with the gentiles. Scripture frequently referred to the gentiles as "Israel." The vocation of the peoples was prior to that of the people of Israel, and from of old, whoever from among the people was pleasing to God was more justified than Israel: Jethro, the Gibeonites, Rahab, Ebedmelech the Ethiopian, Uriah the Hittite. By means of the gentiles God provoked Israel."

First, Aphrahat maintains, "The peoples which were of all languages were called first, before Israel, to the inheritance of the Most High, as God said to Abraham, 'I have made you the father of a multitude of peoples' (Gen. 17:5). Moses proclaimed, saying, 'The peoples will call to the mountain, and there will they offer sacrifices of righteousness' (Deut. 33:19)." Not only so, but God further rejected Israel: "To his people Jeremiah preached, saying to them, 'Stand by the ways and ask the wayfarers, and see which is the good way. Walk in it.' But they in their stubbornness answered, saying to him, 'We shall not go.' Again he said to them, 'I established over you watchmen, that you might listen for the sound of the trumpet.' But they said to him again, 'We shall not hearken.' And this openly, publicly did they do in the days of Jeremiah when he preached to them the word of the Lord, and they answered him, saying,'To the word which you have spoken to us in the name of the Lord we shall not hearken. But we shall do our own will and every word which goes out of our mouths, to offer up incense-offerings to other gods'" (Jer. 44:16-17). That is why God turned to the peoples: "When he saw that they would not listen to him, he turned to the peoples, saying to them, 'Hear O peoples, and know, O church which is among them, and hearken, O land, in its fullness' (Jer. 6:18-19)." So who is now Israel? It is the peoples, no longer the old Israel: "By the name of Jacob [now] are called the people which is of the peoples." That is the key to Aphrahat's case. The people that was a no people, that people that had assembled out of the people, has now replaced Israel.

Like Eusebius, Aphrahat maintained that the peoples had been called to God before the people of Israel: "See, my beloved, that the vocation of the peoples was recorded before the vocation of the people. But because the time of the peoples had not come, and another was [to be] their redeemer, Moses was not persuaded that a redeemer and a teacher would come for the people which was of the peoples, which was greater and more worthy than the people of Israel." The people that was a no-people should not regard itself as alien to God: "If they should say, 'Us has he called alien children,' they have not been called alien children, but sons and heirs...But the peoples are those who hearken to God and were lamed and kept back from the ways of their sins." Indeed, the peoples produced believers who were superior in every respect to Israel: "Even from the old, whoever from among the peoples was pleasing to God was more greatly justified than Israel. Jethro the priest who was of the peoples and his seed were blessed: 'Enduring is his dwelling place, and his nest is set on a rock' (Num. 24:21)." Aphrahat hear refers to the Gibeonites, Rahab, and various other gentiles mentioned in the scriptural narrative.

Addressing his Christian hearers, Aphrahat then concludes, "By us they are provoked. On our account they do not worship idols, so that they will not be shamed by us, for we have abandoned idols and call lies the thing which our fathers left us. They are angry, their hearts are broken, for we have entered and have become heirs in their place. For theirs was this covenant which they had, not to worship other gods, but they did not accept it. By means of us he provoked them, and ours was the light and the life, as he preached, saying when he taught, 'I am the light of the world' (John 8:12)." So he concludes, "This brief memorial I have written to you concerning the peoples, because the Jews take pride and say, 'We are the people of God and the children of Abraham.' But we shall listen to John [the Baptist] who, when they took pride [saying], 'We are the children of Abraham,' then said to them, 'You should not boast and say, Abraham is father unto us, for from these very rocks can God raise up children for Abraham' (Matthew 3:9)."

In *Demonstration Nineteen*, *"Against the Jews, on account of their saying that they are destined to be gathered together,"* Aphrahat proceeds to the corollary argument, that the Israel after the flesh has lost its reason to endure as a nation. Why? Because no salvation awaits them in the future. The prophetic promises of salvation have all come to fulfillment in the past, and the climactic salvation for Israel, through the act of Jesus Christ, brought the salvific drama to its

Who Is "Israel"? 161

conclusion. Hence the Jews' not having a hope of "joining together" at the end of their exile forms a critical part of the entire picture. Here is a summary of the argument: "The Jews expect to be gathered together by the Messiah, but this expectation is in vain. God was never reconciled to them but has rejected them. The prophetic promises of restoration were all fulfilled in the return from Babylonia. Daniel's prayer was answered, and his vision was realized in the time of Jesus and in the destruction of Jerusalem. It will never be rebuilt."

Aphrahat thus stresses that the Jews' sins caused their own condition, a position which sages accepted: "On account of their sins, which were many, he uprooted and scattered them among every nation, for they did not listen to his prophets, whom he had sent to them." The Jews now maintain that they will see salvation in the future, but they are wrong: "I have written this to you because even today they hope an empty hope, saying, 'It is still certain for Israel to be gathered together,' for the prophet thus spoke, 'I shall leave none of them among the nations' (Ex. 39:28). But if all of our people is to be gathered together, why are we today scattered among every people?" But, Aphrahat states, "Israel never is going to be gathered together." The reason is that God was never reconciled to Israel: "I shall write and show you that never did God accept their repentance [through] either Moses or all of the prophets....Further, Jeremiah said, 'They are called rejected silver, for the Lord has rejected them (Jer. 6:30). ...See, then, they have never accepted correction in their lives.."

Aphrahat presents an array of prophetic proof-texts for the same proposition. Then he turns to the peoples and declares that they have taken the place of the people: "Concerning the vocation of the peoples Isaiah said, 'It shall come to be in the last days that the mountain of the House of the Lord will be established at the head of the mountains and high above the heights. Peoples will come together to it, and many peoples will go and say, Come, let us go up to the mountain of the Lord, to the House of the God of Jacob. He will teach us his ways, and we shall walk in his paths. For from Zion the law will go forth, and the word of the Lord from Jerusalem' (Is. 2:2, 3)." Does Israel not hope for redemption in the future? Indeed so, but they are wrong: "Two times only did God save Israel: Once from Egypt, the second time from Babylonia; from Egypt by Moses, and from Babylonia by Ezra and by the prophecy of Haggai and Zechariah. Haggai said, 'Build this house, and I shall have pleasure in it, and in it I shall be glorified, says the Lord (Hag. 1:8)... All of these things were said in the days of Zerubbabel, Haggai, and Zechariah. They were exhorting concerning the building of the house." The house was built – and then destroyed, and it will not be rebuilt (Aphrahat wrote before Julian's proposed rebuilding of the temple, so he could not have derived further proof from that disaster.)

So much for the challenge of those who held such views as Aphrahat expresses. The case is complete: the people which is no-people, the people which is of the peoples, have taken the place of the people which claims to carry forward the salvific history of ancient Israel. The reason is in two complementary parts. First, Israel has rejected salvation, so lost its reason to exist, and, second, the no-people have accepted salvation, so gained its reason to exist. So the threads of the dispute link into a tight fabric: the shift in the character of politics, marked by the epochal triumph of Christianity in the state, bears profound meaning for the messianic mission of the Church, and, further, imparts a final judgment on the salvific claim of the competing nations of God: the Church and Israel. What possible answer can sages have proposed to this indictment? Since at the heart of the matter lies the claim that Israel persists in the salvific heritage that has passed to the Christians, sages reaffirm that Israel persists – just as Paul had framed matters – after the flesh, an unconditional and permanent status. For one never ceases to be the son of his mother and his father, and the daughter is always the daughter of her father and her mother. So Israel after the flesh constitutes the family, in the most physical form, of Abraham, Isaac, and Jacob. And, moreover, as that family, Israel inherits the heritage of salvation hand on by the patriarchs and matriarchs. The spiritualization of "Israel" here finds its opposite and counterpart: the utter and complete "genealogization" of Israel.

IV. The Judaic Response in Leviticus Rabbah

Just as nothing in Aphrahat's case would have struck as alien his Roman-Christian counterparts, so we shall now see that, on the Roman side of the border, the Judaic sages responded just as their counterparts in Iran framed matters. The Judaic position vis a vis Christianity was not affected by political frontiers, even as the Judaic-Christian confrontation had been precipitated by a political event in the conversion of Constantine. Briefly to examine the Judaic side of the issue, we turn to a document framed in what Jews know as the Land of Israel, in the Christian Roman empire of the fifth century, a century beyond the crisis at hand. A cogent and propositional commentary to the book of Leviticus, Leviticus Rabbah, ca. 400-450, reads the laws of the on-going sanctification in nature of the life of Israel as an account of the rules of the one-time salvation in history of the polity of Israel.

To the framers of Leviticus Rabbah, one point of emphasis proved critical: Israel remains Israel, the Jewish people, after the flesh, because Israel today continues the family begun by Abraham, Isaac, Jacob, Joseph and the other tribal founders, and bears the heritage bequeathed by them. That conviction of who is Israel never required articulation. The contrary possibility fell wholly outside of sages' (and all Jews') imagination. To state matters negatively, the people could no more conceive that they were not the daughters and sons of their fathers and mothers than that they were not one large family, that is, the family of Abraham, Isaac, and Jacob: Israel after the flesh. That is what "after the flesh" meant. The powerful stress on the enduring merit of the patriarchs and matriarchs, the social theory that treated Israel as one large, extended family, the actual children of Abraham, Isaac, and Jacob – these metaphors for the fleshly continuity surely met head on the contrary position framed by Paul and restated by Christian theologians from his time onward. In this respect, while Aphrahat did not deny the Israel-ness of Israel, the Jewish people, he did underline the futility of enduring as Israel. Maintaining that Israel would see no future salvation amounted to declaring that Israel, the Jewish people, pursued no worthwhile purpose in continuing to endure. Still, the argument is head-on and concrete: who is Israel? who enjoys salvation? To sages, as we shall see, the nations of the world serve God's purpose in ruling Israel, just as the prophets had said, and Israel, for its part, looks forward to a certain salvation.

The position of the framers of Leviticus Rabbah on the issues at hand emerges in both positive and negative formulation. On the positive side, Israel, the Jewish people, the people of whom Scriptures spoke and to whom, today, sages now speak, is God's first love. That position of course presents no surprises and can have been stated with equal relevance in any circumstances. We in no way can imagine that the authors of Leviticus Rabbah stress the points that they stress in particular because Christians have called them into question. I doubt that that was the case. In fact when we survey the verses important to Aphrahat's case and ask what, in the counterpart writings of sages in all of late antiquity, people say about those same verses, we find remarkably little attention to the florilegium of proof-texts adduced by Aphrahat.[9] While the argument on who is Israel did not take shape on the foundation of a shared program of verses, on which each party entered its position, the issue was one and the same. And the occasion – the political crisis of the fourth century – faced both parties.

Sages delivered a message particular to their system. The political context imparted to that message urgency for Israel beyond their small circle. As to confronting the other side, no sage would concede what to us is self-evident. This was the urgency of the issue. For the definition of what was at issue derived from the common argument of the age: Who is the Messiah? Christ or someone else? Here too, while the argument between Christian theologians and Judaic sages on the present status of Israel, the Jewish people, went forward on the same basic issues, it ran along parallel lines. True, lines of argument never intersected at all. The issue in both topics, however, is what was the same, even though the exposition of arguments on one side's proposition in no way intersected with the other side's.

When Aphrahat denied that God loves Israel any more, and contemporary sages affirmed that God yet loves Israel and always will, we come to a clearcut exchange of views on a common topic. Parallel to Aphrahat's sustained demonstrations on a given theme, the framers of Leviticus Rabbah laid forth thematic exercises, each one serving in a cumulative way to make a given point on a single theme. Therefore in order to describe sages' position, we do well to

---

[9] See my *Aphrahat and Judaism* (Leiden, 1970: E. J. Brill), pp. 150-195.

follow their ideas in their own chosen medium of expression. I can find no more suitable way of recapitulating their reply to the question, Who is Israel? than by a brief survey of one of the sustained essays they present on the subject in Leviticus Rabbah.[10] We proceed to the unfolding, in Leviticus Rabbah Parashah Two, of the theme: Israel is precious. At Lev. R. II:III.2.B, we find an invocation of the genealogical justification for the election of Israel: "He said to him, 'Ephraim, head of the tribe, head of the session, one who is beautiful and exalted above all of my sons will be called by your name: [Samuel, the son of Elkanah, the son of Jeroham,] the son of Tohu, the son of Zuph, an Ephraimite' [1 Sam. 1:1]; 'Jeroboam son of Nabat, an Ephraimite' (1 Sam. 11:26). 'And David was an Ephraimite, of Bethlehem in Judah'" (1 Sam. 17:12). Since Ephraim, that is, Israel, had been exiled, the deeper message cannot escape our attention. Whatever happens, God loves Ephraim. However Israel suffers, God's love endures, and God cares. In context, that message brings powerful reassurance. Facing a Rome gone Christian, sages had to begin with to state the obvious – which no longer seemed self-evident at all. What follows spells out this very point: God is especially concerned with Israel.

II:IV

1. A. Returning to the matter (GWPH): "Speak to the children of Israel" (Lev. 1:2).
   B. R. Yudan in the name of R. Samuel b. R. Nehemiah: "The matter may be compared to the case of a king who had an undergarment, concerning which he instructed his servant, saying to him, 'Fold it, shake it out, and be careful about it!'
   C. "He said to him, 'My lord, O king, among all the undergarments that you have, [why] do you give me such instructions only about this one?'
   D. "He said to him, 'It is because this is the one that I keep closest to my body.'
   E. "So too did Moses say before the Holy One, blessed be he, 'Lord of the Universe: Among the seventy distinct nations that you have in your world, [why] do you give me instructions only concerning Israel? [For instance,] "Command the children of Israel" [Num. 28:2], "Say to the children of Israel" [Ex. 33:5], "Speak to the children of Israel"' [Lev. 1:2].
   F. "He said to him, 'The reason is that they stick close to me, in line with the following verse of Scripture: "For as the undergarment cleaves to the loins of a man, so have I caused to cleave unto me the whole house of Israel"'" (Jer. 13:11).
   G. Said R. Abin, "[The matter may be compared] to a king who had a purple cloak, concerning which he instructed his servant, saying, 'Fold it, shake it out, and be careful about it!'
   H. "He said to him, 'My Lord, O king, among all the purple cloaks that you have, [why] do you give me such instructions only about this one?'
   I. "He said to him, 'That is the one that I wore on my coronation day.'

---

[10] The complete texts are in the Appendix to my *Judaism and Christianity in the Age of Constantine*.

J. "So too did Moses say before the Holy One, blessed be he, Lord of the Universe: 'Among the seventy distinct nations that you have in your world, [why] do you give instructions to me only concerning Israel? [For instance,] "Say to the children of Israel," "Command the children of Israel," "Speak to the children of Israel."'

K. "He said to him, 'They are the ones who at the [Red] Sea declared me to be king, saying, 'The Lord will be king'" (Ex. 15:18).

The point of the passage has to do with Israel's particular relationship to God: Israel cleaves to God, declares God to be king, and accepts God's dominion. Further evidence of God's love for Israel derives from the commandments themselves. God watches over every little thing that Jews do, even caring what they eat for breakfast. The familiar stress on the keeping of the laws of the Torah as a mark of hope finds fulfillment here: the laws testify to God's deep concern for Israel. So there is sound reason for high hope, expressed in particular in keeping the laws of the Torah. Making the matter explicit, Simeon b. Yohai (Lev. R. II:V.1.A-B) translates this fact into a sign of divine favor:

II:V

1. A. Said R. Simeon b. Yohai, "[The matter may be compared] to a king who had an only son. Every day he would give instructions to his steward, saying to him, 'Make sure my son eats, make sure my son drinks, make sure my son goes to school, make sure my son comes home from school.'

   B. "So every day the Holy One, blessed be he, gave instructions to Moses, saying, 'Command the children of Israel,' 'Say to the children of Israel,' 'Speak to the children of Israel.'"

We now come to the statement of how Israel wins and retains God's favor. The issue at hand concerns Israel's relationship to the nations before God, which is corollary to what has gone before. It is in two parts. First of all, Israel knows how to serve God in the right way. Second, the nations, though they do what Israel does, do things wrong. First, Israel does things right. Why then is Israel beloved? The following answers that question.

V:VIII

1. A. R. Simeon b. Yohai taught, "How masterful are the Israelites, for they know how to find favor with their creator."

   E. Said R. Hunia [in Aramaic:], "There is a tenant farmer who knows how to borrow things, and there is a tenant farmer who does not know how to borrow. The one who knows how to borrow combs his hair, brushes off his clothes, puts on a good face, and then goes over to the overseer of his work to borrow from him. [The overseer] says to him, 'How's the land doing?' He says to him, 'May you have the merit of being fully satisfied with its [wonderful] produce.' 'How are the oxen doing?' He says to him, 'May you have the merit of being fully satisfied with their fat.' 'How are the goats doing?' 'May you have the merit of being fully satisfied with their young.' 'And what would you like?' Then he says,

'Now if you might have an extra ten denars, would you give them to me?' The overseer replies, 'If you want, take twenty.'

F. "But the one who does not know how to borrow leaves his hair a mess, his clothes filthy, his face gloomy. He too goes over to the overseer to borrow from him. The overseer says to him, 'How's the land doing?' He replies, 'I hope it will produce at least what [in seed] we put into it.' 'How are the oxen doing?' 'They're scrawny.' 'How are the goats doing?' 'They're scrawny too.' 'And what do you want?' 'Now if you might have an extra ten denars, would you give them to me?' The overseer replies, 'Go, pay me back what you already owe me!'"

If Aphrahat had demanded a direct answer, he could not have received a more explicit one. He claims Israel does nothing right. Sages counter, speaking in their own setting of course, that they do everything right. Sages then turn the tables on the position of Aphrahat – again addressing it head-on. While the nations may do everything Israel does, they do it wrong.

Sages recognized in the world only one counterpart to Israel, and that was Rome. Rome's history formed the counterweight to Israel's. So Rome as a social entity weighed in the balance against Israel. That is why we return to the corollary question: who is Rome? For we can know who is Israel only if we can also explain who is Rome. And, I should maintain, explaining who is Rome takes on urgency at the moment at which Rome presents to Israel problems of an unprecedented character. The matter belongs in any picture of who is Israel. Sages' doctrine of Rome forms the counterpart to Christian theologians' theory on who is Israel. Just as Aphrahat explains both who are the Christians and also who is Israel today, so sages in Leviticus Rabbah develop an important theory on who is Rome. They too propose to account for the way things are, and that means, they have to explain who is this counterpart to Israel. And sages' theory does respond directly to the question raised by the triumph of Christianity in the Roman Empire. For, as we shall see, the characterization of Rome in Leviticus Rabbah bears the burden of their judgment on the definition of the Christian people, as much as the sages' characterization of Rome in Leviticus Rabbah expressed their judgment of the place of Rome in the history of Israel.

To understand that position on the character of Rome, we have to note that it constitutes a radical shift in the characterization of Rome in the unfolding canon of the sages' Judaism. For the treatment of Rome shifts in a remarkable way from the earlier approach to the subject. Rome in the prior writings, the Mishnah (ca. A.D. 200) and the Tosefta (ca. A.D. 300-400), stood for a particular place. We begin with the view of the Mishnah. For matters show a substantial shift in the characterization of Rome from the earlier to the later writings. Had matters remained pretty much the same from earlier, late second century, to later, fourth and early fifth century, writings, we could not maintain that what is said in the fourth century documents testifies in particular to intellectual events of the fourth century. We should have to hold that, overall, the doctrine was set and endured in its original version. What happened later on would then have no bearing upon the doctrine at hand, and my claim of a confrontation on a vivid issue would not find validation. But the doctrine of Rome does shift from the Mishnah to the fourth century sages' writings, Leviticus Rabbah, Genesis Rabbah, and the Talmud of the Land of Israel. That fact proves the consequence, in the interpretation of ideas held in the fourth century, of the venue of documents in that time.

In Leviticus Rabbah, Rome now stood for much more than merely a place among other places. Rome took up a place in the unfolding of the empires – Babylonia, Media, Greece, then Rome. Still more important Rome is the penultimate empire on earth. Israel will constitute the ultimate one. That message, seeing the shifts in world history in a pattern and placing at the apex of the shift Israel itself, directly and precisely takes up the issue made urgent just now: the advent of the Christian emperors. Why do I maintain, as I do, that in the characterization of Rome as the fourth and penultimate empire/animal, sages address issues of their own day? Because Rome, among the successive empires, bears special traits, most of which derive from the distinctively Christian character of Rome.

Rome is represented as only Christian Rome can have been represented: it looks kosher but it is unkosher. Pagan Rome cannot ever have looked kosher, but Christian Rome, with its appeal to ancient Israel, could and did and moreover claimed to. It bore some traits that validate, but lacked others that validate. It would be difficult to find a more direct confrontation between two parties to an argument. Now the issue is the same – who is the true Israel? and the proof-texts are the same, and, moreover, the proof-texts are read in precisely the same way. Only the conclusions differ!

The polemic represented in Leviticus Rabbah by the symbolization of Christian Rome makes the simple point that, first, Christians are no different from, and no better than, pagans; they are essentially the same. Christians' claim to form part of Israel then requires no serious attention. Since Christians came to Jews with precisely that claim, the sages' response – they are another Babylonia – bears a powerful polemic charge. But that is not the whole story, as we see. Second, just as Israel had survived Babylonia, Media, Greece, so would they endure to see the end of Rome (whether pagan, whether Christian). But there is a third point. Rome really does differ from the earlier, pagan empires, and that polemic shifts the entire discourse, once we hear its symbolic vocabulary properly. For the new Rome really did differ from the old. Christianity was not merely part of a succession of undifferentiated modes of paganism. The symbols assigned to Rome attributed worse, more dangerous traits than those assigned to the earlier empires. The pig pretends to be clean, just as the Christians give the signs of adherence to the God of Abraham, Isaac, and Jacob. That much the passage concedes. For the pig is not clean, exhibiting some, but not all, of the required indications, and Rome is not Israel, even though it shares Israel's Scripture. That position, denying to Rome, in its

Christian form, a place in the family of Israel, forms the counterpart to the view of Aphrahat that Israel today is no longer Israel – again, a confrontation on issues. I present only the critical passage at which the animals that are invoked include one that places Rome at the intersticies, partly kosher, partly not, therefore more dangerous than anyone else.

XIII:V

9. A. Moses foresaw what the evil kingdoms would do [to Israel].
   B. "The camel, rock badger, and hare" (Deut. 14:7). [Compare: "Nevertheless, among those that chew the cud or part the hoof, you shall not eat these: the camel, because it chews the cud but does not part the hoof, is unclean to you. The rock badger, because it chews the cud but does not part the hoof, is unclean to you. And the hare, because it chews the cud but does not part the hoof, is unclean to you, and the pig, because it parts the hoof and is cloven-footed, but does not chew the cud, is unclean to you" (Lev. 11:4-8).]
   C. The camel (GML) refers to Babylonia, [in line with the following verse of Scripture: "O daughter of Babylonia, you who are to be devastated!] Happy will be he who requites (GML) you, with what you have done to us" (Ps. 147:8).
   D. "The rock badger" (Deut. 14:7) – this refers to Media.
   E. Rabbis and R. Judah b. R. Simon.
   F. Rabbis say, "Just as the rock badger exhibits traits of uncleanness and traits of cleanness, so the kingdom of Media produced both a righteous man and a wicked one."
   G. Said R. Judah b. R. Simon, "The last Darius was Esther's son. He was clean on his mother's side and unclean on his father's side."
   H. "The hare" (Deut 14:7) – this refers to Greece. The mother of King Ptolemy was named "Hare" [in Greek: lagos].
   I. "The pig" (Deut. 14:7) – this refers to Edom [Rome].
   J. Moses made mention of the first three in a single verse and the final one in a verse by itself [(Deut. 14:7, 8)]. Why so?
   K. R. Yohanan and R. Simeon b. Laqish.
   L. R. Yohanan said, "It is because [the pig] is equivalent to the other three."
   M. And R. Simeon b. Laqish said, "It is because it outweighs them."
   N. R. Yohanan objected to R. Simeon b. Laqish, "'Prophesy, therefore, son of man, clap your hands [and let the sword come down twice, yea thrice]' (Ez. 21:14)."
   O. And how does R. Simeon b. Laqish interpret the same passage? He notes that [the threefold sword] is doubled (Ez. 21:14).

In the apocalypticizing of the animals of Lev. 11:4-8/Deut. 14:7, the camel, rock badger, hare, and pig, the pig, standing for Rome, again emerges as different from the others and more threatening than the rest. Just as the pig pretends to be a clean beast by showing the cloven hoof, but in fact is an unclean one, so Rome pretends to be just but in fact governs by thuggery. Edom does not pretend to praise God but only blasphemes. It does not exalt the righteous but kills them. These symbols concede nothing to Christian monotheism and veneration of the Torah of Moses (in its written medium). Of greatest importance, while all the other beasts bring further ones in their wake, the pig does not: "It does not bring another kingdom after it." It will restore the crown to the one who will truly deserve it, Israel. Esau will be judged by Zion, so Obadiah 1:21. Now how has the symbolization delivered an implicit message? It is in the treatment of Rome as distinct, but essentially equivalent to the former kingdoms. This seems to me a stunning way of saying that the now-Christian empire in no way requires differentiation from its pagan predecessors. Nothing has changed, except matters have gotten worse. Beyond Rome, standing in a straight line with the others, lies the true shift in history, the rule of Israel and the cessation of the dominion of the (pagan) nations.

To conclude, Leviticus Rabbah came to closure, it is generally agreed, around A.D. 400-450, that is, approximately a century after the Roman Empire in the east had begun to become Christian, and half a century after the last attempt to rebuild the Temple in Jerusalem had failed – a tumultuous age indeed. Accordingly, we have had the chance to see how distinctive and striking are the ways in which, in the text at hand, the symbols of animals that stand for the four successive empires of humanity and point towards the messianic time, serve for the framers' message. Rome in the fourth century became Christian. Sages responded by facing that fact quite squarely and saying, "Indeed, it is as you say, a kind of Israel, an heir of Abraham as your texts explicitly claim. But we remain the sole legitimate Israel, the bearer of the birthright – we and not you. So you are our brother: Esau, Ishmael, Edom." And the rest follows.

Sages framed their political ideas within the metaphor of genealogy, because to begin with they appealed to the fleshly connection, the family, as the rationale for Israel's social existence. A family beginning with Abraham, Isaac, and Jacob, Israel today could best sort out its relationships by drawing into the family other social entities with which it found it had to relate. So Rome became the brother. That affinity came to light only when Rome had turned Christian, and that point marked the need for the extension of the genealogical net. But the conversion to Christianity also justified sages' extending membership in the family to Rome, for Christian Rome shared with Israel the common patrimony of Scripture – and said so. The two facts, the one of the social and political metaphor by which sages interpreted events, the other of the very character of Christianity – account for the striking shift in the treatment of Rome that does appear to have taken place in the formative century represented by work on Leviticus Rabbah.

IV. Aphrahat in Iran, Sages in Rome: The Single Issue

The issue is joined, fully, completely, head-on. And well it was. For the stakes, for both sides, were very high. Aphrahat alerts us to the Christians' human problem. They saw themselves as a people without a past, a no-people, a people gathered from the peoples. Then who they can claim to be hardly derives from who they have been. Identifying with ancient Israel – a perfectly natural and correct initiative – admirably accounted for the Christian presence in humanity, provided a past, explained to diverse people what they had in common. One problem from Christians theologians' perspective demanded solution: the existing Israel, the Jewish people, which revered the same Scriptures and claimed descent, after the flesh, from ancient Israel. These – the Jews – traced their connection to ancient Israel, seeing it as natural, and also, supernatural. The family tie, through Abraham, Isaac, Jacob, formed a powerful apologetic indeed. The Jews furthermore pointed to their family record, the Scriptures, to explain whence they come and who they are. So long as the two parties to the debate shared the same subordinated political circumstance, Jewry could quite nicely hold its own in the debate; the pleading tone of Aphrahat's writing opens a window onto the heart of the historical newcomers to salvation, as Christians saw themselves. But with the shift in the politics of the Empire, the terms of debate changed. The parvenu become paramount, the Christian party to the debate invoked its familiar position now with the power of the state in support. Aphrahat's framing of the issue reflects that political fact – even though Aphrahat, living in Shapur II's Iran, did not himself live in a Christian empire. The sages represented by Leviticus Rabbah answered the issues set forth on the agenda represented by Aphrahat, because wherever they lived, they too followed the inner logic of the issue, not the dictates of an ephemeral circumstance, in reflecting on the confrontation with the other Israel.

For Israel what was there to say, but what, in Israel's view, God had said to Israel in the Torah's record of the very beginnings of the world. What now makes that old message matter is simple: the specific context to which, at just this moment, the old words were spoken. That milieu is what imparts meaning to the message: the rise to state recognition and favor of one of the two parties to the dispute of the godly genealogy. And what gives that fact weight for us is the further, equally simple fact that, in the unfolding of the canon of the sages' Judaism, the documents before us contain the first explicit and emphatic statement of the age-old genealogy of God's people. So while the framers of Leviticus Rabbah may have stated in their own medium a familiar and routine message, still, the setting turns out to supply the catalyst of significance. Content, out of political context, is mere theology. But in political context, the theological issues, fully understood in all their awful urgency, focus on matters of social life or death. The doctrines of history and merit, of Israel's identity, selection and grace – these turn out to deal with the very life and identity of a people and its society – a fitting point on which to end this tribute to Howard Kee.

Bibliography

General:

N. H. Baynes, *Constantine the Great and the Christian Church* (New York, 1972: Oxford University Press). Second ed., preface by Henry Chadwick.

Erwin R. Goodenough, *The Church in the Roman Empire* (N.Y., 1931: Henry Holt. Repr, N.Y., 1970: Cooper Square Publishers, Inc.), pp. 41-61.

Adolf Harnack, *The Mission and Expansion of Christianity in the First Three Centuries*. Translated and edited by James Moffatt (London, 1908. Repr. Gloucester, 1972: Peter Smith).

J. R. Palanque, G. Bardy, P. de Labriolle, G. de Plinval, and Louis Brehier, *The Church in the Christian Roman Empire. I. The Church and the Arian Crisis* (N.Y., 1953: Macmillan). With special reference to Pierre de Labriolle, "Christianity and Paganism in the Middle of the Fourth Century," p. 220-257.

Rosemary Radford Ruether, *Faith and Fratricide. The Theological Roots of Anti-Semitism* (N.Y., 1979: Seabury Press).

Rosemary Radford Ruether, "Judaism and Christianity. Two Fourth-Century Religions," *Sciences Religieuses Studies in Religion* 1972, 2:1-10.

Marcel Simon, *Verus Israel. Etude sur les relations entre chrétiens et juifs dans l'empire romain* (135-425) (Paris, 1964: Editions E. de Boccard).

Judaism in the Land of Israel and in Babylonia

Jacob Neusner, *A History of the Jews in Babylonia* (Leiden, 1969) III. *The Age of Shapur II.*

Jacob Neusner, *Judaism in Society. The Evidence of the Yerushalmi. Toward the Natural History of a Religion* (Chicago, 1983: University of Chicago Press), cf. pp. 117-121, 196-197, 247-253.

Aphrahat and Judaism

John G. Gager, *The Origins of Anti-Semitism. Attitudes toward Judaism in Pagan and Christian Antiquity* (N.Y., 1983: Oxford University Press), pp. 247-264.

Adolf Harnack, *The Mission and Expansion of Christianity in the First Three Centuries*. Translated and edited by James Moffatt (London, 1908. Repr. Gloucester, 1972: Peter Smith), pp. 240-278.

Colm Luibheid, *The Essential Eusebius* (N.Y., 1966: Mentor Omega), p.41

Rosemary Radford Ruether, *Faith and Fratricide. The Theological Roots of Anti-Semitism* (N.Y., 1979: Seabury Press).

Marcel Simon, *Verus Israel. Etude sur les relations entre chrétiens et juifs dans l'empire romain* (135-425) (Paris, 1964: Editions E. de Boccard), on Christians as a third type of people, pp. 135-139; on the *Adversus Judaeos* literature in general, pp. 166-176.

Aphrahat and the People Which Is No People

Robert Murray, *Symbols of Church and Kingdom. A Study in Early Syriac Tradition* (Cambridge: Cambridge University Press, 1975).

Jacob Neusner, *Aphrahat and Judaism. The Christian-Jewish Argument in Fourth-Century Iran* (Leiden, 1971: E. J. Brill).